D1110619

No Longer Be Silent

Gender and the Biblical Tradition

The Witch of Endor summons Samuel from Sheol

No Longer
Be Silent

First Century Jewish Portraits
of Biblical Women

Studies in Pseudo-Philo's *Biblical Antiquities*
and Josephus's *Jewish Antiquities*

Cheryl Anne Brown

Westminster/John Knox Press
Louisville, Kentucky

© 1992 Cheryl Anne Brown

All rights reserved. No part of this book may be reproduced or transmitted in any form or by any means, electronic or mechanical, including photocopying, recording, or by any information storage or retrieval system, without permission in writing from the publisher. For information, address Westminster/John Knox Press, 100 Witherspoon Street, Louisville, Kentucky 40202-1396.

Unless marked otherwise, scripture quotations are from the New Revised Standard Version of the Bible, copyright © 1989 by the Division of Christian Education of the National Council of the Churches of Christ in the U.S.A., and are used by permission.

Frontispiece artwork is copyright © 1992 by Pem Pfisterer Clark and is used by permission.

Book design by Ken Taylor

First edition

Published by Westminster/John Knox Press
Louisville, Kentucky

This book is printed on acid-free paper that meets the American National Standards Institute Z39.48 standard. ♾

PRINTED IN THE UNITED STATES OF AMERICA
9   8   7   6   5   4   3   2   1

Library of Congress Cataloging-in-Publication Data

Brown, Cheryl Anne, 1949–
    No longer be silent : first century Jewish portraits of biblical
women / Cheryl Anne Brown.
        p.   cm. — (Gender and the biblical tradition)
    Includes bibliographical references and index.
    ISBN 0-664-25294-X

    1. Women in the Bible.   2. Deborah (Biblical judge)   3. Hannah
(Biblical figure)   4. Jephthah's daughter (Biblical figure)
5. Witch of Endor (Biblical figure)   6. Pseudo-Philo. Liber
antiquitatum biblicarum.   7. Josephus, Flavius. Antiquitates
Judaicae.   8. Bible. O.T.—Criticism, interpretation, etc., Jewish.
9. Misogyny in literature.   I. Title.   II. Series.
BS1199.W7B76   1992
220.9′2—dc20   91-33441

Contents

Preface

     This book is the result of many years of research and reflection on texts that are foundational to Jewish and Christian religious thought and experience. Although I began my journey into this investigative study as an undergraduate, my interest in early Judaism and Christianity and their interrelationship increased significantly when my husband and I served in theological education and interfaith work in Jerusalem for nearly nine years. In that context I had the immensely enriching opportunity of studying Judaism and Christianity with some of the foremost scholars and leaders in both traditions. My quest continued when we moved to Berkeley in 1984, where I was able to build upon graduate work begun at the Hebrew University of Jerusalem and enter a joint Ph.D. program in Near Eastern Religions at the University of California at Berkeley and the Graduate Theological Union. As my studies progressed, so did my interest in those writings that stood outside the sphere of what was accepted as authoritative by either faith—the Dead Sea Scrolls, the New Testament Apocrypha, and the Pseudepigrapha—as well as Jewish midrashic and targumic literature. Through these texts I learned much about the diverse groups within Judaism and early Christianity and gained new perspective upon the development of thought and practice in both traditions.

     I was particularly captivated by the "Rewritten Bible," documents that gave expression to new interpretations by rewriting the biblical text so that these ideas were ac-

corded the authority of divine revelation. It was while
pursuing this interest during my doctoral work that I
discovered Pseudo-Philo's *Biblical Antiquities*. Almost as
soon 'as I read it, I knew I had stumbled onto something extremely important because of the way the author
portrays women biblical figures, which is unparalleled in
other Jewish literature I had studied, and also because
of the overall tendencies of the book, which seems to
reflect a Judaism in transition after the destruction of
Jerusalem. I sensed that it might provide a link with
early Christian tradition that scholars have not yet fully
appreciated.

This book is the fruit of my preliminary investigations of
this intriguing—indeed, amazing—document. As a point
of comparison with my investigation of *Biblical Antiquities*,
I have added a study of the same women figures in another, more familiar, work—Josephus's *Jewish Antiquities*.
This stands in the same literary tradition as *Biblical Antiquities* and dates from the same time period; but it certainly
represents a very different social and religious experience
than *Biblical Antiquities*. The value in a comparative study
such as this is that it highlights the distinctive features of
each author's presentation.

No Longer Be Silent is actually a rewritten text itself:
The basic document was initially presented as my doctoral dissertation, completed in November 1989, but I
have now thoroughly reworked it. It is the product of a
lengthy process, marked by the somewhat tedious disci-
pline of methodical research and writing, as well as the
joyful adventure into new worlds of ideas never explored
before. My primary shepherd in this process was John C.
Endres, S.J., of the Jesuit School of Theology at Berkeley,
to whom I am deeply indebted for his patient guidance
and prodding, encouragement, and always constructive
criticism. He pointed me to my scholarly journey, and
also walked with me on that journey; by word and example, he gave me tools to enable me to analyze, synthesize,
and articulate what I discovered, and he gave me inspi-

ration to continue on the journey that I have really only just begun.

I am also indebted to the four other scholars who served on my doctoral committee and without whose input and encouragement I surely would not have succeeded in completing this work. I acknowledge with deep gratitude the contributions of Jacob Milgrom and William S. Anderson (the University of California at Berkeley); David Winston (the Center for Jewish Studies, Berkeley); and Mary Ann Donovan, S.C. (Jesuit School of Theology, Berkeley). I also wish to express my gratitude to Victor R. Gold (Pacific Lutheran Theological Seminary, Berkeley) for his invaluable guidance and assistance throughout my doctoral studies.

In an age of computers, which are sometimes mysterious and often frustrating to a layperson such as I, a friend who is willing to give advice and help is a friend indeed. I want to acknowledge here my very grateful appreciation of the skills and gifts of William Aram, who generously gave of his time and expertise to help me with the practical side of getting all of this on paper. I am also deeply indebted to Evelyn Mayfield, whose wide knowledge of the intricacies of style and grammar, as well as years of experience as an editor, have been invaluable.

Finally, I am most grateful to my husband, Wesley, and children, Julie Anne and Benjamin Joel, who so graciously shared their wife and mother with this, my third child. With love and gratitude, I dedicate it to them.

Abbreviations

Ant.	*Jewish Antiquities* (Josephus)
Bib. Ant.	*Biblical Antiquities* (Pseudo-Philo)
BJ	*The Jewish Wars* (Josephus)
CAp	*Against Apion* (Josephus)
LA	*Legum Allegoriae* (Philo of Alexandria)
OTP	*The Old Testament Pseudepigrapha*

Introduction

All those who study the Bible, whether ancient interpreters or modern readers, make new interpretations of it and its characters. To both modern Jews and Christians, biblical interpretations by Jewish contemporaries of Jesus have special importance. This was an age that decisively influenced our own, and its outlook on the Hebrew scriptures is a fascinating study in its own right. In the present study, I will examine the portrayal of four biblical women—Deborah, Hannah, Jephthah's daughter, and the witch of Endor—in two first-century Jewish documents, Pseudo-Philo's *Biblical Antiquities*[1] and Flavius Josephus's *Jewish Antiquities*.

Biblical Antiquities recounts biblical history more or less parallel to Genesis through 1 Samuel. The text is also often designated as "Pseudo-Philo" because it was first discovered attached to two texts authored by Philo of Alexandria, the famous first-century Jewish philosopher-exegete. Although early commentators assumed that that Philo was the author of the document, subsequent scholars have universally agreed that its style, vocabulary, and general content preclude Philonic authorship and hence have identified its author as Pseudo-Philo; the true identity of the author remains unknown.

In contrast, we know a great deal about the author of *Jewish Antiquities*, for Flavius Josephus wrote not only many historical works about the Jewish people, but also appended an autobiographical text, "Life," to *Jewish Antiquities*. There we read that he was born Joseph ben

Mattitahu into a priestly family of Jerusalem c. 37 C.E., received a Jewish education as well as some Greek learning, served as an officer in the Jewish army during the first years of the war against Rome, and later defected to Rome, being convinced that a Roman victory was the will of God for the Jewish people. He later took up residence in Rome where, under the patronage of the Flavians, he wrote *The Jewish War*, and subsequently, as a client of Epaphroditus, wrote *Jewish Antiquities*. The latter work is a twenty-volume history of the Jewish people, extending from creation to the last of the Roman procurators. The first ten volumes parallel biblical history.

Both of these works retell biblical narratives as a means of bringing the text up-to-date and communicating ideas not yet developed, or simply not included, at the time of compilation and editing of the biblical text. Each author presents these narratives and characters in his own particular, intriguing way. For example, Pseudo-Philo is clearly sympathetic to women, often introducing feminine imagery and significantly upgrading women's status and roles vis-à-vis the biblical accounts, while Josephus frequently—though not consistently—depreciates women and downgrades their roles. As we will see, these alterations are largely shaped by the authors' perspectives and agendas in writing their respective works.

Certainly, scholars have made great strides in assessing the portrayal of women in the biblical text itself, although with differing opinions as to the significance of the data. Many scholars maintain that biblical religion, the product of these texts, embodies and perpetuates men's dominance of women.[2] Some have opened up possibilities of different interpretations of biblical texts through feminist reinterpretation.[3] The fruit of their work is a new, more positive image of those women portrayed in biblical literature. This is not to say that patriarchalism, men's dominance over women, in Jewish and Christian tradition has been laid to rest simply by the stroke of a feminist pen. In some cases, however, feminist approaches reveal that women in the Bible are not portrayed as negatively as would seem at first glance.[4] In the same way, the study of interpretations of the Bible can open up new possibilities as well as documenting continuing devaluation of women.

Despite considerable interest in women in the Bible, in both the Hebrew and Christian scriptures, not many scholars have expressed interest in the portrayal of women in the literature that developed during the post-biblical period, particularly during the years of formative Judaism and Christianity. Only a few have focused upon those texts designated as deuterocanonical books by Roman Catholics and as the Apocrypha by Protestants, and upon the pseudepigraphic writings, which were not recognized as authoritative by either group.[5]

Negative portrayals of women can be traced through these postbiblical works and into the later interpretations of the ancient Rabbis, texts such as the *Letter of Aristeas*, the *Book of Adam and Eve*, and the *Testaments of the Twelve Patriarchs*.[6] These and other texts reflect a significant movement in the direction of misogyny, as their authors, who were influenced by a Persian dualistic worldview, sought to account for the origin of evil. Indeed, some went so far as to portray women as solely culpable for the origin and perpetuation of evil. For example, one view is based on a reinterpretation of Genesis 6:1–5 and identifies "the sons of God" as rebellious angels (also called Watchers) who had sexual relations with "the daughters of men." The offspring of these unions then became demons after their bodies were destroyed in the Flood (*1 Enoch* 10, 15–16). Frequently, this story was linked with that of the Fall in Genesis 3, and a further element was introduced—that women seduced the angels. A prime example is found in the *Testament of Reuben*, one of the *Testaments of the Twelve Patriarchs:*

> For women are evil, my children, and by reason of their lacking authority or power over man, they scheme treacherously how they might entice him to themselves

by means of their looks. And whomever they cannot en-
chant by their appearance they conquer by a stratagem.
... They contrive in their hearts against men, then by
decking themselves out they lead men's minds astray,
by a look they implant their poison, and finally in the
act itself they take them captive.... For it was thus that
they charmed the Watchers, who were before the Flood
(*T. Reuben* 5:1–3, 5).

Likewise, Philo of Alexandria offered his own interpretations of biblical narratives and characters, including
women, although his main concern was not to interpret
the Bible but rather to conform the Bible to Platonic
philosophy. His governing methodology was to allegorize
the text. Hence, the characters came to stand for philosophical principles or spiritual truths. This can be seen in
Philo's understanding of the process by which a person
is led to sin, which is based upon his interpretation of
the three characters in the story of the Fall in Genesis 2.
According to Philo, Adam, who represents the mind, is
enticed by Eve, who represents the senses and is deceived
by pleasure, the serpent (*De Agricultura* 97). Elsewhere
he comments more directly: "It was the more imperfect
and ignoble element, the female, that made a beginning
of transgression and lawlessness, while the male made
the beginning of reverence and modesty and all good,
since he was better and more perfect" (*Quaestiones et Solu-
tiones in Genesin* 1.43). For Philo, the mind (male) stands
as the highest good, while the senses or sense perception (female) corrupts and destroys the mind. The male
is also consistently portrayed as active, while the female
is passive.

The trend continues into rabbinic Judaism, particularly
in the Midrash. The Hebrew word "Midrash" basically
means "interpretation," and the term "haggadic Midrash"
generally refers to the many homiletic commentaries on
certain biblical books, the earliest of which took the form
of a verse-by-verse commentary. These texts were com-

piled and edited at a much later date (beginning c. 400 C.E.), but are known to incorporate traditions datable to the first century C.E. Although some commentators attempt to persuade us that women are characterized positively[7] in this literature, others demonstrate convincingly that despite a few positive statements about women, the overall portrayal is negative.[8] Nehama Ashkenasay, for example, observes that a comparison of the biblical text and later rabbinic interpretations often reveals a rabbinic tendency to shape the stories according to a sexist bias.[9]

Pseudo-Philo's *Biblical Antiquities* and Josephus's *Jewish Antiquities* are two texts that stand within this same general historical-cultural setting and literary genre, being early Jewish documents that retell the biblical story. Surprisingly, however, neither text's portrayal of women has drawn much interest from scholars. James L. Bailey, who published an article entitled "Josephus' Portrayal of the Matriarchs," points out the need for further scholarly investigation of Josephus's portrayal of women: "Little has been published on the view of women presented in the writings of Flavius Josephus . . . [although] a careful examination of Josephus' writings could yield important results for the study of women in antiquity since these works offer . . . Josephus' own reworked portrayals of women from the biblical tradition."[10]

Josephus gives both direct and indirect expression to his views concerning women. For example, in *Jewish Antiquities* he adds to the biblical text a restriction upon women giving legal testimony: "From women let no evidence be accepted, because of the levity and temerity of their sex" (*Ant.* 4.219). We find a most direct statement in another of his works, *Against Apion*: "The woman, says the Law, is in all things inferior to the man. Let her accordingly be submissive, not for her humiliation, but that she may be directed; for the authority has been given by God to the man" (*CAp* 2.201).

Josephus also often qualifies complimentary material by adding that such commendable conduct is not typical of women, as in the following example from his history of the first Jewish revolt against Rome, called *The Jewish War*. Here, he describes the escape of the only survivors from the mass execution/suicide at Masada during the final days of the war: "But an old woman and another, a relative of Eleazar, superior in sagacity and training to most of her sex, with five children, escaped by concealing themselves in the subterranean aqueducts" (*BJ* 7.399). Note also the implications about women in his description of the Essenes: "They [the Essenes] do not, indeed, on principle, condemn wedlock and the propagation thereby of the race, but they wish to protect themselves against women's wantonness, being persuaded that none of the sex keeps her plighted troth to one man" (*BJ* 2.121; see also *Ant.* 18.21).

In his version of Adam and Eve's fall in Genesis 3, Josephus makes a statement about the place of women through very subtly rewriting the story. According to him, "God imposed punishment on Adam for yielding to a woman's counsel" (*Ant.* 1.49), rather than the biblical "Because you listened to your wife and ate from the tree. . . . " This change transfers the emphasis from condemnation of Adam's specific act that was suggested by his wife, to the general "sin" of letting a woman tell him what to do.[11]

These are some of Josephus's fairly direct statements regarding women and their roles. What about his indirect statements? Do his stated views of women ever color his portrayals of biblical women in the *Jewish Antiquities*? We will see that in some cases he clearly alters the biblical text in order to bring it into conformity with these views, while in one of his portraits he lays aside those opinions in the interest of pursuing the overriding goals of his work.

Likewise, Pseudo-Philo's *Biblical Antiquities,* another first-century Jewish reinterpretation of the Bible, provides a rich resource of information concerning the status and roles of women. Surprisingly, the text has been largely neglected by scholars, in part because a critical edition of the text (*editio princeps*) has only recently become accessible to a wider audience. But the paucity of interest in the portrayal of women in the *Biblical Antiquities* may also reflect the priorities and agenda of most modern scholars, as Ross Kraemer has keenly observed: "There has been very little careful scholarly consideration of women in the varieties of Judaism in late antiquity."[12] Both *Biblical Antiquities* and *Jewish Antiquities* fall into the category of "varieties of Judaism," being neither included in the Bible nor accepted as authoritative by Jews or Christians.

An expression of the variant nature of the *Biblical Antiquities* is its portrayal of women biblical figures. In many cases, the author adds words, phrases, or blocks of material that explicitly include them—or upgrade their character and roles[13]—in the biblical story he retells. The treatise consistently includes women in the genealogical lists and frequently specifies them in worship contexts that in the biblical text involve only men. For example, Dinah is included in the summary of the descendants of Jacob's children: "And Dinah their sister bore fourteen sons and six daughters" (*Bib. Ant.* 8.11).[14] Pseudo-Philo also employs feminine imagery where the Bible does not,[15] and attributes to women key roles that highlight women's spirituality. Miriam takes on special prominence. She predicts Moses' birth through a dream (*Bib. Ant.* 9.10; see 9.15), and the motif of Miriam's Well—itself a variation of Wisdom imagery—occurs repeatedly (*Bib. Ant.* 10.7; 11.15; 20.8). Although these are not unique to *Biblical Antiquities* (many appear also in rabbinic biblical interpretation),[16] the author's inclusion of these Miriam traditions indicates that his own community recognized the special character and value of women's spirituality.

The omissions in *Biblical Antiquities* are equally significant. In an era in which the feminine role in the origin and perpetuation of evil was increasingly emphasized, the author chose to attribute the origin of evil to the invention of musical instruments, which led to sexual sins,[17] and working with metals, which led to idolatry (*Bib. Ant.* 2.7–10).

We can see that a study of the portrayal of women in both of these documents promises to contribute to the overall picture of women in early Judaism, at the time of nascent Christianity. Both characterize women in ways that differ significantly from their biblical counterparts, and thus both open a window into the world of Judaism as it took shape in rabbinic circles soon after the destruction of Jerusalem. Moreover, these texts were preserved not by Jews but by Christians; their preservation reflects the value accorded them in some early Christian circles. Thus, our investigation of the portrayal of women in these two books can result in our gaining some new perspectives on the subject of women in Judeo-Christian tradition during the Greco-Roman period.

To round out the picture, we must hear minority voices as well as majority voices. Hannah speaks for all of these women when she declares: "Speak,... Hannah, and no longer be silent" (*Bib. Ant.* 51.6). Voices too long silent now speak through these significant figures in Jewish and Christian tradition. Their message is worthy of the attention of all who seek to understand the thought-world out of which both Judaism and Christianity emerged.

Overview of *Biblical Antiquities* and *Jewish Antiquities*

Before turning to our analysis of the portrayal of biblical women in these texts, we must first look at the texts as a whole. What are their overall character, purpose, tendencies, and logic?

First of all, they are products of a literary process[18] described as rewriting the Bible,[19] a form related to Jewish midrashic[20] and targumic interpretation, both of which clarify and actualize the biblical text by incorporating new interpretations into the flow of the text itself. While the Midrash generally follows the pattern of quoting a verse followed by commentary, the Targums, which are basically translations of the Jewish scriptures from Hebrew into Aramaic embellished by numerous haggadic traditions, weave the commentary into the fabric of the text so that the distinction between text and interpretation is obliterated.

Authors employ a variety of interpretive techniques in composing this type of literature. Some of these are: (1) wordplay; (2) interpreting one scripture by another, based on a common word or allusion; (3) quoting one part of a verse, assuming that the readers will mentally complete it and even continue with verses that follow in the context; and (4) interpreting a text apart from its obvious meaning in context. Midrashic literature, including the Targums and Rewritten Bible, also often adds dialogue and/or narrative material not found in the biblical text, or removes those elements that are difficult to explain or unacceptable in light of later theological developments. The interpreters' use of the sacred story to communicate their own ideas and messages to their contemporaries gives those ideas and messages a special character and authority, serving to validate their stories as divine revelation in its fullest sense. We will see that both Pseudo-Philo and Josephus employ these techniques in their compositions.

Pseudo-Philo's *Biblical Antiquities*

The author of *Biblical Antiquities*[21] interprets the Bible by modifying the biblical text, either by omissions[22] or additions, the additions taking the form of narrative sections, speeches, hymns, and prayers. Many of the additions correspond to traditions incorporated into targumic lit-

erature or rabbinic Midrash,[23] as well as to some themes
and stories in Greco-Roman literature. But the significant
number that are unique to *Biblical Antiquities*[24] indicate
areas of particular concern for its author.

The text is extant only in Latin manuscripts, although it
was probably originally written in Hebrew (possibly Aramaic) and then translated into Greek before receiving
final form in Latin. It was virtually unknown until it was
edited and published by Johannes Sichardus in 1527. He
based the first published edition upon two manuscripts—
Fulda (eleventh century) and another one not presently
known. The text subsequently fell into obscurity until
1898, when L. Cohn brought it to the attention of the
scholarly world through his article "An Apocryphal Work
Ascribed to Philo of Alexandria."[25] The goal of Cohn's
work was that *Biblical Antiquities* "be rescued from its
obscurity,"[26] and the fruit of that work was the publication
of the first English translation by M. R. James in 1917.[27]
A newer English translation by Daniel J. Harrington appears in volume two of *The Old Testament Pseudepigrapha*
and, unless otherwise noted, serves as the translation for
this study.

Nevertheless, the text remained somewhat out of reach
of most scholars because the first edition in Latin, the
editio princeps, was not accessible. Guido Kisch changed
this situation by publishing the first Latin edition since
Sichardus's *editio princeps*. However, despite the value of
his work, he has been criticized because of his prefer-
ence for the textual readings of a different manuscript
(the Admont) over the *editio princeps*, without giving full
consideration to each individual reading, and the majority of scholars continue to follow the *editio princeps*.[28] The
most complete and reliable resource for studying *Biblical Antiquities* is *Pseudo-Philon: Les Antiquités Bibliques*,[29]
a critical edition of all available manuscripts, including a
critical introduction to the text, as well as translation into
French, literary introduction, and textual commentary.

Both the date and provenance of *Biblical Antiquities*

continue to be debated.[30] On the issue of dating, a majority of scholars accepts a date in the first century, but they do not agree on whether it dates to before or after the destruction of Jerusalem in 70 C.E. Most ascribe it to the period following the destruction of Jerusalem, on the basis of internal evidence and its close correspondence to two other Jewish documents that refer explicitly to the destruction of Jerusalem and the Temple, *2 Apocalypse of Baruch* and *4 Ezra.*

While there is no such unambiguous reference in *Biblical Antiquities,* the treatise certainly reflects a people in crisis, whose very existence is in question.[31] The repeated emphasis upon God's irrevocable covenantal promises and the repeated assurance that God has indeed not abandoned Israel forever, but will ultimately send "the saving power of His covenant" (*Bib. Ant.* 32.15)[32] to destroy Israel's enemies and restore the nation, most naturally point to the circumstances of the Jewish people after the destruction of Jerusalem, when their very existence was threatened.[33]

The people themselves specify that their punishment for sin has included banishment from the Land. As they gather together in repentance at the "mountain of Judah" to seek God's forgiveness and help, they declare, "Now we have been humiliated more than all peoples so that we cannot dwell in our own land" (*Bib. Ant.* 30.4). Other tendencies—concern for proper leadership, communal harmony, keeping of the Torah rather than messianic zealotry,[34] and lack of emphasis upon the Temple cult—also support a postdestruction date, though these in themselves need not relate exclusively to a post-destruction community.

We can detect allusions to the destruction of Jerusalem in two biblical narratives reshaped by the author. He rewrites the biblical story of the Philistines' capture of the Ark (1 Sam. 4) by adding that shortly beforehand, God sent Samuel from Shiloh to "look around Ramathaim" to see where he would live (*Bib. Ant.* 55.1). Hence, Samuel was not present when the battle was lost and the Ark was captured by Israel's enemy. Here, the author adapts a motif commonly associated with legends surrounding both the first and second destruction of Jerusalem, to the effect that because the Temple could not be destroyed while a righteous person was present (the righteous assure divine protection), God deliberately removed such persons from the city to give a free hand to the destroying forces. These legends find basis in the biblical text, primarily in Jeremiah 32:6–15 and Ezekiel 10:1–22, where God (the glory) departs from the Temple shortly before it is destroyed.[35]

Likewise, the author rewrites the story of Israel's slavery in Egypt by adding that in response to pharaoh's oppression, the Israelites decide to refrain from procreation so their children would not become slaves for the Egyptians (*Bib. Ant.* 9.2). Moses' father, Amram, speaks forcefully against this decision and convinces them to continue to have children. His response resembles that of Rabbi Eliezer ben Hyrcannus, who after the destruction of Jerusalem in 70 C.E. rebuked those Jews who abstained from procreation because they did not want to see their children serving as slaves to the Romans.[36]

Besides historical and literary clues, textual evidence also helps to establish some bounds regarding the date. Daniel J. Harrington has argued convincingly that *Biblical Antiquities* was composed before 100 C.E., for behind the Latin text stands a Palestinian Hebrew textual tradition that was suppressed when an official text was established at around the turn of the era. Clearly, this evidence suggests an outer limit for the document; but internal evidence (such as outlined above), along with parallels with *2 Apocalypse of Baruch* and *4 Ezra*, point to a composition sometime after 70 C.E. We should probably look more closely to 70 C.E. because of the general tenor of the book, it being an expression of a nation very much engaged in the process of coming to terms with a nearly fatal crisis and determining its response.

The geographical origins (provenance) of our document are even more difficult to ascertain than its date.[37] Most scholars view it as a Palestinian document on the basis of the underlying text and affinities with rabbinic Judaism. Marc Philonenko argues that its emphasis upon such themes as Torah, knowledge, and light points to an origin among the Jewish sect of the Essenes.[38] Whether or not this is true depends upon his definition of Essene. If he means that branch of Essenism that we know from the apocalyptic priestly community by the Dead Sea at Qumran—as it appears he does[39]—he cannot be correct, for he fails to consider the author's nearly complete lack of interest in cultic matters (including ritual purity and baptism)[40] and the overwhelmingly positive portrayal of women, both of which contradict the philosophy and practices of the Qumran sect.[41] If, rather, he means that branch of Essenism antecedent to the Johannine Christian community, he may not be far from the truth.

Charles Perrot suggests that *Biblical Antiquities* is a product of Palestinian Judaism, but raises in passing the issue of a Diaspora (outside the Land of Israel) provenance,[42] based on its strong polemic against mixed marriages. While mixed marriage and assimilation were very real issues in Jewish communities outside the Land of Israel, this concern need not necessarily point to such a context, for the issue of mixed marriages was also very crucial on Palestinian soil, as evidenced by the strong polemic against them in the Jewish book of *Jubilees* (e.g., *Jub.* 30), which most scholars believe to be a product of Palestinian Judaism.

It appears the cumulative evidence points to a Diaspora provenance, although one with close ties with the Palestinian Jewish community. I would narrow the possibilities even further and suggest that it is probably a Syrian composition, or at least that it received its final editing within a Syrian Jewish community. Certainly, Syria was closely linked with Palestine, both religiously and ad-

ministratively at the turn of the era. Syrian Antioch was
the Roman capital of an administrative district that included Palestine,[43] and at that time relations between Jews
of the two communities were quite good.[44] Indeed, the
ties between Syria and (particularly) northern Palestine
were so close that these areas were often considered one
integral unit.

Because my assumption of a Syrian provenance stands
apart from other interpretations, permit me a brief digression to present some of the evidence in support of
this conclusion. I will not pause at this point to analyze
specific references in the text, but will simply make a few
general observations.

The ideas, practices, and exegetical traditions represented in *Biblical Antiquities* correspond markedly to those
in documents that can be identified with reasonable certainty as Syrian and dated to the turn of the era. These
are by and large Christian documents (though they have
both Jewish and Christian backgrounds); some stand in
continuity with sectarian Judaism of the type represented
in the Qumran scrolls, particularly the hymnbook of the
Dead Sea community, the Thanksgiving Scroll.[45] These
texts are the Gospel of Matthew, the Johannine literature
(the Gospel of John, the epistles of John, and the Apocalypse), the *Odes of Solomon* (an early Christian hymnbook),
and the epistles of Ignatius, bishop of Antioch (c. 35–107
C.E.).

J. H. Charlesworth has carefully traced the parallels between the Qumran scrolls, the Gospel of John, and the
Odes of Solomon, particularly in relation to the theme of
dualism, and concludes that both the odist and the author of the Gospel were strongly influenced by Essene
thought.[46] *Biblical Antiquities* also reflects this tendency.[47]
Other elements that all share in common are the prominence of hymnology[48] and mystical experiences,[49] as well
as an emphasis upon the Word of God (whether by its Hebrew designation, Torah, or its Greek equivalent, Logos)
and its identification with light and water. An impor-

tant element that our document holds in common with the Gospel of John is the prominence of women, and both *Biblical Antiquities* and the *Odes of Solomon* contain feminine imagery that at times is striking.

The combination of emphasis upon the Word of God, with its various metaphors, and the prominence of women and feminine imagery gives expression to a motif that pervades these documents—the motif of Wisdom. Already in Sirach, an early second-century B.C.E. Jewish text, Torah is equated with Wisdom. At the end of his lengthy acclamation of Wisdom, the author declares: "All this is the book of the covenant of the Most High God, the law that Moses commanded us" (Sir. 24:23).[50] Philo of Alexandria identifies the Logos with Wisdom (*LA* 1.63).[51] It is widely held that the prologue to John's Gospel incorporates elements from a Wisdom myth,[52] and elsewhere the Gospel clearly employs Wisdom motifs.[53] This same tendency also pervades the Gospel of Matthew, as James M. Robinson demonstrates in his article "Jesus as Sophos and Sophia": "Scholars today prefer to locate the full identification of Jesus as Sophia incarnate as taking place first in Matthew."[54] Inasmuch as both the Gospel of Matthew and the Gospel of John (in an earlier stage) probably derive from a Syrian Christian community, we may reasonably conclude that "dame Wisdom" had a very high profile in that area.

The preponderance of Wisdom imagery and feminine imagery in general in this literature is in part due to the influence of the worship of goddesses, whether Isis, the ancient Egyptian mother goddess, or other Greco-Roman or Oriental deities.[55] Some Hellenistic Jews adapted qualities and characteristics of Isis to their own descriptions of Wisdom, with the result that Wisdom was soon transformed from an abstract concept into a lifelike entity with a distinctive personality. David Winston points out specific examples of this transference in his commentary on the Wisdom of Solomon, a first-century Hellenistic Jewish text.[56]

Isis was known by a variety of names, many of which identify her using some form of the designation "mother," for example, "mother of the Gods," "mother of all living," "all-mother."[57] Indeed, many scholars maintain that she reappears as "mother of the Church" (*mater ecclesia*), a doctrine rooted in Syrian soil.[58]

Certainly, goddess worship was popular in Syria in the first century C.E. D. S. Wallace-Hadrill notes that on a relief discovered in excavations at Dura Europos, a town on the Euphrates, "the goddess [was] notably bigger and more impressive than the god."[59] Perhaps the goddess's popularity in Syria was the source of some of the imagery employed in the *Odes of Solomon*, which, as we have noted, are of Syrian provenance. Ode 19 describes God, the Father(!), in feminine terms: "A cup of milk was offered to me, and I drank it in the sweetness of the Lord's kindness. The Son is the cup, and the Father is he who was milked; and the Holy Spirit is she who milked him; because his breasts were full, and it was undesirable that his milk should be released without purpose" (19:1–3).

The popularity of goddess worship may also stand behind the positive valuation of women in many Syrian texts. Sarah Pomeroy sees a link between Isis worship in Italy and the increased status and freedom of women: "The establishment of the cult of Isis in Italy in the late Republic coincided with the growing emancipation of women."[60] If that is true, then it is also possible that the significant "feminine element in Syrian Christianity"[61] results from a similar dynamic, a vibrant feminine element in religious experience.[62] Moreover, it is possible that a similar phenomenon occurred with relation to the socio-religious context of *Biblical Antiquities*; that is, the feminine tendencies in the treatise are an expression of a feminine element in the religious experience of its author.

Surely, this factor does not necessarily point to a Syrian provenance, for Isis was worshiped even on Palestinian soil.[63] But the affinities with texts that are clearly identifiable as Syrian weigh the balance in favor of Syria, probably Antioch. We will look more closely at these affinities as we analyze individual portraits in the following chapters. At this point, it is enough to raise the issue as a foundation for our study of *Biblical Antiquities*. We will keep this hypothesis in mind as we examine the document more closely, and determine if the evidence validates or contradicts it. If the hypothesis stands, it follows that our text serves as a link between Jewish and Christian communities at a time when they were going their separate ways. Thus, more than simply being a witness to a side of Judaism sympathetic to women, *Biblical Antiquities* fulfills a broader function of witnessing to the close relation between Judaism and Christianity in their earliest years.

Women are not the only concern—or even the primary concern—of the author of the treatise, who has broader purposes in rewriting biblical history, whether he chooses to accomplish these purposes through women's stories or men's stories. For one, his decision to express his ideas through rewriting segments of the book of Judges[64] reveals a desire to call the people to repentance and assure them of God's continued faithfulness to the divine covenants (solemn pledges made by God to the Jewish people), as well as his concern with proper leadership for the people. Indeed, the most important, overarching theme is God's covenant[65] with Israel, its demands (obedience to the Torah), and its promises (blessings of land and progeny).[66] Within this framework, the author also emphasizes Israel's punishment for failure to live up to covenantal demands, primarily by falling into idolatry and intermarrying with Gentiles,[67] and the sure promise of eventual vindication and restoration, based upon obedience to God's will as revealed in the Jewish scriptures (the Torah).

A further theme concerns Israel's leadership.[68] Israel's leaders cause the people to sin and to disobey the Torah; they are condemned particularly for leading the people astray and for remaining silent in the face of sin or attack by outsiders.[69] The author is also concerned with the issue

of relations among the Jewish people, highlighting inter-
communal conflict[70] and episodes of reconciliation.[71] He
also incorporates information about afterlife, angels, and
the state of the world at the end of the age.[72] All of these
issues are skillfully woven into the biblical narratives; in
the present study, I am particularly interested in how he
weaves them into characterizations and stories of biblical
women.

Josephus's *Jewish Antiquities*

The first ten volumes of *Jewish Antiquities* are a free
rewriting of biblical history. Josephus paraphrases the biblical text, expands it with a variety of legendary material,
and excises those parts that are unacceptable either to
him or to his readers. Some of his legendary material parallels traditions preserved in rabbinic Midrash,[73] in the
works of Philo,[74] in Hellenistic Jewish historiography,[75]
and in *Biblical Antiquities*.[76]

Josephus's own explicit declaration of his twofold purpose in writing *Jewish Antiquities* simplifies the task of
ascertaining his goals for this work. They are (1) to
present the Jewish people and religion in a positive light
to the Greco-Roman world (*Ant.* 1.5–13); and (2) to persuade his readers to conform to the will of God (*Ant.*
1.14–15).

Josephus arranges and presents his material in order
to accomplish these goals. He describes biblical personalities in philosophical categories familiar to Greco-Roman
readers and draws parallels with their own literature and
culture.[77] He also condenses much of the legal and other
nonnarrative material that would not interest a non-
Jewish audience. At the same time, he seeks to draw
lessons, primarily of an ethical nature, from the biblical narratives and often rewrites them to highlight these
lessons.

According to Josephus's own testimony (*Ant.* 20.267), he wrote *Jewish Antiquities* in 93/94 C.E.[78] Its original language was probably Greek,[79] and it was translated into Latin in the fourth century.[80]

Only recently have scholars—even women scholars—shown interest in Josephus's portrayal of women.[81]

Focus and Method of Study

This study provides a descriptive analysis of the portrayals of several women biblical figures in *Biblical Antiquities* and *Jewish Antiquities* and then contrasts those portrayals by the respective authors. I have singled out four characters for study—Deborah, Jephthah's daughter, Hannah, and the witch of Endor. Both authors deal at some length with these particular figures, and their portraits are varied enough to reveal some general attitudes toward women held by each author. Each of the first four chapters in this study will analyze the portrait of one biblical woman according to the following method:

1. Those elements in the story that are unique to the respective authors will be isolated. I will compare those elements first of all with the biblical text and then with other interpretive works of nearly the same period: that is, those in the Pseudepigrapha, Targums, Midrash, Hellenistic Jewish works, or the literature of the broader Greco-Roman world.

2. These elements in the portrait will be evaluated based upon the data gained from this comparative analysis.

3. I will draw conclusions concerning the individual author's overall portrayal of the character and apparent aims of that characterization, in light of the author's background, purpose, and audience.

4. I will compare the portraits in *Biblical Antiquities* and *Jewish Antiquities*.

Chapter 5 will include a summary description of both authors' portraits and general conclusions concerning the overall portrayal of women in each document.

Notes

1. This text is known by several titles. M. R. James suggests that the title *Biblical Antiquities* may have been given by its first editor, Johannes Sichardus, "due to a recollection of Josephus' great work, the *Jewish Antiquities*" (M. R. James, *Biblical Antiquities of Philo*, 27). Another title, *Liber Antiquitatum Biblicarum* (in Eng.: *Book of Biblical Antiquities*), does not appear in any manuscript of the text but is used frequently by scholars, especially in its abbreviated form, *Bib. Ant.*, for referencing specific passages in the text. I will follow this general usage when referencing *Biblical Antiquities* in this study.

2. Such a view is articulated by Nehama Ashkenasay although she does not exactly hold to this view in her book: "Some . . . argue that social patriarchy and all its accompanying evils were buttressed by monotheism, which they describe—with some justification—as essentially a father religion" (*Eve's Journey*, 9). See also Fiorenza, "Will to Choose or Reject"; Ruether, "Feminist Interpretation."

3. In addition to the works cited above, see, for example, Trible, *Texts of Terror*; Sakenfeld, "Feminist Uses," 63ff.

4. Ashkenasay attempts to look beyond the traditional interpretations to the stories themselves: "Still, a close reading of many biblical tales that revolve around women yields mixed results as to the Bible's conception of women. . . . Even those stories that throughout the ages have been read as paradigms of female subordination may sometimes reveal a surprisingly unbiased attitude to women and an egalitarian conception of the roles of the sexes" (*Eve's Journey*, 10).

5. For example, Warren C. Trenchard (*Ben Sira's View of Women*) investigated the portrayal of women in the book of Sirach and argues convincingly that Ben Sirah was a misogynist.

Gilbert ("Ben Sira et la femme") maintains the opposite view in his study of the same book. Likewise, the book of Judith has been the focus of a number of studies. See Craven, *Artistry and Faith*; Alonso-Schökel, "Narrative Structures"; C. Moore, "Judith."

6. The development of thought concerning women in these and other texts is surveyed by Leonard Swidler in his book *Women in Judaism*. He concludes that "the attitude toward women . . . is very strongly, even overwhelmingly, negative, reaching at times the peaks of hatred" (p. 45).

7. Raphael Loewe (*Position of Women in Judaism*, 26) is one who concludes that on the whole women are characterized positively.

8. See Swidler, *Women in Judaism*, 70–82; Lachs, *Women in Judaism*, 105–8.

9. Ashkenasay, *Eve's Journey*, 11.

10. Bailey, "Josephus' Portrayal," 154.

11. For further references, see Feldman, "Josephus' Portrait of Deborah," 116–20.

12. Kraemer, "Women in the Religions," 131. For further discussion of the "varieties of Judaism," see Neusner, "Varieties of Judaism."

13. In a very few cases, the modifications serve to portray women more negatively. We will see this process at work in the portrayal of the witch of Endor; however, the negative portrayal is not directed against women per se, but against the role played by a particular woman.

14. Interestingly, the author presents Dinah as the wife of Job (*Bib. Ant.* 8.8). Although another Jewish text, the *Testament of Job*, incorporates this tradition (e.g., *T. Job* 36:33), *Biblical Antiquities* is unique in its assertion that she remained Job's wife throughout his ordeal and bore him twenty children.

15. For example, *Bib. Ant.* 12.5; 21.6; 39.5; 62.10. Note that when God recounts Israel's sins, quoting a commandment and then stating how Israel has disobeyed it, God declares: "Whereas I have told them to love father and mother, they have dishonored me, their Creator" (*Bib. Ant.* 44.7). "Father and mother" stands in parallelism with "Creator," thus suggesting that God is both mother and father (see Deut. 32:18; Isa. 49:15).

16. See Ginzberg (*Legends,* 3:50–54) for a fuller treatment of the legend of Miriam's Well in Jewish thought.

17. We find a similar polemic by early Christians who opposed the use of musical instruments in worship. Note the close parallel to our text in the Clementine *Recognitions,* a Jewish-Christian document that states that after the Flood unbelieving and wicked men "introduced false and perverse religions and contrived banquets with food and drink. Led astray by feasts and festivities, the greater part of mankind gave itself over and followed the playing of flutes, shepherd's pipes, citharas and all sorts of musical instruments.... With this every error had its beginning" (*Recognitions* 4.13). This example and others are quoted in Quasten, *Music and Worship,* 60–62.

18. I use the term "process" rather than "genre" based on Daniel J. Harrington's suggestions and conclusions in "Palestinian Adaptations." Harrington distinguishes "Rewritten Bible" from a Targum or Midrash, describing it rather as "a free rewriting of parts of Israel's sacred history" (p. 242). For further information, see Vermes, *Scripture and Tradition*; Patte, *Early Jewish Hermeneutic,* 233–36; Endres, *Biblical Interpretation*; and Nickelsburg, "Bible Rewritten."

19. The phrase "Rewritten Bible" was introduced to the scholarly world in 1961 by Geza Vermes (*Scripture and Tradition*), who published a collection of studies that built upon the foundation laid by Renée Bloch in her seminal work on Midrash (see Bloch, "Midrash"). Unfortunately, Vermes never defines the phrase.

20. There is no consensus on the definition of Midrash. See, for example, the article by Roger Le Deaut: "Apropos a Definition of Midrash." Addison G. Wright has devoted a book to the subject (*The Literary Genre Midrash*); his definition, which some regard as too narrow, has not been accepted as definitive. For an extensive bibliography on Midrash, see Haas, "Bibliography on Midrash."

21. For general introductory information, see M. R. James, *Biblical Antiquities of Philo*; Feldman, "Prolegomenon," vii–clxix; Kisch, *Pseudo-Philo's Liber Antiquitatum Biblicarum*; Cohn, "An Apocryphal Work"; and *OTP,* 297–303.

22. For example, see Nickelsburg, "Good and Bad Leaders," 49.

23. Numerous parallels to other Jewish and early Christian literature are cited by Feldman, "Prolegomenon," li–lxx.

24. Ibid., lxx–lxxvi.

25. For publication data, see the Bibliography.

26. Cohn, "Apocryphal Work," 279.

27. It has also been translated into German, French (see Bibliography under *Pseudo-Philon*), modern Hebrew, and Spanish.

28. Feldman, "Prolegomenon," xix–xx; Vermes, *Scripture and Tradition,* 9 n. 2; Harrington, "A Decade of Research," 4.

29. For publication data see the Bibliography under *Pseudo-Philon.*

30. The various positions are summarized by Davies and Chilton, "Aqedah," 517 n. 7.

31. *Bib. Ant.* 19.6; 23.7–13; 24.2; 26.13; 39.7.

32. *Bib. Ant.* 32.12, 13; 35.2–3; 39.16; 49.3.

33. See Nickelsburg, "Good and Bad Leaders," 63.

34. *Bib. Ant.* (Anchor Bible) 56.2; 57.3–4; 58.4; 62.9. Murphy ("2 Baruch and the Romans," 663, 667–68) discusses a similar concern in *2 Apocalypse of Baruch.*

35. See Ginzberg, *Legends,* 4:322–23. See also Josephus, *BJ* 7.299–300; and *2 Apoc. Bar.* 8:2.

36. *Yebam* 63b: "R. Eliezer said, 'Anyone who does not engage in the propagation of the race is as though he sheds blood; for it is said, "Whoso sheddeth man's blood," and close upon it follows, "And you, be fruitful etc."' R. Eleazar b. Azariah said, 'As though he diminished the Divine Image.'"

37. Charles Perrot (in *Pseudo-Philon,* 2:65) discusses various scholarly positions on this issue.

38. Philonenko, "Une paraphrase"; idem, "Essénisme et gnose."

39. He refers to "l'essénisme quomrânien" ("Essénisme et gnose," 406) and otherwise compares *Biblical Antiquities* with Qumran texts in his section on the Essenes. Elsewhere ("Une paraphrase," 158) he clearly associates the author with Qumran literature: "Le Pseudo-Philon se révèle ainsi comme un maître du midrash essénien, genre illustré par le livre des Jubilés et l'Apocryphe de la Genèse."

40. The one reference to baptism appears in the story of Kenaz, who, after killing the Amorite, "took off his clothes and threw himself into the river and washed himself" (*Bib. Ant.*

27.12). But this is a special case and in no way represents a major concern with ritual purity on the part of the author.

41. For an example of Essene attitudes concerning women, see Allegro, "Wiles"; Philo, *Hypothetica* 11.14–17; Josephus, *BJ* 2.120–21.

42. Perrot, in *Pseudo-Philon*, 2:65 n. 2.

43. See Kraeling, "Jewish Community."

44. Ibid., 146–47.

45. A Jewish text that fits into this category is the Syriac *Apocalypse of Baruch* (*2 Apoc. Bar.*). Moreover, many scholars believe that Gnosticism was a pre-Christian Jewish movement that began in Syria. See, for example, Pearson, "Jewish Elements"; Koester, *Introduction*, 1:209–11. Although *Biblical Antiquities* employs some vocabulary and other motifs sometimes associated with Gnosticism, it is not a Gnostic text; it reveals no negative valuation of the Creator God of the Hebrew scriptures and no interest in cosmic speculation.

46. Charlesworth, "Qumran."

47. For example, *Bib. Ant.* 32.10; 51.5; 61.6 (implied). Also note Pseudo-Philo's peculiar use of parental imagery to give expression to his dualistic tendency. He categorizes David and Goliath according to their two mothers: "And David went out to Goliath and said, . . . 'Were not the two women, from whom you and I were born, sisters? And your mother was Orpah, and my mother Ruth. And Orpah chose for herself the gods of the Philistines and went after them, but Ruth chose for herself the ways of the Most Powerful and walked in them'" (*Bib. Ant.* 61.6).

48. *Bib. Ant.* 18.6; 19.16; 21.8; 32.1–18; 40.1; 51.3–6; 59.4; 60.1–3. Certainly, hymnology was not limited to religious communities in Syria. Note, for example, the levitical hymns in Chronicles and Nehemiah, the hymns of Qumran, the *Psalms of Solomon*, as well as the hymns of Egyptian Jewish communities such as the Theraputae (see Philo, *Vita* 11, 83) and that which produced the *Testament of Job* (see *T. Job* 46–52). *Biblical Antiquities* probably did not originate in either of those communities, because it contains no explicit ascetic tendencies or evidence of the highly speculative, philosophical, and allegorical biblical interpretation so characteristic of Egyptian Judaism and Christianity. We know that women played a significant role in hymn singing in some early Christian communities. See

Quasten, *Music and Worship,* 75–87, and Koester, *Introduction,* 1:214.

49. *Bib. Ant.* 12.1; 28.6–10; 53.1–7; 60.1–3. This list does not include the many references to dreams in the text.

50. See *2 Apoc. Bar.* 48:24: "We . . . received one Law from the One. And that Law that is among us will help us, and that excellent wisdom which is in us will support us."

51. For further references, see Winston, *Wisdom of Solomon,* 59 n. 83; Fiorenza, "Wisdom Mythology," 34.

52. Koester (*Introduction,* 1:188) comments: "The term 'word' (*logos*) has replaced the older term 'wisdom' (*sophia*), something which also happened with Philo of Alexandria under Greek influence. Like the Jewish figure of Wisdom, the Logos is pre-existent with God, who creates the world through him. He appears in the world as the revealing light, is not understood, but gives to those who accept him the right to become God's children."

53. For example, John 6:35ff.; 7:33ff.; 8:21–23; 16:16ff.

54. Robinson, "Jesus as Sophos," 9. He cogently argues that this identification of Jesus with Wisdom occurred at the level of Matthean redaction rather than being present in Q (8, 10) and is based upon an identification of Jesus with Torah. See also Suggs, *Wisdom.*

55. Hans Conzelmann, among others, notes that as Isis worship spread throughout the Greco-Roman world, she became identified with local gods and goddesses and "hence represents syncretism itself" ("Mother," 234).

56. Winston, *Wisdom of Solomon,* 37; see also Witt, *Isis,* 194–95; Conzelmann, "Mother," 234–42.

57. See Witt, *Isis,* 130–35.

58. For example, see Plumpe, *Mater Ecclesia:* "It is . . . probable that in Asia Minor at about the half-way mark of the second century the *mater ecclesia* was received, fully developed, from the great center of Eastern Christianization, Antioch, through the gates of Syria" (p. 124).

59. Wallace-Hadrill, *Christian Antioch,* 15.

60. Pomeroy, *Goddesses,* 225.

61. Wallace-Hadrill, *Christian Antioch,* 167. In addition to describing God in feminine as well as masculine terms, valuing the gifts of women and allowing them to be used, and describing the church as "mother," Theophilus (Bishop of Antioch,

c. 180) conceives of the Trinity in a way that is a very interesting expression of this feminine element. He refers to the "'triad' of God, his Word and His Wisdom," where Wisdom stands in place of the Holy Spirit (quoted in Grant, "Problem of Theophilus," 188). Certainly this analogy between the Holy Spirit and Wisdom appears elsewhere, but Theophilus actually names Wisdom as the third Person of the Trinity.

62. Wallace-Hadrill, *Christian Antioch*, draws a similar parallel in his discussion of the feminine element in Syrian Christianity. My conclusions were arrived at independently of his work.

63. See Hengel, *Judaism and Hellenism*, 1:158.

64. Nickelsburg ("Bible Rewritten," 107) notes that one third of the material in *Biblical Antiquities* is parallel to the book of Judges. See also Nickelsburg, "Good and Bad Leaders," 49.

65. *Bib. Ant.* 2.43–44.

66. For example, *Bib. Ant.* 8.3; 10.2; 11.9; 23.7.

67. See Murphy, "Retelling the Bible."

68. Nickelsburg, "Good and Bad Leaders," 60.

69. For example, *Bib. Ant.* 45.4; 47.4, 8; 63.3.

70. For example, *Bib. Ant.* 6; 10.3; 39.4–5; 45.3.

71. For example, *Bib. Ant.* 6.18; 62.11; 65.5.

72. These are discussed by Perrot, in *Pseudo-Philon*, 2:52–63.

73. For examples, see Rappaport, *Agada und Exegese*. But see also Feldman's criticism in "Flavius Josephus Revisited": "[He] attempts to be exhaustive, but he is far from complete and suffers from the attempt to force parallels with rabbinic midrashim where they are sometimes far-fetched. He fails to realize that many of Josephus' changes may be due to a conscious appeal to his audience of Greek-speaking Jews and non-Jews" (p. 790).

74. See Heinemann, "Josephus' Method," 202; Smallwood, "Philo and Josephus," 114–32.

75. See Rajak, "Moses in Ethiopia"; Shinan, "Moses and the Ethiopian Woman."

76. Feldman, "Prolegomenon," lviii–lxvi.

77. Martin Braun discusses rather thoroughly the conventions and style of this type of literature in *History and Romance*.

78. There is some speculation about a second edition, published after 100, but the prevailing view is that there was only one edition. See Attridge, "Josephus," 210–11; Rajak, *Josephus*, 237–38.

79. The standard Greek text with English translation (based on the *editio maior* of Niese) is that of H. St. J. Thackeray, in the Loeb Classical Library series, which, unless otherwise noted, serves as the basis for my inquiry.

80. The text of the first half (the focus of my study) is rather corrupt, due to several factors, among which is the work of Christian censors and interpolators during the Middle Ages. Feldman ("Flavius Josephus Revisited," 770–71) remarks that the Latin text predates the oldest extant Greek manuscript by nearly five hundred years and is thus a valuable aid in reconstructing the Greek text.

81. The *Jewish Antiquities* has been studied extensively, as evidenced by the numerous related entries in Louis Feldman's mammoth annotated bibliography and supplement. On the subject of women in the *Antiquities,* note Feldman's comments ("Josephus' Portrait of Deborah," 115): "With the tremendous rise in recent years of interest in the portraits of women in ancient literature it is surprising that scholarship has neglected Josephus' portraits of women in Jewish history." The following are studies related to Josephus's portrayals of women: Amaru, "Portraits"; Bernstein, "Josephus"; Feldman, "Josephus' Portrait of Deborah"; idem, "Hellenizations in Josephus' Version of Esther"; Le Deaut, "Miriam"; Trencsényi-Waldapfel, "Die Hexe"; Wiseman, "Rahab of Jericho."

1

Deborah

Deborah stands out as a unique figure in the Hebrew Bible. Although scripture designates three other women as prophetesses (Miriam, Huldah, and Noadiah), none of them displays so many leadership capabilities and roles as Deborah. She is at once a prophetess, a poetess,[1] a great military leader on a par with male military leaders, and even a judge, not simply like others,[2] but a judge to whom Israelites turned for legal counsel and settling of court cases (Judg. 4:5). This is the only case in which the Bible presents a woman in this role. Indeed, Deborah is the only judge who was already serving in a leadership role when God commissioned her to lead the people to deliverance from their enemy (Judg. 4:4–5).

Deborah in the *Biblical Antiquities:*
A Leader Like Moses

Pseudo-Philo significantly upgrades this already prominent and illustrious biblical figure. Indeed, we will see that in *Biblical Antiquities,* she becomes the feminine counterpart to the greatest leader in all of Israel's history—Moses.

Setting the Stage:
Zebul and Kenaz's Daughters (*Bib. Ant.* 29)

Pseudo-Philo begins to lay the foundation for his portrayal of Deborah in the section preceding Deborah's story (*Bib. Ant.* 29); he does this by introducing a story that points to a transfer of power, deriving from land ownership, from male recipients to female recipients. Here, he has inserted the story of Zebul, a character of his own creation, although the name does occur in Judges (Judg. 9:20–34), where he is named as a leader of the Israelite city of Shechem during Abimelech's rule (Judg. 9:28–57). In the biblical account, the king totally destroys the city when his people rebel against him and then captures a neighboring city, Thebez (vv. 50ff.). Its citizens had fled to a tower, and as he moved to set it on fire, a woman dropped a millstone on him, cracking his skull (v. 53). We are told that Abimelech immediately directed his armor-bearer to kill him so no one could say, "A woman killed him" (v. 54). The allusion to the story of Abimelech at this point hints at what is to come in Deborah's story. Pseudo-Philo's audience would have been aware of the way in which Abimelech died—his head having been crushed by a woman (Judg. 9:54)—and would likely have turned their thoughts to another great enemy (Sisera) who was defeated by a woman (Jael), his own head crushed by a tent peg.

In *Biblical Antiquities,* Zebul follows the most important male judge, Kenaz, a figure created by the author (*Bib. Ant.* 25–28). Zebul is chosen by the people as leader— not judge—after Kenaz's death, and his first act in that capacity is to apportion Kenaz's property to Kenaz's three daughters: "And Zebul gave to the firstborn all that was around the land of the Phoenicians, and to the second he gave the olive grove of Ekron, but to the third he gave the tilled lands that were around Ashdod" (*Bib. Ant.* 29.1–2).[3]

Pseudo-Philo appears to build this episode around the account of Moses' ruling concerning Zelophehad's daughters, who were given their father's inheritance (Num. 36).[4] Outside of this case, in biblical practice women did not inherit property; in postbiblical Jewish practice, they generally were excluded from inheritance and ownership of property. Hence, this episode reflects the author's more positive perception of women, and his placing the story immediately before he introduces Deborah also serves to set the stage for a woman filling a role traditionally reserved for men.

Deborah's Leadership: God's Response to Israel's Repentance (*Bib. Ant.* 30)

Deborah's crucial ministry begins more or less as it does in the Bible. The people have fallen into apostasy and subsequently have been punished by God through enslavement by Jabin. In *Biblical Antiquities,* however, the brief biblical account is expanded by many interpretive elements; most of these modifications either point directly to Deborah or hint at her role before she is introduced into the narrative. This editorial activity, which serves to increase Deborah's status and build expectations about her leadership, reveals the author's intention to upgrade Deborah's role significantly.

We see that at the very outset of his version of the story, Pseudo-Philo introduces the element of crisis of leadership that is so characteristic of *Biblical Antiquities*;[5] according to him, the Israelites fall into apostasy because they "did not have anyone to appoint for themselves as judge" (*Bib. Ant.* 30.1). Without proper leadership, Israel cannot observe the commandments and thereby be liberated from those God sends to punish them. The fact that Deborah is the one chosen by God as capable of providing the needed leadership is indicative of her highly commendable character and abilities.

The author also expands the stereotypic formula that "the Israelites did what was evil in the sight of the Lord" (Judg. 4:1). He describes the evil first in general terms and then more specifically (*Bib. Ant.* 30.1):

(1) "Their heart fell away."

(2) "They forgot the promise."

(3) "They transgressed the ways that Moses and Joshua . . . had commanded them."

(4) "They were 'led astray after the daughters'[6] of the Amorites and 'served their gods.' "

Israel's Punishment (*Bib. Ant.* 30.2–3)

God's response to Israel's sin is (1) to become angry, (2) to send an angel to reprove them and promise them a leader, and (3) to punish them by "arousing against them Jabin," the Canaanite king who attacks them through Sisera (*Bib. Ant.* 30.2). We see that Pseudo-Philo expands the rather terse biblical statement that "the Lord sold them into the hands of King Jabin of Canaan" (Judg. 4:2) to include a promise—mediated by an angel—that God would send them a leader. Pseudo-Philo creates the angel's speech to increase the authority of the message. The angel first draws attention to—and emphasizes—the narrator's statement that Israel has transgressed God's ways and then goes on to make several additional assertions about the people and God's dealings with them. At the climax of it all, he announces: "A woman will rule over them and enlighten them forty years." The rhetorical effect of the last statement is striking, coming as it does not only from God's angel, but also at the end of the message, after the announcement that the people will repent.

The mission of Deborah is to "rule over" and "enlighten" the people, both of which are highly unusual roles for a Jewish woman around the turn of the era.[7] The second role (enlightener), which refers to her role as Torah teacher, in *Biblical Antiquities* is reserved for leaders of the stature of Moses, Kenaz, and Samuel.[8]

Pseudo-Philo designates Deborah as one who "enlightens" on at least two bases. The first derives from an element in the biblical story, that is, the appositional phrase *'eseth lapidoth* (Judg. 4:4). It has long been debated whether this describes Deborah (a fiery woman) or names her husband (she is the wife of Lapidoth). The ambiguity stems from both the word *'eseth,* meaning "woman" or "wife," and the word *lapidoth,* possibly a proper name or a noun meaning "torches."[9] The author obviously interprets it as a reference to Deborah herself (she will "enlighten" the people), rather than to her marital status. The second basis upon which Pseudo-Philo describes Deborah as an enlightener is that he associates her with Moses, whom he also describes as enlightening the people (*Bib. Ant.* 11.2). God's messenger draws this parallel by clearly juxtaposing Deborah with Moses—God sent Moses to the people to declare to them the divine laws and statutes, and now "a woman will rule over them and enlighten them forty years" (*Bib. Ant.* 30.2). Like Moses, Deborah calls Israel to observe the Torah, leads them in their miraculous deliverance (*Bib. Ant.* 32.17), and shepherds them for forty years.

The language the author employs and his associating of Moses with Deborah give expression to another aspect of his interpretation of both figures, one which makes its first appearance at this point in his portrait—and will reappear in later segments. Light is a metaphor of Wisdom; and both Deborah and Moses, as "enlighteners," are clearly Wisdom figures according to *Biblical Antiquities*. But Moses is male. How does he come to be identified with the feminine figure of Wisdom?

The groundwork for this transference was laid early in the first century B.C.E. by the Alexandrian Jewish philosopher Aristobulus. He identified Logos with Wisdom, "the primal light of creation, [which is] symbolized by the number seven [and which] gives true Sabbath rest to those who follow her."[10] Philo of Alexandria also equated Wisdom with Logos (*LA* 1.63) and Logos with Moses;[11] that is, Logos, the masculine counterpart to Wisdom, is identified with Moses. Pseudo-Philo not only reflects a similar interpretation but also builds certain aspects of his portrayals of both Deborah and Moses upon its foundation. He develops the idea of Wisdom's identification with Logos into real-life, flesh-and-blood characters. Deborah and Moses are counterparts, as are Wisdom and Logos. What is particularly noteworthy is that this interpretation is unique to the *Biblical Antiquities*; no other text develops Deborah's character and role in quite this way. We will encounter other expressions of this perception of Deborah as a Wisdom figure further in the story.

According to *Biblical Antiquities,* Deborah leads Israel "forty years." Although this reference to forty years could derive from the summary statement at the close of the Song of Deborah (Judg. 5:31), the text does not state that Deborah actually led Israel all that time, only that "the land had rest forty years." Here, the author attributes this forty-year period of peace to Deborah's leadership, which further elevates her character and role and again associates her with Moses, who likewise led Israel for forty years.

Israel Repents and Deborah's Mission Begins (*Bib. Ant.* 30.4–7)

Biblical Antiquities expands the Bible's simple statement that the people "cried out to the Lord" (Judg. 4:3) into a dramatic repentance scene (*Bib. Ant.* 30.4):

> All the sons of Israel gathered together to the mountain of Judah and said, "We say that we are more blessed than other nations, and behold now we have been humiliated more than all peoples so that we cannot dwell in our own land and our enemies have power over us. And now who has done all these things to us? Is it not our own wicked deeds, because we have forsaken the Lord of our fathers and have walked in these ways that have not profited us? And now come, let us fast for seven days. . . . And who knows, perhaps God will be reconciled with his inheritance so as not to destroy the plant of his vineyard."

The gathering takes place on the mountain of Judah, rather than Mount Tabor (Judg. 4:6). The "mountain of Judah" could refer to the specific mountain on which the Jewish Temple stood (Mount Moriah) or to Jerusalem in general. The purpose of the gathering is to "seek reconciliation" rather than to prepare for battle (Judg. 4:6–7). These significant alterations indicate that the author wishes to make a particular point through retelling the story. A close parallel to his version is the biblical narrative of Israel's miraculous deliverance from its enemies during the reign of King Jehoshaphat, who reigned from 872 to 848 B.C.E. In that account (2 Chron. 20:1–30), the enemies prepare to attack, and Jehoshaphat responds by "[inquiring] of the Lord" and "[proclaiming] a fast throughout all Judah" (v. 3). Accordingly, all the people gather at the Temple in Jerusalem to pray for God's intervention and await divine counsel as to how to respond (vv. 4–13). After some time, God speaks through a prophet, indicating that they are not to fear, for "the battle is not [theirs] but God's" (vv. 14–15). They are instructed to go out and take up positions for the battle, but then to "stand still and see the victory of the Lord on [their] behalf"; they themselves will not have to fight the battle (v. 17).

The people obediently march out to battle, praising God for granting them victory (vv. 20–22). While they are singing, God sends ambushes against the enemies and they destroy one another without engaging in battle with Israel (vv. 22–24). Jehoshaphat and his army gather the spoil, and the king leads the people in triumphal procession to the Jerusalem Temple, where they all rejoice in the victory (vv. 27–28).

I have paused to summarize this biblical story because it so closely parallels our story in *Biblical Antiquities,* as will soon become more apparent. At this point, we encounter only two parallels—the Israelites find themselves in a crisis and they respond by gathering at the Temple in Jerusalem to fast and pray for deliverance.

The correspondence to the story in 2 Chronicles may explain why the author locates this gathering in Jerusalem rather than on Mount Tabor, although it is strange that he does not place it in Shiloh, which normally serves as the cultic center in the document (*Bib. Ant.* 22.1; 23.1; 32.18; 45.5). Yet, it is possible that he situates it in Jerusalem in order to introduce an eschatological element into the account, for the eschatological element certainly is prominent in his version of Deborah's story.

The expression "gathering together" as used in this context recalls the Jewish doctrine of the gathering of exiles (a corollary to the return to the Land), which by and large emerged in the postbiblical period, although it was present to some extent in biblical literature. The basic belief was that the exiles (the dispersed) would once again be gathered together in their land (or Jerusalem), either as a prelude to redemption or as a result of it (see Jer. 31:10 and Ezek. 39:25–29). Repentance plays a very important role in this whole schema of events; indeed, it serves as a prelude to redemption.[12]

The author's alteration of the biblical scene from one in which Israel prepares for battle (literally) to one in which they repent and prepare for reconciliation is consistent with these beliefs. Israel is engaged in a spiritual battle and must prepare spiritually; this, too, corresponds to the example of Israel's experience under Jehoshaphat's leadership. Moreover, the allusion to the themes of the gathering of exiles, as well as repentance and redemption, indicates Pseudo-Philo's concern to place the story of Deborah in an eschatological framework. The eschatological element will appear more explicitly later in the story.

Deborah Is Sent: Reproof and Promise
(*Bib. Ant.* 30.5–7)

Pseudo-Philo has introduced some very dramatic material into these opening scenes whereby he heightens expectations concerning God's promised deliverer: Who will she be and when will she come? Only after presenting such extensive background does he introduce Deborah. She stands out as the only leader—male or female—introduced in this way in all of *Biblical Antiquities*.

Deborah is sent by the Lord. Although this is implied in the biblical text by the connection between the Israelites' crying out to the Lord for help and the subsequent introduction of Deborah as their judge (Judg. 4:3–4), the explicit statement is Pseudo-Philo's own comment that furthers his upgrading of Deborah's importance as Israel's leader. Equally significant is the notice that she was sent on the seventh day. The number seven[13] holds special meaning in its present context. We have already seen that in some Jewish texts, Wisdom is identified with the primordial light, the number seven, and Logos. We have also seen that Deborah is portrayed as a Wisdom figure in *Biblical Antiquities*. Hence, Deborah's coming to the people on the seventh day may serve as further manifestation of Deborah's character as a Wisdom figure.

Deborah demonstrates her true character and calling as more than a political liberator by her first activity among the people. She comes initially as a prophetess, a role that she plays also in the biblical version (Judg. 4:4), although here this aspect is greatly amplified. Deborah speaks the words of God to the people—words of reproof and words of hope.

She begins with an image drawn from Isaiah 53:7, appropriately a feminine image—a ewe, who is about to be slaughtered, is silent, as is her slaughterer (*Bib. Ant.* 30.5). The ewe (Israel) "cannot answer her slaughterer" (God); the slaughterer's silence should not be mistaken for lack of grief over what must happen. Deborah then explicitly compares Israel to a flock that has been blessed in many ways. This metaphor is repeated in *Biblical Antiquities* 31.5 and (more remotely) in 32.3. The reference to Israel as a flock points to Deborah's role as a "shepherdess," and again to her equality with Moses.

Deborah then begins her reproof (*Bib. Ant.* 30.6), employing another image: Israel is like iron, which is pliant in the fire (when punished) but becomes hard again when removed from the fire. This signifies that the people obey their leader but soon fall into apostasy after the leader's death. Deborah includes herself in the list of illustrious leaders (with Moses and Kenaz) by predicting that the people will also sin after her death (*Bib. Ant.* 30.7).

This recalls Moses' final speech to the Israelites, when he predicted the people's lapse into sin: "For I know that after my death you will surely act corruptly, turning aside from the way that I have commanded you" (Deut. 31:29). These words—with minor variation—are placed in the mouth of Deborah. Her words of hope—"God will take pity on you today . . . because of his covenant that he established with your fathers and the oath that he has sworn not to abandon you forever" (*Bib. Ant.* 30.7)—also recall Moses' words before his death (Deut. 30:6, 8; 31:8). Her affirmation—"Our fathers are dead, but the God who established the covenant with them is life"—echoes Deuteronomy 30:20: "For the Lord is your life."

Thus, Deborah, from her very first appearance, is an extremely impressive figure, certainly greater than the already remarkable heroine of Judges 4–5. Her first activity is prophetic, which corresponds to her role in Judges 4. But the explicit statement that she is "sent from the Lord on the seventh day" and her association with Moses, even to the point of speaking his words, increase her stature beyond anything we find in Judges. Here, the author also highlights God's covenantal relationship with Israel, and because of this concern, he transforms Deborah into a "covenantal preacher," in every way equal to her masculine counterpart in biblical tradition.

Israel's Deliverance under Deborah's Leadership (*Bib. Ant.* 31)

In chapter 31, Pseudo-Philo retells the story of Israel's deliverance and the demise of Sisera "by the hand of Jael." Here, he follows the biblical account more closely than in other sections; yet he clearly shapes the story to accentuate the lessons he wishes to draw from it.

In the narrative introducing Deborah's exhortation to Barak (*Bib. Ant.* 31.1), the author rather faithfully quotes Judges 4:6. But he creates the exhortation that follows, incorporating some material from Judges 4–5. Notably, he omits the dialogue containing Barak's refusal to go into battle without Deborah and her subsequent rebuke and moves the prediction that Sisera would be handed over to a woman into another context. He reworks this and replaces it in the context of Sisera's punishment for boasting that he would attack the Israelites and plunder them, taking for himself their women as spoil (*Bib. Ant.* 31.1).

In the lines that follow, Deborah takes on a new role; she is a visionary:[14] "I see the stars moved from their course and ready for battle on your side. Also I see the lightning that cannot be moved from its course going forth to hinder the works of the chariots of those who glory in the might of Sisera" (*Bib. Ant.* 31.1). Although the notion of cosmic warriors derives from the poetic version of the biblical story (Judg. 5:20), Pseudo-Philo clearly amplifies and expands this element, thereby introducing an apocalyptic element into the story. The battle is announced by a visionary and takes on cosmic proportions and significance. The thunderstorm is not merely a timely phenomenon that helps the Israelites to overcome their enemies; the lightning and the stars become actual figures who join the battle, winning it for Israel by "burning up their enemies":[15]

> And when Deborah and the people and Barak went down to meet the enemies, immediately the Lord disturbed the movement of his stars. And he said to them, "Hurry and go, for your enemies fall upon you; and confound their arms and crush the power of their heart, because I have come that my people may prevail. For even if my people have sinned, nevertheless I will have mercy on them" (*Bib. Ant.* 31.2).

Deborah's final words before the battle are significant. She sets up a series of reciprocal actions that point to the reason for the specific and unusual conditions of the victory. Sisera has boasted about three things he will do, and he will accordingly be punished in three ways, all of which are duly humiliating to a "powerful" male:

Sisera's Boast (*Bib. Ant.* 31.1b)	Sisera's Punishment (*Bib. Ant.* 31.1c)
1. I am going down to attack Israel with my mighty arm.	1. The arm of a weak woman will attack him.
2. I will divide their spoils among my servants.[16]	2. Maidens will take his spoils.
3. I will take for myself beautiful women as concubines.	3. Even he will fall into the hands of a woman.

The author transfers Deborah's assertion that Sisera would die by the hand of a woman from the context of her rebuke of Barak to her description of Sisera's punishment; moreover, he reworks it so that it becomes part of a reciprocal action whereby Sisera is punished according to his own act or intent. This notion of reciprocal punishment, common in early Judaism, appears frequently in *Biblical Antiquities.*[17]

Here, the first and last points derive from the biblical account, but Pseudo-Philo's particular way of interpreting the story is interesting. Commentators have long debated whether "the woman" in Deborah's statement that the Lord would "sell Sisera into the hand of a woman" (Judg. 4:9) refers to Deborah or to Jael. Pseudo-Philo divides this power between the two women: Deborah will attack him (and presumably also his forces) and he will fall into the hands of Jael.

The middle element (2) is not specifically biblical[18] but was added to emphasize the point that the weakest are the strongest if righteous, for then God enables them to overcome their enemies.[19] In other words, "The Lord... does not need a great number but only holiness" (*Bib. Ant.* 27.14). The author emphasizes this central point in the remaining material in the Jael-Sisera narrative, thereby encouraging his audience that even in their weakness they can overcome their enemies, when God fights for them.

Sisera's Death "by the Hands of" Jael
(Bib. Ant. 31.3–9)

Pseudo-Philo leads into these scenes by commenting that the stars "did not destroy Sisera, because so it had been commanded them" (*Bib. Ant.* 31.2), thus heightening the miraculous element and emphasizing that God is in charge of the situation. Sisera does not simply escape on his own initiative, which we could infer from the biblical account. He is destined to be killed by a woman, and the circumstances all direct him to that end.

All that follows turns upon the themes of the strength and weakness of Jael and Sisera and, by analogy, of the people of Israel and their enemies. Pseudo-Philo skillfully makes use of irony to create nuanced scenes that serve to dramatize his point that true strength comes from God and that it is God's power that enables Israel to triumph over its enemies.

The scene begins with Sisera fleeing "on a horse to save his life" (*Bib. Ant.* 31.3). The detail that he was on a horse is unique to *Biblical Antiquities*; other versions state that he was on foot. Possibly, this modification reflects a word-play on the Hebrew word for horse (*sus*) and Sisera. On another level, however, it indicates that Sisera is powerful and strong, because such are those that ride horses. Sisera flees (a sign of weakness), but he flees in strength, or so it would seem. The contradiction implied points to the author's use of irony; we are aware from the beginning that reality is not as it appears.

The following phrases describing Jael correspond some-what to the biblical text: "Jael the wife of Heber the Kenite adorned herself and went out to meet him" (*Bib. Ant.* 31.3). The author omits, however, the notice that the Kenites had a covenant with Jabin, likely because his high valuation of covenants rendered Jael's disregard of it un-thinkable, or at least embarrassing. He also adds the detail that Jael was "very beautiful in appearance," which, along with the note that Jael "adorned herself," recalls the great heroine Judith.[20] Like Judith, Jael will use the weapons at her disposal—her gender (*'eśeth ḥeber,* meaning woman/ wife of Heber), beauty,[21] and adornment. These are traditional women's "weapons." But Jael possesses a fourth weapon, a hint of which we detect in the allusion to Judith—her piety.[22] What is merely a hint at this point will become more evident as the scene unfolds.

Jael lures Sisera inside (her tent)[23] and makes him feel secure and comfortable. Pseudo-Philo focuses upon the couch, strewn with roses, waiting to receive Sisera and— both he and we imagine—Jael. Jael demonstrates her ingenuity and proficiency in strategizing and deploying her weapons as clearly here as when she hammers a tent peg through his head. Sisera is totally in her power, although he thinks he is in control; he is weak, *she* is strong. As he approaches the couch, he fantasizes that he will take Jael home to be his wife: "If I am saved, I will go to my mother, and Jael will be my wife" (*Bib. Ant.* 31.3).

But Sisera's words inject a disquieting element into the scene. His remark, "If I am saved," reveals an uncertainty in his mind, despite his seeming confidence and control of the situation. His reference to his mother points ahead to the final scene of the biblical drama (Judg. 5:28–30), to a mother peering through a lattice, looking expectantly for a son who does not come home. The third phrase hints at what is to come. Deborah had said that because Sisera had boasted "I will take beautiful women as concubines," he would "fall into the hands of a weak woman" (*Bib. Ant.* 31.1). As Sisera fulfills the first part of the prophecy by stating that Jael will be his wife, we are alerted to look for the fulfillment of the second part.

This same dramatic use of irony continues in the following scene (*Bib. Ant.* 31.3–6). Sisera is passive; Jael is active. He admits his weakness: "I am faint" and "my soul burns with the flame that I saw in the stars." In the second phrase, we detect a hint of irony due to the ambiguity about whether he is weak because he is sexually aroused[24]—and thus vulnerable to Jael—or because he is already in the process of dying, a process set in motion at the battle with the stars and moving toward its climax, which occurs when he burns in Gehenna (*Bib. Ant.* 31.7). The scene closes with Sisera sleeping (and vulnerable), in all likelihood dreaming about Jael.

He has asked Jael for water (*Bib. Ant.* 31.4), and she now goes to get a drink, although one that is not exactly what he requested. She will instead give him milk and wine (*Bib. Ant.* 31.5). In *Biblical Antiquities,* Israel is repeatedly likened to a flock or a vine,[25] and milk and wine represent Israel under the care of God. Note also that milk represents Torah/Wisdom in the document (e.g., *Bib. Ant.* 51.3) and that this imagery is central in Jael's prayer:

> And when she was milking, she said, "... Did you not choose Israel alone and liken it to no animal except to the ram that goes before and leads the flock? ... And I will take from the milk of these animals to which you have likened your people, and I will go and give him to drink. And when he will have drunk, he will be off guard, and afterward I will kill him."

The milk is a crucial weapon in Jael's arsenal. It will weaken Sisera so that she will effortlessly overcome him and slay him. Hence, through this imagery, the author suggests that Israel will conquer its enemies by relying upon the Torah/Wisdom.

In the milking scene, Jael first reveals her inner thoughts. Here, as she is alone, milking the sheep, she speaks in prayer to God.[26] She speaks of strength and weakness (*Bib. Ant.* 31.4–5): (1) Israel was destined to be the leading nation in the world, but finds itself in bondage to Sisera. (2) Jael acknowledges her own weakness by asking God for signs as assurance of divine help; here also, she follows the example of Judith. Although she is weak, with God's assistance, she will be strong enough to defeat Sisera.

Pseudo-Philo employs the motif of the signs given to

Jael not only to emphasize the miraculous aspect and to heighten the dramatic effect of the story, but also to assure his audience that Jael did not have intercourse with Sisera—surely a major concern for them.[27] He emphasizes that Sisera was asleep alone. He did not fall between her legs, as the biblical text could imply (Judg. 5:27), but she threw him off the couch on to the ground. Jael's action also corresponds to Judith's treatment of Holophernes and thus—by analogy—communicates the same message concerning what transpired in Jael's tent.

As Jael drives the tent peg through Sisera's skull, he awakens long enough to utter his last words, which acknowledge his weakness: "Behold pain has taken hold of me, Jael, and I die like a woman" (*Bib. Ant.* 31.7). Jael then emphasizes the important point (*Bib. Ant.* 31.7): "Go boast before your father in hell and tell him that you have fallen into the hands of a woman." This is repeated by Barak, who upon arrival at the scene, exclaims, "Blessed be the Lord, who sent his spirit and said, 'Into the hand of a woman Sisera will be handed over'" (*Bib. Ant.* 31.9). Finally, the same is suggested in the scene in which Sisera's mother awaits his arrival (*Bib. Ant.* 31.8). She refers to the concubines that Sisera will bring, to the exclusion of the other items named in the biblical account. This again points back to Deborah's prophecy and Sisera's own words (*Bib. Ant.* 31.1).

Thus, every character in the climax of the drama communicates—explicitly or implicitly—the same message: Those who boast in their own strength, although they appear strong, are not as strong as those who, although appearing weak, trust in God and rely on divine strength to give them victory. This message must have been crucial for Pseudo-Philo's audience, for he communicates it through both Deborah and Jael, indeed, through all characters in the story. His community, in their weakness, needed to know that God would strengthen them to overcome their enemies. Again, this would fit well into a post-70 C.E. time frame for *Biblical Antiquities,* when the

Jewish people were nearly overwhelmed by their weakness and despaired of ever becoming sufficiently strong to overcome their enemies and once again "dwell in their land" (*Bib. Ant.* 30.4) as a free people.

Response to God's Deliverance (*Bib. Ant.* 32.1–17)

Deborah and all the people respond to God's deliverance by singing a hymn. Although this hymn stands in the same place in her story as the biblical Song of Deborah and alludes (remotely at times) to events or phraseology in the biblical story or hymn, *Biblical Antiquities*'s version could be more precisely identified as a sermon. From a form-critical standpoint, it corresponds most closely to the levitical sermons in the books of Chronicles.[28] Deborah and the people recount God's saving acts in Israel's history, emphasizing God's choosing of Israel and faithfulness in fulfilling covenantal promises. Then, on the basis of these "witnesses," Deborah assures them of God's future deliverance, even the ultimate renewal of creation.

The hymn is quite lengthy and deals with many issues; for the sake of brevity, I will highlight mainly those elements that pertain to the portrayal of Deborah.

God's Mighty Acts in Israel's History (Bib. Ant. 32.1–12)

The hymn begins with a significant introduction, which in part corresponds to the biblical version:

Judg. 5:1	Bib. Ant. 32.1
Then Deborah and Barak son of Abinoam sang on that day....	Then Deborah and Barak the son of Abino and all the people together sang a hymn to the Lord on that day.

Here, the author inserts the phrase "and all the people together sang a hymn to the Lord," which he draws from the Song of the Sea (Ex. 15:1), thereby linking the victory over Sisera with the victory over the Egyptians. He again associates the two at the end of the hymn (*Bib. Ant.* 32.16–17) and thus frames the entire hymn with references to these two great salvific events in Israel's history. This editorial activity enhances Deborah's role, in that her leadership is once again equated with that of Israel's greatest liberator and shepherd.

The hymn focuses first of all upon God's work in the lives of the patriarchs (*Bib. Ant.* 32.1–6). Particularly highlighted are God's election of Abraham and Abraham's faithfulness (32.1); Abraham's "sacrifice" of Isaac (32.2–4), emphasizing its beneficial value for Israel (32.4); and the birth of Jacob in the third year of Rebecca's marriage (32.5). We must look for some special significance in this last element because it so clearly contradicts the biblical statement that Jacob and Esau were born in the twentieth year (Gen. 25:21, 26). Instances of other such subtle changes in chronology in *Biblical Antiquities* indicate that Pseudo-Philo attaches significance to the number three, or to the third in a series.[29] Similarly, he intentionally places Deborah as the third judge of Israel, while, according to the Bible, she is the fourth[30]— a subtle innovation that further upgrades her status in *Biblical Antiquities*.

Then follow other significant events—the establishment of the covenant with Israel at Sinai (*Bib. Ant.* 32.7–8), Moses' "vision" of Israel's future (*Bib. Ant.* 32.9), Joshua's victory over Israel's enemies (*Bib. Ant.* 32.10), and finally Deborah's victory over Sisera, although Deborah is not mentioned by name, only Jael (*Bib. Ant.* 32.11–12). The element of cosmic "witnesses" (earth and heaven) and "servants" (moon, sun, stars) ties together this last series of events, and the last two episodes demonstrate that Israel was protected while the enemy was destroyed.[31] The key message the author endeavors to communicate through this recitation of Israel's history is that "he [God] has remembered both his recent and ancient promises and shown his saving power to us" (*Bib. Ant.* 32.12). He reminds Israel of what God has done as an encouragement that God will again act on their behalf. This message is again highlighted in the following section.

Assurance of God's Saving Help for Israel (Bib. Ant. 32.13–17)

The subject matter changes abruptly at this point. The hymn changes from third person to second person in a series of directives to various natural elements and to Deborah, all of which are designated as "witnesses." Also, Pseudo-Philo incorporates eschatological material not present in the biblical version of the narrative and hymn.[32] Although this element has already appeared, here it becomes more explicit. Finally, we will see that this section contains three rather difficult passages, there being two significant textual problems and one rather complex metaphor.

In the beginning of this section (v. 13), Deborah first reassures "the fathers" in "the chambers of souls"[33] that God will indeed fulfill the covenant promises made to Israel. She does not speak this message herself but commands the earth, heavens, lightnings, and angels to give it; here, Deborah's address to such elements recalls Moses' final speech in which he likewise addressed heaven and earth in his hymn regarding Israel (Deut. 32:1). Her assurance that the promises will be fulfilled repeats the statement in the previous verse and thus emphasizes the point.

The promise ("Many wonders will I do for your sons") alludes back to Deborah's reassurance when she was first sent to the people: "The Lord will work wonders among you and hand over your enemies into your hands" (*Bib. Ant.* 30.7). At that time, she told them that God would do this "because of his covenant that he established with your fathers," and that even though their fathers are dead, "the God who established the covenant with them is life." Now, after recalling significant events, she turns directly to "the fathers" with these words of hope and comfort. The reference to those in "the chambers of souls" (awaiting judgment day) builds upon and continues to develop the eschatological aspect of Pseudo-Philo's presentation.[34]

In this section, Deborah's role is enhanced in two ways: (1) She has command over cosmic elements, and even angels. Her power over the elements places her in a category with Joshua (*Bib. Ant.* 32.10), although she commands elements over which even he did not have control. This aspect of Deborah's role in *Biblical Antiquities* resembles that of the goddess Isis, who likewise commands cosmic elements, and perhaps represents a syncretistic incorporation of an important feature of the goddess's capabilities and role. A further—very interesting—parallel is found in Philo's portrayal of Moses. He, too, holds command over these elements (*Mos.* 1.55–56). Earlier in this chapter, we noted that in some exegetical traditions Wisdom was equated with Logos, and Moses was identified with Logos. If the concept of Wisdom in Hellenistic Jewish tradition was derived in part from characteristics attributed to Isis, we can see how both Moses in Philo's works and Deborah in *Biblical Antiquities*—both Wisdom figures—could take on such characteristics and roles. Hence, Pseudo-Philo's incorporation of this element significantly increases the extent of Deborah's power and authority. (2) Deborah serves as God's special messenger, sent to assure Israel's great ancestors of God's eventual vindication on their behalf.

Deborah then assures Israel of God's faithfulness to covenant promises (*Bib. Ant.* 32.14–17). In the beginning of this section, she exhorts herself to praise God for these mighty acts: "But you, Deborah, sing praises, and let the grace of the holy spirit[35] awaken in you, and begin to praise the works of the Lord" (*Bib. Ant.* 32.14a).

Biblical Antiquities combines two statements in the biblical Hymn of Deborah: "Awake, awake, Deborah! Awake, awake, utter a song!" (Judg. 5:12); and "To the Lord I will sing; I will make melody to the Lord, the God of Israel" (Judg. 5:3). Although neither biblical verse specifies the content of the song, the author explains that it was a song in praise of "the works of the Lord." This recounting of God's salvific acts, which characterizes both Hebrew psalmody and levitical sermonizing, continues the theme of the first part of the hymn and emphasizes again Deborah's role as a covenantal preacher, although the song takes on a new dimension as a call to worship.

In her words of praise, Deborah refers to the stars' fighting for Israel as evidence of the surety of God's aid in future distress: "If Israel falls into distress, it will call upon those witnesses along with these servants [the stars], and they will form a delegation to the Most High, and he will remember that day and send the saving power of his covenant" (*Bib. Ant.* 32.14).

This assertion derives in part from the author's identification of the stars as "witnesses" and "servants" and also reflects the common belief in antiquity that stars were angels. The notion of angels as intercessors was greatly developed in the postbiblical period and is present in *Biblical Antiquities*.[36] The phrase "the saving power of his covenant" points again to covenantal concerns in this book.

Next, Deborah recounts what God has done under her leadership: "And you, Deborah, begin to tell what you saw in the field, how the people were walking about and going forth in safety and the stars fought for them" (*Bib. Ant.* 32.15a). She summarizes the story of the battle, highlighting again the role of the stars and God's protection of Israel while the enemy was destroyed. Deborah fills the role of a witness; she observes God's fulfillment of covenantal promises and she declares what she has seen. Thus, she once again in the book plays a role similar to that of Moses: "And everything that the Most Powerful said, this he fulfilled,[37] having Moses his beloved as a witness" (*Bib. Ant.* 32.8).

Deborah next addresses the earth, which is also a "witness":

Rejoice, earth, over those dwelling on you, because the assembly of the Lord that builds a tower on you[38] is present. Not unjustly did God take from you the rib of the first-formed,[39] knowing that from his rib Israel would be born. Your forming will be a testimony of what the Lord has done for his people (*Bib. Ant.* 32.15; cf. 32.9).

This section contains both a major textual variant and a somewhat obscure analogy. Why does Deborah tell earth that God took from it the rib of Adam (the first-formed)? What is the meaning of the metaphor of the rib? Why does she declare that the earth's forming would be a "testimony of what the Lord has done for his people"?

First, the textual difficulty centers on the phrase *quoniam adest concio Domini que turrificat in te*. Here, I have combined elements from the two readings suggested by Kisch and Harrington into a new reading. Kisch's text reads: "because the assembly of the Lord that burns incense among you" (*quoniam adest concio Domini que thurrificat in te*),[40] and Harrington's reads: "because the knowledge of the Lord that builds a tower among you" (*quoniam adest conscientia Domini que turrificat in te*).[41]

The variation between "assembly" (*concio*) and "knowledge" (*conscientia*) possibly stems from a confusion of the Hebrew original text, for both terms derive from the same consonants, although metathesized: "assembly" (*'dh*); "knowledge" (*d'h*). Possible evidence that *'dh* stands behind "assembly" is suggested by the word "testimony" (Heb.: *'d*), which perhaps reflects a wordplay with *'dh*.

The imagery of an "assembly of the Lord" building a tower recalls a passage in the *Shepherd* of Hermas, a late first-century Christian text. The passage contains a vision of angels building a tower, a symbol of the church:

"The six young men that build, who are they, lady?" "These are the holy angels of God.... By their hands therefore the building of the tower will be accomplished." "And who are the others who are bringing the stones?" "They also are the holy angels of God. . . . The building of the tower [i.e., the church] then shall be accomplished, and all alike shall rejoice in heart (as they stand) round the tower, and shall glorify God that the building of the tower was accomplished" (5.3.4).

The similar imagery in *Biblical Antiquities* suggests that earth is to rejoice because God's angels (the assembly of the Lord) continue to build up the tower (Israel) by fighting for Israel against its enemies (*Bib. Ant.* 32.15a).

In the second metaphor, Pseudo-Philo states that God took from earth "Adam's rib," knowing that from "his rib" Israel would be born. Because earth is the ultimate source of Israel's life, earth is therefore a "testimony" of Israel's continued existence.[42] As surely as earth exists, Israel will continue to exist. We see here another expression of encouragement to Israel at a time when its continued existence must have been in question.

The imagery the author employs in this message is striking. He speaks of Adam's rib as having been taken from earth and having given birth to Israel. "Adam's rib" is an appellation for "woman," or more specifically Eve, in the Hebrew language.[43] Thus, the author sets up the complex: earth–woman (or Eve)–Israel. This is interesting, particularly because in early Christian and Gnostic literature we find a similar notion of "Mother Earth" giving birth to Eve (sometimes Mary), who then gives birth to the church.[44] We perhaps have here a non-Christian witness to this type of exegetical tradition. Additionally, the use of feminine imagery in this section gives expression to interest in and positive valuation of women in *Biblical Antiquities* and especially suits the present context—a sermon-hymn by Israel's premier female leader.

After affirming the surety of Israel's continued existence, Deborah turns to Israel's future and that of all creation:

Wait, you hours of the day, and do not wish to hurry, in order that we may declare what our mind can bring forward, for night will be upon us. It will be like the night when God killed the firstborn of the Egyptians on account of his own firstborn.[45] And then I will cease my hymn, for the time is readied for his just judgments. For I will sing a hymn to him in the renewal of creation. And the people will remember his saving power, and this will be a testimony for it. And let the sea with its abyss be a witness, because not only has God dried it up before our fathers, but also he has diverted the stars from their positions and attacked our enemies (*Bib. Ant.* 32.16–17).

In her references to "the day" and "the night" that would soon be upon them, Deborah recalls the eschatological imagery of light and darkness, mentioned earlier in the hymn (*Bib. Ant.* 32.10). She also looks ahead to judgment day. Her next two statements highlight this theme, both by direct allusion to "the renewal of creation" (v. 17) and by two analogies—between the coming "night" and Passover, and between the drying up of the sea (the Red Sea) and the stars fighting for Israel against Sisera. While no such eschatological element is present in the biblical Hymn of Deborah, the later rabbinic Targum incorporates the tradition that Judges 5:31 refers to the eschatological judgment of God's (and Israel's) enemies and the reward of the righteous: "As Sisera, so will all the enemies of Your people perish, O Lord; and those who love Him are destined to shine with splendor, and their glory will be sevenfold" (*Tg. Neb. Judg.* 5:31; my trans.).

Rejoicing at Shiloh (Bib. Ant. 32.18)

In this closing paragraph of chapter 32, Pseudo-Philo also reveals his intention to associate the victory over Sisera with the day of judgment and final redemption. Following the hymn, Deborah and all the people go to Shiloh and sacrifice "to the accompaniment of trumpets." Then Deborah declares, "This will be as a testimony of trumpets between the stars and their Lord."[46]

There is no symbol in Judaism that more clearly represents judgment than the trumpet (*shofar*). In the Jewish New Year (Rosh Hashanah) liturgy, it is blown to recall, among others: the creation of the world, the revelation and covenant at Sinai, the binding of Isaac (the Akedah), the future judgment of the world, and redemption of Israel. Rosh Hashanah is known as the "Feast of Trumpets," "Day of Memorial," and "Day of Judgment." In later liturgy,[47] it became customary to recite scriptures that speak of God as King and Judge and also of memorials. The themes of memorials and judgment have already appeared in Pseudo-Philo's retelling of Deborah's story, and the allusion here accords with his portrayal of her as an eschatological figure.

Summary of the Portrait of Deborah in the Hymn

Although the hymn does not often focus directly upon Deborah, several aspects of her character and role are presented in this passage:

1. She is a poetess, inspired by the Holy Spirit.

2. She is a prophetess, who directs that God's message be given even to "the fathers" in Sheol.

3. She is a covenantal preacher, who recounts the works of God in Israel's past and assures the people of God's continued faithfulness to covenantal promises.

4. She is a witness, counterpart to Moses.

5. She has command over natural and cosmic elements and angels, an authority elsewhere attributed to Moses, as well as the goddess Isis.

6. She is an apocalyptic visionary.

7. She is chronologically placed as the third judge, which enhances her status.

Thus, in the hymn, Pseudo-Philo continues to upgrade Deborah as previously. Only the roles of judge, prophetess, and poetess are biblically based; all of the others are additions or modifications, and, moreover, are unique to *Biblical Antiquities*. Through this refashioned figure of Deborah, the author reminds the Israelites of God's saving acts in their history and assures them of eventual and final restoration.

The Testament of Deborah (*Bib. Ant.* 33)

The Bible contains no counterpart to the testament of Deborah. The book of Judges contains no further mention of Deborah or her activity after the summarizing statement that "the land had rest forty years" (Judg. 5:31). The author of *Biblical Antiquities,* by contrast, has chosen to complete her story with a testament scene worthy of so great a figure as Deborah—a scene that also provides a vehicle for him to communicate his own message to his audience.

Deborah's testament conforms to a specific literary genre that developed considerably during the postbiblical period as it took on specific characteristics that became stereotypic.[48] A testament is the final discourse of an important figure, delivered to those gathered around him or her[49] (children or disciples) and generally incorporating both ethical and apocalyptic teaching. The testament became a popular vehicle for expounding such doctrine due to the authority conferred upon the solemn last words of a righteous person. The testament of Deborah fulfills all the criteria for a true testament, except that it includes no apocalyptic vision as such. She does, however, speak of the world to come, and thus the absence of an apocalyptic vision is not significant.

Deborah begins by admonishing the people. In this context, she announces her imminent death in order to encourage them to repent immediately: "Only direct your heart to the Lord your God during the time of your life, because after your death, you cannot repent of those things in which you live" (*Bib. Ant.* 33.2).

The author leads into the message of Deborah's final sermon in a manner that highlights the degree of its importance. He builds upon a series of analogies—all but one employing specific feminine imagery—to stress the authority of her words:

1. "I am warning you as a woman of God."

2. "[I] am enlightening you as one from the female race."

3. "Obey me like your mother."

4. "Heed my words as people who will also die."

The charge to "obey me like your mother" recalls the phrase "a mother in Israel," attributed to Deborah in Judges 5:7. Although that text possibly inspired its specific mention here, the phrase also recalls references to mothers in the Pentateuch and Proverbs,[50] as well as Wisdom imagery in a variety of texts. For example, Ben Sirah states that "She [Wisdom] will come to meet him like a mother" (Sir. 15:2), and Philo of Alexandria declares that Wisdom is "the mother and nurse of the All."[51]

Deborah announces her death by (nearly) quoting the words of Joshua before his death, which highlights her stature and role as a major covenantal figure:

Joshua 23:14	*Bib. Ant.* 33.2
Behold, I am going today on the way of all the earth.[52]	Behold, I am going today on the way of all flesh.

These words would have reminded Pseudo-Philo's audience not only of Joshua's exhortation to obey the Torah and his promise of blessing, but also of the Israelites' response, expressed by solemn oath in a covenant-renewal ceremony at Shechem (Josh. 23:15–24:27). They knew the story and the speech, and they knew that they were being encouraged to follow the example of their ancestors.

Deborah exhorts the people to obey the Torah and to do so immediately rather than wait until it is too late:

> Only direct your heart to the Lord your God during the time of your life, because after your death you cannot repent of those things in which you live. For then death is sealed up and brought to an end.... For even if you seek to do evil in hell after your death, you cannot, because the desire for sinning will cease and the evil impulse will lose its power,[53] because even hell will not restore what has been received and deposited to it unless it be demanded by him who has made the deposit to it. Now, therefore, my sons, obey my voice; while you have the time of life and the light of the Law, make straight your ways (*Bib. Ant.* 33.2–3).

This section ends with Deborah repeating the exhortation to obey her by repenting. The literary device of repetition serves to emphasize the admonition and to summarize the most important point of her message.

Deborah's Death (*Bib. Ant.* 33.4–6)

The final scene of Deborah's earthly life is highly dramatic and emotional. Even while Deborah is speaking with the people, they all raise up their voices together and weep (*Bib. Ant.* 33.4a). Rather than respond to her admonition with an oath that they will indeed obey her (see Joshua 24), they summarize their deepest fear and most urgent

concern in the simple question: "To whom do you commend your sons whom you are leaving? Pray therefore
for us, and after your departure your soul will be mindful of us forever" (*Bib. Ant.* 33.4). Who will lead them
after she dies? Who will intercede for them? Lying behind this query is the conviction that she has been of
such stature and so greatly loved and respected that no
one could succeed her.

Moreover, Pseudo-Philo records a similar response in
Moses' deathbed scene: "Who will give us another shepherd like Moses or such a judge for the sons of Israel
to pray always for our sins and to be heard for our in-
iquities?" (*Bib. Ant.* 19.3). Note the parallelism between
"shepherd" and "judge." In *Biblical Antiquities*, these
function primarily as intercessors, which differs completely from the role of a judge in the book of Judges,
where he or she is essentially a liberator.

This description of Moses' death resembles his deathbed scene in the *Assumption of Moses* (also known as the
Testament of Moses), where Joshua asks Moses basically
the same question. I quote it here at length because
of its correspondence to Deborah's testament in *Biblical
Antiquities*:

Now, Master, you are going away, and who will sustain
this people? Or who will have compassion on them,
and will be for them a leader on (their) way? Or who
will pray for them, not omitting a single day, so that
I may lead them into the land of their forefathers?
How, therefore, can I be (guardian) of this people, as
a father is to his only son, or as a mother is to her
virgin daughter (who) is being prepared to be given to
a husband; a mother who is disquieted, guarding (the
daughter's) body from the sun and (seeing to it) that
(the daughter's) feet are not without shoes?... Can I be
responsible for food for them as they desire and drink
according to their will? (*Asm. M.* 11:9–13).

Most of these roles—clothing, feeding, and giving drink—are characteristically feminine. According to the *Assumption of Moses*, Moses fills masculine and feminine roles on behalf of the people; according to *Biblical Antiquities,* Deborah fills many of the more traditionally masculine roles (leading, liberating, teaching Torah, shepherding) attributed to Moses, as well as more traditionally feminine roles. Again, we see that she is portrayed as Moses' counterpart.

Deborah's response to their query affords the author an opportunity to emphasize once more the importance of repenting immediately, in this case, by reminding the people that they must not trust in their ancestors to intercede for them because no one can pray for another after his or her death.[54] Deborah then dies and is "buried in the city of her fathers" (*Bib. Ant.* 33.6).

The Dirge (*Bib. Ant.* 33.6)

Pseudo-Philo introduces the dirge with a striking comment: "And the people mourned for her for seventy days." Although it was customary to mourn no more than thirty days,[55] the great patriarch Jacob was mourned for seventy days (Gen. 50:3). Perhaps this extended mourning period expresses again the degree to which Deborah was revered and loved by "her children."[56]

The dirge makes four statements about Deborah:

1. She is a "mother from Israel." This corresponds to Judges 5:7. The phrase does not signify physical motherhood, but a role and quality of character. The mother's role is to nourish, protect, admonish, teach, and guide; she is compassionate and always mindful of her children.

2. She is "the holy one." This is a striking appellation. Although Jewish literature from this period refers to "holy men," the expression "holy woman" is unusual, although not unique (see Judith 8:31: *mulier sancta*). In

early Jewish usage, "holy one" was primarily a synonym for prophet or prophetess; it highlighted one's special calling and character (piety) as well as ability to work miracles, to have visionary experiences, and to intercede before God for the community. In *2 Apocalypse of Baruch* 85:1–2, the terms "holy men," "prophets," and "intercessors" are employed interchangeably. In *Biblical Antiquities* 59.2, the term "holy one" (masc.) stands in parallelism with "anointed one of the Lord." Wisdom of Solomon 11:1 speaks of "the holy prophet" in a passage based on Hosea 12:13, where we read simply "a prophet."

3. She is a "leader in the house of Jacob." The author has certainly portrayed Deborah in this role in all its aspects, with the exception of priest in the cultic sense. She has indeed fulfilled the angel's promise that "a woman will rule over them and enlighten them for forty years" (*Bib. Ant.* 30.2).[57]

The designation of Deborah as "leader" possibly derives from a wordplay on the Aramaic root of the name Deborah, *dbr*, which denotes (among other meanings) to "lead (the flock)." Hence, a *dbr* is a leader—specifically a leader of the flock (a shepherd or shepherdess); and Deborah, in true Semitic fashion, lives up to her name. Note also the similarity between Deborah and Moses suggested by this interpretation—both served as shepherds of the "flock" of Israel.

4. She has "firmed up the fence about her generation." I would suggest several possible bases for this statement: (a) The image of the "fence" may derive from the biblical version of Deborah's story. Judges 5:7 refers to the "unwalled cities"—signifying lawlessness, vulnerability, and confusion—in Israel before Deborah's arrival on the scene. She has now restored those walls by her "enlightening" leadership. (b) A righteous leader is called a "fence-maker" in the Midrash.[58] Louis Ginzberg relates a Midrash concerning the scribe Baruch's distress at not having received the prophetic spirit. God tells Baruch, "Baruch, there is no need of a fence if there is no vine-

yard; of what use is the shepherd, if there is no flock?"[59] Thus, a "fence" equals a shepherd. Note also the parallelism between "vineyard" and "flock" in this passage, which also appears in *Biblical Antiquities* (23.12; 28.4–5). (c) According to Ezekiel, a prophet "builds up a wall" and "stands in the gap" for God's people, that is, intercedes for them (Ezek. 22:30).

Whatever the specific basis for this expression, it is clear that Deborah's role has been to strengthen, protect, guide, and intercede for the people. She has accomplished this by her "enlightening" leadership under the guidance and authority of the Torah.

Deborah in *Jewish Antiquities:* Spiritual Leader in Time of Crisis

Josephus's account of Deborah's story is abbreviated in comparison with the biblical narrative; it spans merely ten paragraphs (*Ant.* 5.200–209). The biblical material Josephus chooses to include and what he adds and omits are all indicators of his perspectives and concerns. His characterization of Deborah is in some cases positive, but on the whole it is more negative than that of the Bible. We will see that he ascribes to her the role of prophetess but omits mention of the other biblical roles (poetess, military leader, judge). Although Josephus's disregard of Deborah's role as poetess naturally results from his omission of the entire Hymn of Deborah,[60] we may not so easily excuse his lack of reference to her leadership in the political, military, and legal realms.[61] It is at this point that Josephus's stated bias against women in these roles shapes his portrayal of Deborah.

Background (*Ant.* 5.198–200)

Josephus more or less follows the biblical narrative in relating the stories of the judges; he names four judges
before Deborah,[62] although he uses the term "judge"
only in reference to Keniaz (5.184). Otherwise, they
are called "rulers" (*archon*) or "governors" (those who
exercise hegemony). In every case, the people acclaim
the man[63] as ruler after his demonstration of ability to
rule. The supernatural element of God's sending the
judge, so prominent in the Bible, is downplayed.[64] It
is also significant that Josephus consistently interprets
the biblical statements to the effect that "the Land
had rest for X years" as a reference to the length of
time the particular judge ruled. These are important
points to keep in mind as we analyze his portrait of
Deborah.

In the paragraphs leading into the story of Deborah, Josephus describes the spiritual condition of the
people and resultant enslavement by the Canaanites:
"Again, however, the Israelites, who had learnt no lesson of wisdom from their previous misfortunes, since
they neither worshipped God nor obeyed the laws, . . . fell
under the yoke of Jabin, king of the Canaanites"
(*Ant.* 5.198). He later adds that Israel remained in
this condition for twenty years while God continu-
ally tried to "tame their insolence" and make them
"wise" (*Ant.* 5.200). The description here and in *Jewish Antiquities* 5.198 translates into Greco-Roman terms
the biblical phrase "The Israelites again did what was
evil in the sight of the Lord" (Judg. 4:1). Moreover,
Josephus indicates his interest in military and geographical matters in his expansion of the description
of Jabin's city, his military might, and his general (5.
200).

Restoration: Deborah as Prophetess (*Ant.* 5.201)

Josephus completely changes the section that introduces Deborah and describes her role. When the people learn that "their calamities are due to their contempt of the laws" (*Ant.* 5.200), they ask Deborah to intercede with God for them, because she is a prophetess: "They besought a certain prophetess named Dabora—the name in the Hebrew tongue means 'bee'—to pray to God to take pity on them and not to suffer them to be destroyed by the Canaanites" (*Ant.* 5.201). The designation of Deborah as prophetess accords with the biblical account ("Deborah, a prophetess, wife of Lapidoth" [Judg. 4:4]) although we detect some editorial activity here. First, the biblical account immediately names Deborah, whereas Josephus first names her profession; she is one of a class: "a certain prophetess named Dabora." Second, Josephus explains the meaning of the name Deborah in Hebrew; it denotes "bee." He translates *deborah* by the Greek word for bee, which is *melissa*. This simple editorial note may be more significant than it first appears, for two reasons:

1. The word *melissa* also denotes a priestess of Delphi. Sarah Pomeroy briefly describes these *melissae*: "A group of priestesses *panageis* (sacrosanct), also known as *melissae* (bees), lived together in segregated dwellings and had no contact with men. The name 'bees' probably alludes to the asexuality associated with these insects. The function of these priestesses is unknown."[65] Josephus's allusion to the *melissae* perhaps explains his reference to Deborah interceding for the people because that is a priestly function,[66] as well as a prophetic function. We have already seen that the intercessory role was a very important aspect of the prophet's or prophetess's ministry in *Biblical Antiquities* and other contemporary literature.

2. The analogy to the bee implies that Deborah is asexual. Pomeroy also notes that the Greek poets Semonides (seventh century) and Phocylides (sixth century) both

likened women to various types of animals, among which only the woman represented by the bee was positively characterized. She comments, "The bee was notable not only for its industrious nature but for its asexual manner of reproduction."[67] In this regard, is it perhaps significant that Josephus omits the biblical phrase *'ešeth* (wife of) *lapidoth?*

Josephus omits reference to Deborah as "judging Israel" (Judg. 4:4), as well as the subsequent description of her popularity and judicial activity. The omission is noteworthy because of the importance of that particular role. We know that Josephus maintained that women could not even testify in court—"because of the levity and temerity of their sex" (*Ant.* 4.219)—much less serve as judges. Hence, he deals with this "incongruity" in the biblical text by simply omitting the problematic phrases.

Very interestingly, the problematic reference does appear in *Jewish Antiquities.* In telling the story of Gideon (which immediately follows the story of Deborah), Josephus adds this postscript: "Gideon then . . . continued for forty years to administer justice;[68] all men resorted to him concerning their differences, and all his pronouncements had binding weight" (*Ant.* 5.232). This statement adds to the biblical narrative about Gideon what too closely corresponds to the biblical description of Deborah.

Josephus has difficulty accepting that a woman could be not only a judge, in the legal sense, but also a political leader. Elsewhere, he states plainly that women are inferior to men. In *Jewish Antiquities,* the judges are given the mandate to rule because of the outstanding leadership qualities they exhibit through delivering the people from their enemies. Besides omitting the biblical reference to Deborah's leading the people, Josephus further reveals his prejudice against women leaders by excluding this element in the story of Deborah. Moreover, he interprets the biblical statement that "the land had rest forty years" as "then he [Barak] held command of the Israelites for forty years" (*Ant.* 5.209).[69] In every other case, Josephus interprets the phrase as a reference to the period of ruling or governing by the judge who has proven himself worthy to rule. It is all the more striking that Josephus would designate Barak as such a leader because Barak behaved so unadmirably when given the commission to liberate his people (*Ant.* 5.203).

Although Josephus omits reference to some of Deborah's roles, he appears to be comfortable with maintaining her role of prophetess. What did the term mean to him? To answer this question, we must look briefly at the role of a prophet or prophetess in the biblical world, in the Greco-Roman world, and in Josephus's own writings. We will see that because of Josephus's understanding of prophecy, both as a Jew and as one at home in Greco-Roman culture, he would have no problem presenting Deborah in this role, including the intercessory aspect.

Prophecy was a common phenomenon in antiquity. Its basic character was oracular; that is, it involved the communication of the will of the god regarding a specific matter. Hence, the prophet or prophetess spoke for (*pro* = for; *phete* = speak) the god. In ancient Greece, the god was consulted at public oracles—the most famous being the oracle at Delphi—concerning important decisions related to national or international policy, including going to war. The prophet or prophetess was believed to be momentarily an incarnation of the god, who then spoke the message through the human medium. This type of prophecy was ecstatic in nature and was interpreted to the inquirer by a third party, usually a priest. On the whole, these spokespersons were female; at Delphi, the prophetesses were known as the *Pythiae*.

Another famous class of prophetesses was the *Sibyllae*. Their role was similar to that of the *Pythiae*; they spoke on behalf of a god when "possessed with a spirit of divination,"[70] although they were not associated with a particular oracular seat, as were the *Pythiae*. Many of their prophecies were brought together in a series of books called the *Sibylline Books* (not to be confused with the

Sibylline Oracles). Although these collections originated in Greece, they were early brought to Rome, where they played a significant role in Roman national life:

> The use of these oracles was from the outset reserved for the State, and they were not consulted for the foretelling of future events, but on the occasion of remarkable calamities, such as pestilence, earthquake, and as a means of expiating portents. It was only the rites of expiation prescribed by the Sibylline books that were communicated to the public, and not the oracles themselves.[71]

In ancient Israel, in the preclassical period, prophecy was primarily oracular. Both men and women filled this role and played a prominent role in the political life of the nation by delivering oracles in the name of God. The prophet or prophetess was consulted for advice and often mediated between God and the people. Although forbidden to engage in many forms of divination practiced by their neighbors,[72] the people of ancient Israel were permitted to consult the urim and thummim (Ex. 28:30; Lev. 8:8; Num. 27:21) and the ephod (1 Sam. 23:9ff.)—both a kind of lots—when in need of specific guidance. Often the will of God was revealed through dreams, and there were limited occurrences of ecstatic prophecy (Num. 11:16ff.; 1 Sam. 10:9–13; 1 Kings 18:28–29).

Generally, Josephus holds prophecy in high regard,[73] especially when he deals with the biblical narratives. For Josephus, a true prophet or prophetess is primarily one who communicates God's message—whether predictive or revelatory—and serves as an intercessor. Despite his generally negative portrayals of women, he portrays them positively in this role, even as intercessors. A good example is that of the prophetess Huldah, who ministered during the time of King Josiah (see 2 Chron. 34:22–28): "The king sent... [envoys] to the prophetess Oolda [Huldah]..., commanding them to go to her and tell

her to appease God and attempt to win His favor" (*Ant.*
10.59–61). In the continuation of the passage in *Jewish
Antiquities,* Huldah delivers an extended prophecy to the
king, with Josephus uncharacteristically adding no negative commentary about women. In *Jewish Antiquities,*
Deborah functions as a true prophetess, for next Josephus implies that she delivers an oracle concerning the
outcome of the battle: "God thereupon promised them
salvation and chose for general Barak of the tribe of
Nephthali; *barak* denotes 'lightning'[74] in the tongue of
the Hebrews" (*Ant.* 5.202).

Israel Delivered (*Ant.* 5.202–9)

In Deborah's oracle, God promises victory and designates
who is to command the troops. Now, Deborah summons
Barak and commissions him to go into battle against Sisera, adding details about the number of troops and the
promise of victory.

Although Josephus portrays Deborah positively (as in
the Bible) as a prophetess, at the same time he betrays
his aversion to a woman serving in a leadership role. We
have already seen that he rewrote Judges 4:4–5 to elim-
inate any reference to Deborah judging or leading the
people. Now, here, he is careful to make the point that
Deborah is merely God's spokesperson. God designates
Barak as general before Deborah summons him. When
she specifies details about the campaign, Josephus makes
it clear that it is God who "prescribes it" (*Ant.* 5.202).
When Barak responds that he will not take command unless Deborah goes with him, Josephus has her retort, "You
resign to a woman a rank that God has bestowed on you!"
(*Ant.* 5.203). All of these subtle variations point to Josephus's bias against women exercising authority over men
or playing any leadership role outside of the spiritual
realm.

Josephus's version of Barak's response to Deborah's call differs considerably from that of the Hebrew and Greek versions of the Bible:

Judg. 4:8–9 (Heb.)	Judg. 4:8–9 (Gr.)	*Ant.* 5.203
Barak said to her, "If you will go with me, I will go; but if you will not go with me, I will not go." And she said, "I will surely go with you; nevertheless, the road on which you are going will not lead to your glory, for the Lord will sell Sisera into the hand of a woman."	Barak said to her, "If you go with me, I will go, but if you do not go with me, I will not go, because I do not know the day in which the help of the angel of the Lord is with me." And Deborah said to him, "I will surely go with you, but know that yours shall not be the honor on the way in which you go, because into the hand of a woman the Lord will hand over Sisera."	But Barak declared that he would not take command unless she shared it with him; whereto she indignantly replied, "You resign to a woman a rank that God has bestowed on you! Howbeit, I do not decline it."

Barak's unmanly behavior contrasts sharply with Deborah's willingness to do what is needed. Absent is any reference to the cause-effect relationship between Barak's unwillingness to obey God and Sisera's death "by the hand of a woman," which is a central feature of the biblical story. Josephus chooses instead to emphasize that a man has resigned to a woman a task given him to do. He wants to assure his audience that God does not place women in positions of political or military leadership.[75]

Although Josephus rewrites Deborah's reply, omitting the prediction that the battle would be won by a woman, it is interesting that he refers to it later in the story as if he had mentioned it previously: "Thus, did this victory redound, as Dabora had foretold, to a woman's glory" (*Ant.* 5.209). Unless his readers had access to a biblical version, this would have had no meaning for them. Josephus's reference to the statement at a later point indicates that he deemed it important; thus, his replacing it by a statement that it was not God's will for Deborah to take a leadership role points to intentional rewriting for polemical purposes.

It is also striking that even after Barak has behaved so unimpressively (he declined to take the lead, even with victory assured), according to Josephus, he still "commands" Israel for forty years. As we have seen, Josephus would not normally portray such a person as meriting a leadership role. Moreover, he again refers to Barak's lack of bravery in his account of the battle, described in the following paragraphs.

Josephus devotes three paragraphs to his description of the battle (*Ant.* 5.204–6), incorporating elements not present in the biblical versions, including emotional responses and military details. He also excludes (or briefly mentions) other biblical material.

First of all, he sets the scene in a way that emphasizes the impossibility of an Israelite victory. The two armies do not simply meet on the battlefield (as in the Bible); they are first encamped opposite one another, which allows the Israelites to become duly overwhelmed at the prospect of entering into battle with their opponents. Josephus heightens the dramatic impact of the scene by noting that the Israelites and Barak were panic-stricken[76] by the multitude of the enemy and resolved to retreat. He singles out Barak as responding in this way, which we would not expect of a general in command of an army. It is Deborah who restrains them from retreating and orders them to do battle that very day[77] (cf. Judg. 4:14), "for they would be victorious and God would lend them aid" (*Ant.* 5.204). She had prophesied earlier that God would indeed deliver the people and that Barak was to be the commander, and she now delivers an oracle about the timing of the victory, which encourages the Israelites and spurs them on to victory.

Josephus's version of the battle, although heightened dramatically by very vivid description, downplays the supernatural element; it follows more closely the narrative portion of the Bible (Judg. 4) than the poetic version

(Judg. 5). Josephus does, however, allude to the role of
the storm, although he treats it as no more than a well-
timed "great tempest" (*Ant.* 5.205) that worked to Israel's
advantage, because it was "at their back" (*Ant.* 5.206).
Also, he interprets the timing and direction of the storm
as signs of God's assistance (*pronoia*), which encourages
Israel to fight all the harder. Once the description of the
actual battle begins, Deborah is no longer mentioned,
which accords with the biblical account.

The scene depicting Sisera's death (*Ant.* 5.207–8) is abbreviated considerably. Josephus omits the dialogue and
specific imagery that serve to create the nuanced story
recounted in the Bible. This feature is puzzling, given
Josephus's penchant for introducing (or heightening) the
erotic element in his versions of other biblical stories (e.g.,
those of Joseph and Moses). Here, in a scene in which it
would be natural, he almost completely ignores it.[78]

Josephus introduces Jael as "a woman of the Kenites"
(*Ant.* 5.207); he does not name her husband (Heber); nor
does he mention the alliance the Kenites had with the
Canaanite king, Jabin. The latter alteration probably derives from Josephus's concern to avoid presenting Jewish
heroes and heroines unfavorably, as those who do not
keep faith in commitments. We see this same tendency
in the way Josephus adjusts the scene of the initial encounter between Sisera and Jael. While in the Bible Jael
goes out to meet him and then coaxes him into her tent,
all the while admonishing him not to be afraid (Judg.
4:18), in *Jewish Antiquities* he comes to Jael's tent and she
takes him in "at his request to conceal him" (*Ant.* 5.207).
Thus, the embarrassing element of her disregard for the
protocol of hospitality is moderated considerably, if not
entirely eliminated.

The remainder of the story more or less follows the
biblical account. Sisera drinks the milk and falls asleep,
whereupon Jael drives a tent peg through his mouth and
jaw. Then Barak's soldiers[79] arrive on the scene and dis-
cover what has happened. Josephus's commentary is an

addition: "Thus did this victory redound, as Dabora had foretold, to a woman's glory" (*Ant.* 5.209). The fact that her prophecy has come to pass validates her as a true prophetess. On a larger scale, it also confirms the validity of the Jewish religion, which is likely one of the primary points that Josephus endeavors to communicate through this story. The reliability of the Jewish prophets and prophetesses testifies to the providence (*pronoia*) of the Jewish God.[80]

Josephus closes his account with the notice that Barak "held command of the Israelites for forty years" (*Ant.* 5.209). He adds this element to the biblical narrative in spite of Barak's initial refusal to carry out his commission and his cowardly behavior before the battle. That Josephus nevertheless portrays Barak in this role reveals the degree of opposition to a woman filling such a role. Even a bad male leader is better than a good female leader.

Josephus does, however, make one final reference to Deborah, which indicates that she is not entirely off the scene. In introducing the following judge, he remarks that Barak and Deborah "died simultaneously" (*Ant.* 5.210). Although he gives the most important place to Barak, mentioning him first, he implies that she continued to serve in some capacity—probably prophetic—alongside Barak. Not only in one battle, but for forty years, Barak cannot function without her.

Comparison of the Portraits of Deborah in *Biblical Antiquities* and *Jewish Antiquities*

The similarities between the portraits of Deborah in these two documents are for the most part limited to the basic details and story structure drawn from the biblical text. Beyond this, we find considerable divergence between the two authors' accounts. Although Josephus agrees that Deborah is a great prophetess and even expands upon this by incorporating elements from the Greco-Roman perception of that role, at the same time, he alters the story to bring it into conformity with his stated opinion that women should not hold authority over men. He moves the reference to Deborah serving as judge in a legal sense (Judg. 4:4–5) into the story of Gideon (*Ant.* 5.232). He also elevates Barak to commander of Israel throughout the forty-year period of "rest" that the Land enjoyed.

By contrast, the author of *Biblical Antiquities* significantly upgrades the character and roles of Deborah to the point that she becomes the feminine counterpart to the greatest prophet in Israel's history, Moses himself. As with Moses, God sends Deborah to the people to "enlighten them for forty years" (*Bib. Ant.* 30:2). She speaks and acts like Moses, calling the people back to their covenantal commitment to God, leading them from bondage to freedom, interceding for them, and teaching them the way of God. She leads a mighty apocalyptic battle that corresponds to the exodus from Egypt and the eschatological battle of the forces of light and darkness. She commands not only humans but also angels and the natural elements, thus taking on a superhuman character. This is primarily a function of the author's portrayal of Deborah as a Wisdom figure.

He also enhances her character and role by adding two sections of material that are unique to *Biblical Antiquities*—Deborah's testamentary address upon her deathbed and the dirge after her death. In both cases, the scenes are interwoven by a significant amount of feminine imagery: woman of God, one of the female race, mother. The designation "mother," although rooted in the biblical text (Judg. 5:7), is developed into a metaphor of the special relationship between Deborah and her people—a relationship that in many ways corresponds to aspects of

Moses' relationship with Israel highlighted in other Jewish literature.

Deborah also takes on typological character, personifying Wisdom, sent by God, who enlightens Israel and gives it "rest" for forty years. This transformation into the metaphorical realm represents a perspective and approach unique to *Biblical Antiquities*. It derives in part from the prominence of Torah in the document, for Torah is equated with Wisdom in many Jewish texts. But Pseudo-Philo could have chosen to communicate the message through the masculine figure of Logos, represented in the character of Moses, as for example does Philo of Alexandria, who identifies the Logos with Moses.[81] But Pseudo-Philo chooses to return, as it were, to the feminine figure of Wisdom and to express significant truths through women in Israel's history.

We may understand this unique portrait of Deborah in light of the concerns of the Jewish people after 70 C.E. Deborah in every way conforms to the qualities of character and ability that the people needed in a leader—one who would call them back to Torah observance (with the promise of vindication for those who obey) and lead them in the battle against their enemies—and longed for in a leader, one whose motherly care and compassion would offer them healing and hope in their time of national crisis. This portrait certainly reveals Pseudo-Philo's uniquely positive valuation of women and the roles they could or should play in the life of Israel.

Notes

1. It is not clear whether Deborah or Barak is the author of the Hymn of Deborah. Judg. 5:1 states that both sang, but the verb is feminine singular (*wetašar*). It appears that "and Barak, son of Abinoam" is an addition. See G. Moore, *Critical and Exegetical Commentary*, 132.

2. All of the others are only military leaders, or "deliverers."

3. According to Josh. 14:6ff., Caleb, the brother of Kenaz's father (see Judg. 3:9), received Hebron as a reward for his faithfulness to God, and the land around Ashdod was given to the tribe of Judah (Josh. 15:45). It is not clear why the author so blatantly alters the biblical text.

4. Note that, according to the *Testament of Job*, Job gave to his three daughters an inheritance "better than that of [their] seven brothers." Although the statement is based on Job 42:15, in the biblical story, they are simply granted an inheritance with the brothers. In the *Testament of Job*, this "inheritance" proves to be the ability to prophesy, compose and sing hymns, and see visions (*T. Job* 48–52).

5. See Nickelsburg, "Good and Bad Leaders," 49–66. This depiction of the spiritual crisis at that time is also found in targumic and rabbinic literature. The Targum, for example, interprets Judges 4–5 (along with the entire book of Judges) in terms of worship, Torah study, and Torah observance. The *Targum of Judges* 5:2 (Heb.: "They chose new gods") reads: "When the House of Israel rebelled against the Torah, the nations came upon them and drove them out of their cities" (my trans.). This interpretation resembles Israel's confessional prayer in *Biblical Antiquities*: "We have been humiliated more than all peoples so that we cannot dwell in our own land and our enemies have power over us" (*Bib. Ant.* 30.4).

6. The Latin text contains two alternative readings. The *editio princeps* reads: *filias Amorreorum,* while the Admont MSS read: *filios Amorreorum.* I prefer *filias* because of the imagery suggested by the verb *seducti sunt,* as well as the obvious parallel to the incident in Numbers 25, when the Israelites were seduced by Moabite women and led to worship their gods. The author employs similar phraseology in his version of that story: "And the people were seduced [*seductus est*] after the daughters of Moab" (*Bib. Ant.* 18.14).

7. There are a few references to women serving in one role or the other, but in no figure are both combined. The Hasmonean queen Salome (Alexandra) ruled over Israel (*Ant.* 13.320, 405; 20.242; *BJ* 1.76–77, 85, 107–19); and Imma Shalom (sister of R. Gamaliel II and wife of R. Eliezer b. Hyrcannus) and Beruria (wife of R. Meir) were teachers of Torah. See Swidler, *Women in Judaism,* 105.

8. For example, *Bib. Ant.* 9.8; 11.2; 15.6; 19.4; 51.3–4, 6. See also *2 Apoc. Bar.* 17:4, and Ginzberg, *Legends,* 4:35, and 5:397 nn. 42 and 44.

9. Ginzberg (*Legends,* 4:35) presumes it refers to Deborah's husband and even goes so far as to equate Lapidoth with Barak: "God appointed Deborah and her husband Barak. . . . " He bases his assumption on the similarity of meaning between the Hebrew words *baraq* (lightning, flash) and *lapidoth* (torch).

10. Winston, *Wisdom of Solomon,* 37. For further information about Aristobulus, see Hengel, *Judaism and Hellenism,* 1:163–68.

11. See Winston, *Wisdom of Solomon,* 59 n. 83; Fiorenza, "Wisdom Mythology," 34.

12. See Urbach, *Sages,* 668ff.

13. The number seven is surely symbolic. Some Rabbis saw special significance in the fact that the benediction for redemption was the seventh (of eighteen) benediction, commenting that "Israel will be redeemed only in the seventh year (of the Messiah's advent)" (Urbach, *Sages,* 655). See Philo, *De Opificio Mundi* 89–128; *LevR* 29.11.

14. Susan Niditch examines the role of the visionary in her article "Visionary." She writes, "He suffers acutely from the crises of his community and sees visions in response to shared crisis situations" (p. 159). "[He] receives information about salvation for the blessed, destruction for the cursed, about the

passage of time, and the demise of empires" (p. 169). See also
1 Sam. 9:9, 18; *Bib. Ant.* 56.4; Philo, *Moses* 2.252, 281.

15. Belief in the interchange between stars, angels, and fire
(even lightning) was common in antiquity and was closely related to the also ubiquitous belief (derived from the Persians) in
a judgment of the world by fire. The motif appears repeatedly
in the *Sibylline Oracles*. The author of *2 Apocalypse of Baruch*
describes angels as "a flame and a fire" (21:6) and maintains
that the world will be judged by fire (44:15; 53:7; ch. 70). Note
also the parallel in Wis. 5:17–21, which describes the role of
the cosmos in the battle of final vindication of the righteous:
"The Lord will . . . arm all creation to repel his enemies; . . . and
creation will join with him to fight against his frenzied foes.
Shafts of lightning will fly with true aim, and will leap from
the clouds to the target, as from a well-drawn bow." See also
Mo'ed Qat. 16a, and Ginzberg, *Legends*, 6:197 n. 8es1; Perrot
and Bogaert, in *Pseudo-Philon*, 2:167. In the present passage,
Pseudo-Philo does not even mention the Kishon River, whereas
water plays the decisive role in the biblical version. He obviously
plays upon the Hebrew words *baraq* (lightning) and *'eśeth lapidoth* (fiery woman). On Deborah as "mistress of the stars" in the
Bible and Ugaritic Anat cycle, see Craigie, "Deborah and Anat,"
379–80. Note also that Isis takes on a similar role, being identified as "Sovereign of the stars" (Witt, *Isis,* 23; Conzelmann,
"Mother," 238). Deborah's role in *Biblical Antiquities* does not
correspond precisely to this, because she does not actually direct the stars herself at this point, although later she commands
the "lightnings" (meaning stars) to move on behalf of God (*Bib.
Ant.* 32.13).

16. The words of Sisera's mother (Judg. 5:30) are put into
Sisera's mouth. This could, however, be based on Ex. 15:9:
"The enemy said, 'I will pursue, I will overtake. I will divide
the spoil.'"

17. *Bib. Ant.* 43.5; 44.10; 45.3; 53.10; 63.4. See also Winston,
Wisdom of Solomon, 232–33.

18. In Judg. 5:30, the women tell Sisera's mother that Sisera
will bring spoils.

19. This message is also central in the Targum (see *Tg. Neb.
Judg.* 5:2, 4, 8, 10, 13).

20. Pseudo-Philo's portrayal of Jael is based on Judith, whose

portrayal, in turn, is based on the biblical story of Jael. See also Frölich, "Historiographie," 389–94.

21. On Judith's beauty, see Judith 10:7, 14, 19, 23; 11:21, 23.

22. Jael's piety is also highlighted in the Targum, for example, *Tg. Neb. Judg.* 5:24: "Good is Jael, wife of a scholar [reading *ḥaber*, fellow scholar, rather than the biblical *ḥeber*, a proper name], righteous, as one of the women who serve in the *beth midrash* [house of study], may she be blessed" (my trans.).

23. Pseudo-Philo assumes his audience's knowledge of the biblical story; he makes no reference to a tent or any dwelling in his account.

24. See Judith 12:16: "Holophernes' heart was ravished with her and his passion was aroused, for he had been waiting for an opportunity to seduce her from the day he first saw her."

25. For example, *Bib. Ant.* 18.10; 23.12; 28.4–5; 39.7.

26. Pseudo-Philo employs this literary technique for communicating messages through characters elsewhere in *Biblical Antiquities*. See, for example, Hannah's prayer (*Bib. Ant.* 50.4–5).

27. In *Biblical Antiquities* note the repeated polemic against sexual intercourse with Gentiles, for example, 9.6; 18.13; 21.1; 30.1; 44.7; 45.3.

28. A levitical sermon consists of instruction and exhortation, setting forth a doctrine and applying it to Israel's history, and then exhorting the community to act in accordance with that doctrine. Harrington (in *OTP*, 345 n. b) notes that "even though what follows is called a hymn, we cannot now detect a hymnic structure."

29. For example, when the people ask Samuel for a king, he replies, "Behold, your king will come to you after three days" (*Bib. Ant.* 56.7), whereas the biblical version (1 Sam. 10:8) specifies seven days. See also *Bib. Ant.* 11.1, 2; 18.6; 19.6; 28.4. The same motif is highlighted by Ben Sirah (Sir. 45:23) in connection with Phinehas: "Phinehas son of Eleazar ranks third in glory for being zealous in the fear of the Lord."

30. The biblical order is Othniel, Ehud, Shamgar, and Deborah; in *Biblical Antiquities*, it is Kenaz, Zebul, Deborah.

31. The motif of God guarding Israel while judging the wicked occurs in the story of the plagues in Egypt (the plague of hailstones [Ex. 9:26], darkness [Ex. 10:23], and death of the

firstborn [Ex. 11:7]). Cf. *Bib. Ant.* 7.4 and *2 Apoc. Bar.* 29:2.
David Winston (*Wisdom of Solomon*, 228–29) discusses various
rabbinic views as to whether the Israelites suffered from the
plagues. The opinions are divided between limited suffering
during all of the plagues and merely some of them. By contrast, Philo declares that they were not touched by any plague
(*Mos.* 1.143), which accords with the presentation in *Biblical
Antiquities*.

32. This eschatological element is present also in the Targum
(*Tg. Neb. Judg.* 5:31): "As Sisera, so may all the enemies of Your
people perish, O Lord; but all those who love him are destined
to shine like the sun; their glory will be more than 343 times,
as the going-forth of the sun in its strength" (my trans.).

33. The literal expression is "storehouses of their souls"
(Lat.: *promptuariis animarum eorum*). The same expression is
found in *2 Apoc. Bar.* 21:23 and 30:2.

34. There is a textual variant at the end of verse 13 and
the beginning of verse 14. The question centers upon whether
to read "... even if a man die [*morior*]. Sing a Hymn to God,
Deborah" (so Kisch); or "... even if a man delay [*moror*] to
sing a Hymn to God. But you, Deborah, sing a Hymn" (so
Cazeaux in *Pseudo-Philon* and Harrington in *OTP*). The first
reading better suits the context because Deborah is speaking
to "the fathers in their chambers of souls."

35. *Tg. Neb. Judg.* 5:3 reads: "I, Deborah, spoke in prophecy
before the Lord; I praised, thanked, and blessed [before] the
God of Israel" (my trans.). Note the similarity between the Targum and *Biblical Antiquities*, considering that the Holy Spirit is
equated with the Spirit of prophecy in many Jewish texts.

36. See *Dictionnaire de la Bible, Supplément* (1966), s.v. "Philon
(Pseudo-)," by M. Delcor.

37. The verb is actually *custodivit*, which is more literally
translated as "observed" (so Harrington in *OTP*) or "kept." I
have rendered the Latin more literally, as "fulfilled."

38. Latin: *in te*. *OTP* reads: "among you"; I have rendered
it "on you," in accordance with my translation of the entire
phrase.

39. See Wisd. Sol. 10:1 and 7:1 for parallel usage of this
term.

40. Feldman ("Prolegomenon," cxviii–ix) accepts this reading.

41. Harrington (in *OTP*) emends *thurificat* (burns incense) to *turrificat* (builds a tower).

42. Note that this interpretation of earth as a testimony of Israel's continued existence differs from Deut. 32:1, where earth is called upon to testify against Israel.

43. See *Apoc. Mos.* 42:1; *4 Macc.* 18:7.

44. See Plumpe, *Mater Ecclesia*, 11. Note also his discussion of Tertullian's illustration that just as Eve was formed from Adam's side during sleep, so the church was formed from Christ's side during the sleep (of death) (pp. 56–57).

45. See Wisd. Sol. 18:6; *Tg. Yer. Ex.* 12:32: "Four nights are there written in the Book of Memorials before the Lord of the world. Night the first, when He was revealed in creating the world; the second, when He was revealed to Abraham; the third, when He was revealed in Miṣraim, His hand killing all the firstborn of Miṣraim, and His right hand saving the firstborn of Israel; the fourth, when He will yet be revealed to liberate the people of the house of Israel from among the nations" (quoted in Winston, *Wisdom of Solomon,* 315.)

46. Note the parallel with the story of Israel's liberation under Jehoshaphat's leadership (2 Chron. 20:27–28): "Then all the people of Judah and Jerusalem, with Jehoshaphat at their head, returned to Jerusalem with joy, for the Lord had enabled them to rejoice over their enemies. They came to Jerusalem, with harps and lyres and trumpets, to the house of the Lord." Pseudo-Philo relocates the cultic center from Jerusalem to Shiloh.

47. We do not know how far back this practice dates, although it is possible—even probable—that it began already in the Second Temple period.

48. The genre finds its roots in Genesis 49, and underwent significant development at the hands of the Deuteronomist (Deut. 31–34; Josh. 23–24). Other testaments, or texts that include testaments, are these: Tobit, *Jubilees*, 1 Maccabees, *2 Enoch*, the *Testaments of the Twelve Patriarchs*, the *Testament of Moses* (*Asm. M.*), and the *Testament of Job*. For further discussion, see Collins, "Testaments."

49. The only other case of a woman giving a testament is that of Rebecca in *Jub.* 35:1–27. For an excellent discussion of Rebecca's testament, see Endres, *Biblical Interpretation*, 173–76.

50. For example, Ex. 20:12; Lev. 19:3; Deut. 5:16; Prov. 6:20; 31:1.

51. This is found in Philo's commentary on Prov. 8:22. Winston (*Wisdom of Solomon*, 177) remarks that Philo follows the terminology of Plato's *Timaeus* 49A–50D.

52. My translation, which more closely parallels *Biblical Antiquities*.

53. Harrington notes (*Bib. Ant.* 33.3 n. c in *OTP*) that the expression "evil impulse" corresponds to *yeṣer haraʿ* in Jewish thought and that the notion that the evil impulse ceases after death is "unique to Pseudo-Philo." But see *GenR* 9.5: "Why was death decreed against the wicked? Because as long as the wicked live, they anger the Lord...; but when they die they cease to anger him.... Why was death decreed against the righteous? Because as long as the righteous live, they must fight against their evil desires, but when they die, they enjoy rest."

54. A different view is expressed through the midrashic story of Rachel interceding for Israel after the destruction of the Temple (see Ginzberg, *Legends*, 4:304–10). One by one, many of the great patriarchs and prophets implore God to have mercy on Israel, all to no avail. Finally, Rachel pleads her case, whereupon God is moved to forgive the sins of the people and restore them. The motif is drawn from Jer. 31:15–16, where Rachel "weeps for her children" and subsequently is promised that her "work will be rewarded" by Israel's eventual restoration (v. 16). See also Ginzberg, *Legends*, 2:135–36, and Perrot and Bogaert, in *Pseudo-Philon*, 2:177.

55. See *The Tractate "Mourning,"* p. 27.

56. It is also possible that the number seventy is to be understood as symbolic.

57. Note the parallelism between "judges, rulers, and leaders" in *Jub.* 31:15, where Jacob prophesies that Levi will fulfill all of these roles. These same leadership roles are highlighted in *Biblical Antiquities*, and Deborah—a woman—fills them all.

58. See *LevR* s.1, interpreting the name Avigdor (1 Chron. 4:4), based on the Hebrew root *gdr*, meaning, among others, "fence": "Israel had many fence-makers (guardians) against sin." A fence-maker is a protector.

59. Ginzberg, *Legends*, 6:411 n. 65.

60. Josephus consistently omits poetic material in the *Antiq-*

uities; for example, the omission of the Song of Hannah (*Ant.* 5.347).

61. See Betsy Amaru's comments in "Portraits": "Female characters such as Deborah and Naomi pose another kind of problem for Josephus. In their cases he does not need to defend virtuous character so much as limit an assertiveness that potentially goes beyond his sense of propriety in a female, even a prophetess. Thus he deletes from his characterization of Deborah any references to her activities as a judge (Judg. 4:4). Instead he has her, more maternally, seek God's 'pity' on behalf of the beleaguered Israelites (5.200)" (p. 162). My own observations were arrived at independently of this article.

62. He names the first Judge as Keniaz, rather than Othniel (Judg. 3:9), which accords with the tradition preserved in *Bib. Ant.* 25–28.

63. I use the word "man" deliberately, for Josephus never portrays a woman in such a role.

64. On Josephus's downplay of the supernatural, see Feldman, "Introduction," 44–45; idem, "Hellenizations in Josephus' *Jewish Antiquities*," 145–46.

65. Pomeroy, *Goddesses*, 76.

66. Feldman ("Josephus' Portrait of Deborah," 122) maintains that Josephus's designation of Deborah as "bee" points to a negative portrayal of her, based on *Meg.* 14b, which indeed interprets her name negatively: "R. Nahman said, 'Haughtiness does not befit women. There were two haughty women, and their names are hateful, one being called a hornet and the other a weasel. Of the hornet it is written, "And she sent and called Barak," instead of going to him.'" But Josephus's reference to "bee" in *Jewish Antiquities* is not negative.

67. Pomeroy, *Goddesses*, 49. She also quotes (p. 51) from the poet Juvenal's notoriously misogynist satire on women where he likens the only positively portrayed woman to a bee.

68. Greek: *brabeuōn*, to judge or umpire, arbitrate, direct, govern.

69. Note that *Biblical Antiquities* states that Deborah ruled the people (*Bib. Ant.* 32.18); like *Jewish Antiquities*, the epistle to the Hebrews (11:32) mentions only Barak: "And what more should I say? For time would fail me to tell of Gideon, Barak, Samson, Jephthah, of David and Samuel and the prophets—

who through faith conquered kingdoms, administered justice, obtained promises."

70. *A Dictionary of Classical Antiquities: Mythology, Religion, Literature, Art,* rev. ed. (1958), s.v. "Sibyllae," 583.

71. Ibid., 584.

72. Ibid., 1153–54.

73. For example, *Ant.* 8.418–20. Negative valuations refer primarily to those "false prophets" in the last days before the fall of Jerusalem (70 C.E.) who led the people astray by telling them that it was God's will that they resist the Romans and that God would miraculously deliver the city. See Betz, "Miracles," 226–35.

74. Perhaps Josephus points out this detail because of Roman superstitions about lightning. Romans believed it was "divine fire" and thus an omen to be deciphered. See *A Dictionary of Classical Antiquities: Mythology, Religion, Literature, Art,* rev. ed. (1958), s.v. "Puteal," 529, and "Haruspex," 270.

75. See Pomeroy's discussion (*Goddesses,* 185–89), and note particularly her comments that "Romans, unlike the Macedonians, believed that the battlefield was no place for a woman" (p. 188); and "Roman women were given no true political offices and were forced to exert their influence through their men" (p. 189).

76. The Greek verb *kataplessō* may denote a stronger response than the Loeb translation "dismayed."

77. My translation, more literal than the Loeb rendering, attempts to express the contrast in behavior between Barak and the Israelites, on one hand, and Deborah, on the other.

78. We must remember, however, that Josephus omits the poetic version (Judg. 5:24–27), which is truly the artistic masterpiece in this regard. He does allude to the biblical hymn when he states that Iale (Jael) gave Sisera "milk that had turned sour" (*Ant.* 5.207/Judg. 5:25).

79. According to Judg. 4:22, it was Barak who came.

80. See Attridge, "Josephus," 223–24; Feldman ("Introduction," 44) attributes Josephus's great emphasis upon *pronoia* to his affinities with Stoicism, of which *pronoia* was a cardinal doctrine. Many Stoics maintained that the validity of divination was proof of *pronoia.*

81. Fiorenza ("Wisdom Mythology," 34) notes that Philo identifies Logos with Moses, Isaac, and Israel.

2

Jephthah's Daughter

The daughter of Jephthah is one of the great tragic figures in biblical literature. Her choice to submit willingly to her father's "word,"[1] innocent as she is, and the violent nature of her death are tragic enough.[2] But her saga is even more poignant because of its context. It is an *Israelite* story. The vow is made to the God of Israel (Judg. 11:30), who categorically opposes human sacrifice (Jer. 19:5),[3] and—most poignant of all—God, by remaining silent, allows it to be fulfilled.[4]

God is not the only silent one. The narrator, too, passes over the story without comment, perhaps marking an ancient belief that such acts were an ultimate expression of piety and devotion to God. Moreover, the silence is not confined only to the biblical narrative. As Phyllis Trible has keenly observed, "Throughout the centuries, patriarchal hermeneutics has forgotten the daughter of Jephthah but remembered her father, indeed exalted him."[5] The ultimate silence is that of the author of the

epistle to the Hebrews, who includes Jephthah in his panegyric on great heroes of the faith, without reference to
his rash vow or the fulfillment of it (Heb. 11:32).[6] Perhaps the tragedy greater than her untimely death is its
meaninglessness, attested to by the embarrassed, or simply unconcerned, silence of commentators throughout
the centuries.

Yet, the example of this nameless Israelite girl became a
paradigm for later Jewish and Christian martyrology. This
did not occur directly; it developed, rather, through incorporating into the story of Abraham's sacrifice of Isaac
the motif of willing submission to death. This element is
absent from Genesis 22, but becomes a primary motif in
later interpretations.[7]

This element was combined with two other elements—
the belief that Isaac was actually sacrificed, willingly, and
that his death had atoning value for the Jewish people
of future generations—into a cardinal doctrine in Jewish
thought called "the Akedah." The term "Akedah" derives
from the Hebrew '*qd*, meaning "to bind," a verb describing Abraham's action in the biblical account. According
to Genesis 22:9, Abraham binds Isaac, but the later
interpretation focuses upon Isaac's attitude and role, emphasizing that he allowed himself to be bound; that is, he
willingly submitted to his father and to God. The doctrine further developed the aspect that Isaac truly died
as a burnt offering unto God. Texts speak very graphically of "the ashes of Isaac," or "the blood of the binding
of Isaac,"[8] which were understood to have atoning value
for the Jewish people.[9] Some texts expressly link Isaac's
sacrifice with the whole burnt sacrifice (*tamid*) offered on
behalf of the people twice daily in the Jerusalem Temple.

Neither the idea that Isaac was a willing sacrifice nor
the notion that his sacrifice had value for the good of
the people is found in the Genesis account. Both are suggested, however, in the story of Jephthah's daughter, who
responds to her father's announcement, "Do to me according to what has gone out of your mouth, now that

the Lord has given you vengeance against your enemies"
(Judg. 11:36). She must die because her people's enemies have been subdued, and she willingly submits to her
fate. Thus, two central elements in the Akedah doctrine
not present in the biblical story correspond to features of
the story of Jephthah's daughter. Although, as a nameless
female, her voice is muffled, she speaks through the life
of one of the most significant figures in Israelite history.

Jephthah's Daughter in *Biblical Antiquities:* A Worthy Sacrifice

In his portrait of Jephthah's daughter, Pseudo-
Philo heightens and expands the basic elements in the
biblical account and introduces additional motifs. Rather
than denying her tragedy, or worse, ignoring it, he focuses
upon it and explores the various nuances of its meaning.
He interprets it, to be sure; but in the process, he invests
her sacrifice with a significance unparalleled in other interpretations, thus bestowing upon her life and death a
unique significance. The author's treatment of her story
is sometimes shocking, sometimes puzzling, but wholly
intriguing.

Background: Jephthah's Vow (*Bib. Ant.* 39.10)

Pseudo-Philo portrays Jephthah differently than does the
biblical narrator, except for the most basic elements in
the story. As in Judges 11:1, Jephthah is a "mighty warrior" (*Bib. Ant.* 39.2) whom the Israelites solicit to be
their leader (Judg. 11:4ff./*Bib. Ant.* 39.3ff.), a role that
he only reluctantly accepts. But the author omits the reference to Jephthah's ignominious parentage (Judg. 11:1)

and instead explains that his brothers expelled him because they "envied him" (*Bib. Ant.* 39.2).[10] He apparently did not want to portray Jephthah as any less than a full Israelite.

A major variation in *Biblical Antiquities* is that Jephthah comes to the people as a prophet, exhorting them to repent and reminding them of God's promises to forgive them and deliver them from their enemies (*Bib. Ant.* 39.6). The people repent and pray for deliverance (*Bib. Ant.* 39.7). To this point, Jephthah functions very much like a "good leader." God then duly "repent[s] of his wrath and strengthen[s] the spirit of Jephthah" (*Bib. Ant.* 39.8), who delivers an ultimatum to the king of Ammon.[11] As in the Bible, when the king refuses to listen to Jephthah, he goes into battle against the Ammonites (Judg. 11:28–29/ *Bib. Ant.* 39.10).

In both accounts, Jephthah makes a vow to God before going to battle, though the specific wording differs between the two texts:

Judges 11:30–31	*Bib. Ant.* 39.10
And Jephthah made a vow to the Lord, saying, "If you give the Ammonites into my hand, then whoever[12] comes out of the doors of my house to meet me, when I return victorious from the Ammonites, shall be the Lord's, to be offered up by me as a burnt offering."	Jephthah rose up...to go out and fight in battle array, saying, "When the sons of Ammon have been delivered into my hands and I have returned, whoever meets me first[13] will be a holocaust to the Lord."

In *Biblical Antiquities* the vow is not couched in formal language and form. Jephthah merely "says" it, almost as an aside. Although the same is true in Judges, there he verbalizes it more formally. A corollary to the absence of a formal wording of the vow is the impersonal character of the phraseology. Jephthah does not speak to God; nor does he speak directly of himself; he states only that whoever meets him "will be a holocaust to the Lord."

Biblical Antiquities describes God's response to Jephthah's vow: "And God was very angry and said, 'Behold

Jephthah has vowed that he would offer to me whatever meets him first on the way; and now if a dog should meet Jephthah first, will the dog be offered to me?' " (*Bib. Ant.* 39.11). God is angry, primarily because of Jephthah's carelessness in making his vow, for its unspecific wording could lead to his sacrificing something unclean. We find a similar commentary on Jephthah's vow in both the Midrash and Talmud:

> Jephthah made a request in an improper manner, as is proved by the text, "Then it shall be that whatsoever cometh forth of the doors of my house to meet me . . . I will offer it up." Said the Holy One, blessed be He: "If a camel, or an ass, or a dog had come out, would you have offered it for a burnt-offering?" So the Holy One, blessed be He, answered him accordingly by bringing him his daughter to hand (*LevR* 37:4).[14]

Indeed, God is furious with Jephthah. This is right; this is how we expect God to respond. But the unexpected turn comes when God responds to the vow not by decreeing that Jephthah be punished, but by declaring another, more radical, vow: "And now, let the vow of Jephthah be accomplished against his own firstborn, that is, against the fruit of his own body, and his request against his only-begotten" (*Bib. Ant.* 39.11). Jephthah's notorious vow has become God's vow. God is angry at Jephthah, but it is the *daughter* who will die. We are compelled to ask why Pseudo-Philo would represent God in this way. At a time when commentators on the whole sought to censure Jephthah's vow or to devise the means to annul rash vows,[15] he has chosen to portray God as responsible for the sacrifice of Jephthah's daughter.[16] This alteration surely points to a significant element in his presentation of the story.

God's directive that Jephthah would sacrifice his daughter recalls the story of the Akedah. In Genesis 22, as here,

God is responsible for the sacrifice of the child. In both cases, the child is very dear to his/her father.

One could argue that a major contrast between the two stories is that in the case of the Akedah, God does not intend that the child be actually sacrificed. But the Akedah was understood as an actual sacrifice, particularly by later commentators. This aspect of the doctrine is present also in *Biblical Antiquities,* for God declares: "And I demanded his [Abraham's] son as a holocaust. And he brought him to be placed on the altar, but I gave him back to his father and, because he [Isaac] did not refuse, his offering was acceptable before me, and on account of his blood, I chose them" (*Bib. Ant.* 18.5). Indeed, Jephthah's daughter herself refers to Isaac's example as a model for her own response to her fate: "And who could be sad in death, seeing the people freed? Or do you not remember what happened in the days of our fathers when the father placed the son as a holocaust, and he did not refuse him but gladly gave consent to him, and the one being offered was ready and the one who was offering was rejoicing?" (*Bib. Ant.* 40.2).

Moreover, there are echoes of Isaac's story in the wording of God's decree. Pseudo-Philo uses three terms or phrases to describe Jephthah's daughter—"firstborn" (*primogenitum*), "fruit of his own body" (*fructum ventris sui*), and "only-begotten" (*unigenita*); only the last of these is found in the biblical text. His use of the first term is significant, for there is no compelling reason for him to designate her as such, unless perhaps he plays upon the word "first," used, though adverbially, by Jephthah in his vow. The term "firstborn," by analogy, links Jephthah's daughter with Isaac. Isaac was "firstborn" in the sense that he was the designated heir, even though he was not Abraham's actual firstborn son.

The third phrase, which appears in both Judges 11:34 and Genesis 22:2, 19, denotes one who is unique and beloved or precious.[17] It occurs in combination with "firstborn" in Zechariah 12:10: "They will...mourn as one mourns for an only child [*hayyahid*] and weep bitterly over him as one weeps over a firstborn [*habbakor*]."[18] The only other occurrence of the term in reference to a daughter is found in a postbiblical text, Baruch 4:16: "They have led away this widow's cherished sons, and of [my] only-begotten daughter they have made me desolate."[19]

The second phrase, "fruit of his own body," appears elsewhere in *Biblical Antiquities* in reference to Isaac (*Bib. Ant.* 32.2, 4). Thus, Pseudo-Philo draws a parallel between Isaac's offering and that of Jephthah's daughter and develops her story in such a way as to incorporate elements that would enhance this correspondence.

After declaring that Jephthah would sacrifice his daughter, God adds a promise: "But I will surely free my people in this time, not because of him [Jephthah] but because of the prayer that Israel prayed" (*Bib. Ant.* 39.11). This introduces an element not present in the Bible. Israel will be liberated not because of Jephthah, but because of Israel's prayer. This alone is what moves God to act on behalf of the people, not overzealous leaders who make rash vows and thus treat lightly God's holiness. The author wants to assure his audience that Jephthah's vow and the fulfillment of it are censured, despite the tone and direction he gives to the story.

Jephthah Returns in Victory (*Bib. Ant.* 40.1)

Although Pseudo-Philo basically follows the biblical account in his summary of the ensuing battle against the Ammonites (Judg. 11:32–33), he moves quickly to the dramatic moment—the meeting between Jephthah and his beloved daughter. We are already aware of who will meet him.[20] Hence, the dramatic question is not, Who will meet him? Rather the questions are: How will it come to pass? and How will the daughter respond? The moment is hardly less dramatic because the subject has already been identified; indeed, it is intensified, as we await the unfolding of the inevitable.

Unaware that the scene has been orchestrated by God so that the decree be fulfilled, Jephthah falls apart[21] when he catches sight of the one who first meets him. But he quickly gathers himself together enough to tell his daughter of her fate:

> Rightly was your name called Seila, that you might be offered in sacrifice. And now, who will put my heart in the balance and my soul on the scale? And I will stand by and see which will win out [lit., weigh more], whether it is the rejoicing that has occurred or the sadness that befalls me. And because I opened my mouth[22] to my Lord in song with vows, I cannot call that back again (*Bib. Ant.* 40.1).

This differs greatly from the biblical account, in which Jephthah chides his daughter for meeting him even though his intense sorrow indicates the depth of his affection for her. Here, too, his rejoicing quickly turns to sadness, but Jephthah openly describes the struggle within and the emotions that accompany his dilemma, which is characteristic also of Hellenistic drama.

The beginning of Jephthah's speech is built around his daughter's name, announced here for the first time—and the only time in history. This tendency to name the Bible's unnamed characters is typical of *Biblical Antiquities*.[23] Her name is Seila, a name "rightly" given her at birth because she would one day "be offered in sacrifice." Leopold Cohn suggests that the name derives from the Hebrew root *s'l*, to ask, demand; thus, *se'ila* denotes "she who was demanded."[24]

But is the conjectured etymology wholly appropriate to the text that states that she is thus named because she "would be offered [*offeraris*] in sacrifice"? Perhaps the form of the Hebrew word that stands behind Seila (*s'l*) should be understood according to its meaning of "to lend, or dedicate," in the sense that it is used in 1 Samuel 1:28: "I have lent him to the Lord; as long as he lives, he is given to the Lord." *Offeraris* in this case would denote "she who was dedicated, or offered," to God.

Seila is described as a sacrificial offering, an analogy that further links her story with the Akedah—as to the meaning and significance of her death, she is the feminine counterpart to Isaac. In this regard, note the parallelism encompassing both genders in Isaiah's description of the Suffering Servant who was killed on behalf of the people: "Like a lamb [*se*] that is led to the slaughter, and like a sheep [*rahel,* ewe] that before its shearers is silent..." (Isa. 53:7).[25] Geza Vermes discusses the relationship between Isaiah 53 and reflection on Genesis 22 recorded in the Targum:

> The leading idea of Isaiah 53 is parallel in *leitmotif* to the targumic tradition on Genesis 22. Isaac freely offered his life and it was accepted by God in favour of his descendants, and even of the Nations, according to Ps-Philo (*Bib. Ant.* 32.3). The Servant is compared to a lamb brought to the slaughter (53:7); Isaac was also a holocaustal lamb. Isaac's sacrifice was ordained by God; so also was the Servant's (53:10). These common features of the two stories are on the scriptural level. On the targumic level, the resemblances are plainly realized and the nature and effect of the Servant's passion are applied to the sacrifice of Isaac so that Genesis 22 becomes the story of a just man who offered himself for the sake of sinners.[26]

Vermes misses the parallels between the Suffering Servant and Seila, which are intriguingly similar to those he names in relation to Isaac. Elsewhere, he deals briefly[27] with the reference to Isaac in Seila's response to her father, but concludes that Pseudo-Philo contrasts Isaac's willingness to be a sacrifice with Seila's reluctance,[28] and that the purpose of her story in *Biblical Antiquities* is to underline the contrast between Abraham's sacrifice and Jephthah's.[29] His final comment is that "Jephthah's offering was valueless."[30] This we may not dispute, but not so Seila's offering. According to Pseudo-Philo, it is indeed "valuable," because it is given willingly, as is Isaac's offering (*Bib. Ant.* 40.3). Later, God declares, "Her death will be precious [Lat.: *preciosa*/Heb.: *yeqarah*, valuable] before me always" (*Bib. Ant.* 40.4).[31]

As in the biblical narrative, Jephthah closes his speech with an assertion that he cannot revoke his vow. From his perspective, his daughter must die because she has been the first to meet him; the conditions of his simple, though drastic, vow have been met. He is unaware of just how irrevocable is his vow, for it has intersected with God's vow. He does not seem to be aware of God's role in the course of events.

In contrast to Jephthah's statement that he cannot revoke his vow, the Rabbis taught that one could indeed annul a rash or unacceptable vow by finding a "door of regret," something that one was unaware of when making the vow and that rendered it invalid. Specifically, concerning Jephthah, they applied the text, "Is there no balm in Gilead? Is there no physician there?" (Jer. 8:22). They replied that he could have gone to the priest Phinehas and had the vow annulled had he not been too proud to do so (see nn. 15–16). Although they asserted that God arranged that Jephthah's daughter came out to meet him, they also declared in the same passage that he could have had the vow annulled.

According to *Biblical Antiquities*, Jephthah's vow was irrevocable because it was in truth God who vowed that Seila's life be offered in sacrifice. Indeed, this central feature of Pseudo-Philo's treatment of the story is unique to this document, and extremely significant, as evidenced by his further development of it later in the story.

Seila's Response (*Bib. Ant.* 40.2-3)

From a literary standpoint, the moment of truth has arrived. Seila has been informed of her father's vow; now she must determine how she will respond. She must choose, and her choice will determine the validity of her sacrifice. This element of choice is pivotal in Greek tragedy, as demonstrated by Richard Lattimore: "[These plays] pre-set a pattern in which death, whether or not by divine orders, is seen to be necessary, and in which the hero sees this, consents, and makes the act his own."[32] He notes that in Aeschylus's *Iphigenia in Aulis* (which at points closely parallels our story) the heroine's choice to offer herself willingly "supports the entire play, in which the climax comes when the heroine chooses death of her own free will."[33]

Although it is not a classical Greek tragedy as such,[34] Seila's story is structured in part around a similar pattern. At this point, her response is the crucial issue, evidenced by Pseudo-Philo's expansion of the terse biblical statement:

Judges 11:36	*Bib. Ant.* 40.2
My father, if you have opened your mouth to the Lord, do to me according to what has gone out of your mouth, now that the Lord has given you vengeance against your enemies.	And who is there who would be sad in death, seeing the people freed? Or do you not remember what happened in the days of our fathers when the father placed the son as a holocaust, and he did not refuse him but gladly gave consent to him, and the one being offered was ready and the one who was offering was rejoicing? And now do not annul everything you have vowed, but carry it out.

In *Biblical Antiquities,* Seila actively embraces her fate, drawing an analogy between her offering and that of Isaac. Just as Isaac's readiness to be offered gave his offering meaning and value, so her readiness is crucial to the value of her own offering.[35] She seems to know that it was possible to annul a vow, for she directs her father not to annul his vow; her will accords with the divine will (*Bib. Ant.* 40.4).

Seila then requests permission to go and mourn her youth, which corresponds to her response in Judges, although with a few variations:

Judges 11:37	*Bib. Ant.* 40.3
Grant me two months, so that I may go and wander on the mountains, and bewail my virginity, my companions and I.	[Grant] . . . that I may go into the mountains and stay in the hills and walk among the rocks, I and my virgin companions, and I will pour out my tears there and tell of the sadness of my youth. And the trees of the field will weep for me, and the beasts of the field will lament over me.

The request is expanded to include a statement about nature's mourning over her death. It omits the time period,[36] as well as the notice that Seila "bewail[s] [her] virginity," replacing it with the statement that with her "virgin companions" she will mourn the "sadness of [her] youth." This element of mourning appears strange because she has just affirmed her readiness to be a "willing sacrifice," but mourning does not necessarily imply reluctance. Indeed, Seila's next words reveal that she does not mourn because she must die: "For I am not sad because I am to die nor does it pain me to give back my soul, but because my father was caught up in the snare of his vow" (*Bib. Ant.* 40.3). Through Seila's words, Pseudo-Philo also makes a statement about Jephthah (Israel's leader)—he is not wise but foolish; for in biblical thought, fools are ensnared by the words of their mouth.[37] This motif will appear again when the author (in a comment attributed to God) contrasts Jephthah's foolishness with Seila's wisdom (*Bib. Ant.* 40.4). Hence, it appears that Seila mourns the sin of her father, Israel's leader, and what must occur because of his folly.

Then, Seila states once more that she must offer herself willingly or her "death would not be acceptable" or she "would lose [her] life in vain." There can be no doubt that she willingly gives her life; she has affirmed this again and again. Why, then, does she declare that she will "tell [these things to] the mountains" (40.3) and later tell them "to the wise men of the people," who could not "respond to her word" (40.4)? She seems to search for some escape from death, although this contradicts her (repeatedly) stated position of willing acceptance.

To reconcile this apparent contradiction, we must first examine the motif of Seila's journey to the "mountains." The "mountains" correspond to the "wise men of the people" by an exegetical process that is typically midrashic. We find similar interpretations in rabbinic literature. A Midrash that specifically identifies the "mountains" of Judges 11:37 with the "elders" (corresponding to the "wise men of the people") is recorded in *ExodR* 15:4: "And 'mountains' refers to the elders, for so does the daughter of Jephthah say to her father: 'That I may go down upon the mountains.' Did she then go upon the mountains? No, she went to the elders to prove to them that she was a pure virgin."[38] The translator[39] notes that she did this "in hope that they would absolve her father from his vow; otherwise they might have thought that her father's vow had been intentional."

We might likewise interpret Seila's actions in *Biblical Antiquities,* if not for her repeated affirmations of her willingness to die. Pseudo-Philo incorporates this tradition of her visit to the elders but uses it differently. His particular purpose for including it will become clear in the following section when God speaks about Seila's life and death.

God's Response (*Bib. Ant.* 40.4)

In this section, unparalleled in other literature, God speaks on behalf of Seila, affirming that she indeed must

die but also affirming her special qualities of character
(vis-à-vis her father and the rest of Israel's leadership)
and the value of her death:

> And afterward she came to Mount Stelac,[40] and the
> Lord thought of her by night and said, "Behold now I
> have shut up the tongue of the wise men of my people
> for this generation so that they cannot respond to the
> daughter of Jephthah, to her word, in order that my
> word be fulfilled and my plan that I thought out not
> be foiled. And I have seen that the virgin is wise in
> contrast to her father and perceptive in contrast to all
> the wise men who are here. And now let her life be
> given at his request, and her death will be precious
> before me always, and she will go away and fall into
> the bosom of her mothers" (*Bib. Ant.* 40.4).

Seila's pilgrimage to Mount Stelac (Mount Hermon) is
a very intriguing element in her story. Mount Hermon, as
George W. E. Nickelsburg has cogently demonstrated, is
traditionally a place of revelation[41] and commissioning.[42]
Here, Seila is, in essence, commissioned to die. In this,
her experience is not unlike that of Jesus, whose visit
to Mount Hermon before his martyrdom involved a discussion about his death (Luke 9:31), and resulted in a
"witness" from God about his status and value in relation
to God (Matt. 17:5, and par.).

While Seila is at Mount Stelac, God "thought of"
her "by night." The temporal element is significant because divine revelations often come at night in *Biblical
Antiquities*.[43] God's thinking of Seila stands in contrast to
the wise men, who ignored her. At this point, we expect
God to do what they did not—annul the vow. But God has
already declared that Seila must die. Will God change the
vow?

God not only does not annul the vow, but also claims
responsibility for the silence of the wise men: "I have
shut up the tongue of the wise men of my people for this

generation so that they cannot respond to the daughter of Jephthah...in order that my word be fulfilled and my plan that I thought out not be foiled" (*Bib. Ant.* 40.4). Seila must die; the decree will not be altered. Her only choice is to die in a way that will give her death meaning and purpose. Because she chooses this, God later declares that her death "will be precious before me always" (*Bib. Ant.* 40.4).

The notion that God requires a human death contradicts biblical religion (Jer. 19:5; Micah 6:6–8) and the overwhelming majority of rabbinic dictums on the subject. The notion that the elders could not annul the vow also contradicts rabbinic interpretation. The notion that Seila attempted to have the vow annulled (which we could infer from this text) contradicts her stated intention to give herself willingly (*Bib. Ant.* 40.3). So, then, what is the purpose of Seila's visit to the wise men? And why does God declare that God has "shut up the tongue of the wise men" so that she would die?

To begin with, the motif of Seila's visit to the wise men makes a subtle statement about Israel's leadership. Their silence in the face of this unthinkable vow corresponds to that of the Israelites when Micah led Israel into idolatry and Israel's subsequent punishment (*Bib. Ant.* 44–47). In this extrabiblical story, Israel's silence, especially the leaders' silence, is roundly condemned as a sin comparable to murder and idolatry. God declares that those who were silent would be destroyed because "they acted wickedly" (*Bib. Ant.* 47.8).[44] Thus, the silence of the leaders in Seila's story points to their apostasy. The author expresses his condemnation of them more explicitly in God's statement that Seila is "perceptive in contrast to all the wise men who are here" (*Bib. Ant.* 40.4). She is "perceptive" because she is willing and obedient to God's will.

Inasmuch as Pseudo-Philo indicates that God is responsible for the silence of the wise men, how then can they be indicted? We could perhaps understand this as an example of irony, in the same vein as the biblical statement that "God hardened Pharaoh's heart" (Ex. 10:20; 11:10) and Isaiah's call to preach to the people so their hearts would be hardened (Isa. 6:10). God does not actually harden the heart; it is hardened already.[45] In the case of Pharaoh, God uses the hardness of heart to accomplish the divine purpose for Israel. In contrast, we find a strong tendency toward determinism in *Biblical Antiquities* (e.g., *Bib. Ant.* 12.3). Thus, the emphasis upon God's word being fulfilled and plan being carried out represents this overall tendency in the document.

The motif of Seila's visit to the wise men functions to highlight the absolute necessity of her death. She did not die because her father would not have the vow annulled, or even because "the scholars forgot they could annul it."[46] She died because God decreed it, and God could not and would not change the decree. Pseudo-Philo has Seila go to the wise men primarily as a means of emphasizing this point and censuring Israel's leadership; her primary purpose in going to the wise men is not to have them annul the vow.

Even though Seila must die, God praises her in a eulogy unique to *Biblical Antiquities*. God declares that she is "wise in contrast to her father and perceptive in contrast to all the wise men who are here" (40.4). Regarding the qualities highlighted, note the parallel in the Song of Moses, where Moses uses forms of the terms "wise" and "perceptive" as contrasts to the qualities of apostate Israel (Deut. 32:28–29): "They are a nation void of sense; there is no understanding in them. If they were wise, they would understand [perceive] this; they would discern what the end will be." Moreover, these qualities characterize two of Israel's greatest figures—Joseph (Gen. 41:33) and Solomon (1 Kings 3:12)—and are particularly demonstrated here in Seila's willing submission to God's will, because it expresses her covenant faithfulness.

In this section, God clearly attests to the value of Seila's death: "Her death will be precious before me always, and she will go away and fall into the bosom of her mothers" (*Bib. Ant.* 40.4; cf. Lam. 2:12). Pseudo-Philo quotes from Psalm 116:15: "Precious in the sight of the Lord is the death of his faithful ones [Heb.: *hasidim*]." By describing Seila with the words of this Psalm, he highlights her piety, intimating that she is faithful to the covenant, indeed a saint (Heb.: *hasid*).

The insertion of the word "always" into the text of Psalm 116 is significant, representing as it does the Hebrew word *tamid*, which recalls the twice-daily burnt offering at the Temple. As noted above, this offering came to be identified with Isaac's sacrifice, the Akedah,[47] and we may infer that the word's introduction here further marks the author's intention to link Seila's sacrifice with the Akedah.

Seila's Lament (*Bib. Ant.* 40.5–7)

Here, Pseudo-Philo introduces and develops new imagery. He portrays Seila as a virgin weeping because she will never be a bride, a motif suggested by the biblical account, where Jephthah's daughter requests to go and mourn her "virginity" (Judg. 11:37). But the entire lament is extrabiblical and has no counterpart in other postbiblical literature;[48] its significance is indicated by the amount of material Pseudo-Philo includes in the lament. In Seila's great lament, set upon Mount Stelac (*Bib. Ant.* 40.5), he amasses mourning terms to create a scene of intense lamentation: "She began to weep, and this is her lamentation, weeping over herself before she departed" (*Bib. Ant.* 40.5). Nature's involvement in the lament, though remotely linked to Judges, is developed significantly in *Biblical Antiquities*.

Seila begins by addressing three elements of nature (mountains, hills, and rocks), exhorting them to hear her lament. She had mentioned the same three elements when requesting to go away and mourn (*Bib. Ant.* 40.2). Now she addresses them, describing her fate and her resolve to offer herself willingly so that "not in vain" would her "life be taken away":

> Behold how I am put to the test! But not in vain will my life be taken away. May my words go forth in the heavens, and my tears be written in the firmament! That a father did not subdue by force his daughter whom he had devoted to sacrifice,[49] so that her ruler approve of the only-begotten, promised as a sacrifice.[50] But I have not made good on my marriage chamber, and I have not retrieved my wedding garlands. For I have not been clothed in splendor, according to my nobility.[51] And I have not used the sweet-smelling ointment, and my soul has not rejoiced in the oil of anointing that has been prepared for me (*Bib. Ant.* 40.5–6).[52]

In this section, Seila affirms her willingness to die and also declares the personal cost the death will entail. I have translated the Latin text accordingly (in some cases differing from *OTP*) because of the author's consistent emphasis upon Seila's perspective and self-sacrifice rather than Jephthah's willingness to offer her.

Seila next addresses her mother:

> O Mother, in vain you have borne your only-begotten daughter[53] because Sheol has become my bridal chamber,[54] though my people [dwell] on earth.[55] And may all the blend of oil that you have prepared for me be poured out, and the white robe that my mother has woven,[56] the moth will eat it. And the crown of flowers that my nurse plaited for me for the festival, may it wither up; and the coverlet that she wove of hyacinth and purple in my nobility,[57] may the worm devour it. And may my virgin companions tell of me in sorrow and weep for me through the days (*Bib. Ant.* 40.6).

Here, Pseudo-Philo employs the same imagery as in the previous section, with some variation. He specifies again the wedding chamber, the crown of flowers, the bridal garments, and the anointing oil. Again, Seila refers to herself as the "only-begotten daughter." As I have already noted, her status as the only-begotten child is central to the story, as its emphasis suggests. Not only does this compound the sense of parental grief at her fate, but it also serves to associate her with Isaac. The extraordinary value accorded her death is expressed in her statement that although Sheol is her bridal chamber, her nation dwells upon earth; her death is truly an acceptable offering for the good of the nation. We will return to this point later.

Finally, Seila addresses trees and animals, bidding them join in her lament: "You trees, bow down your branches and weep over my youth, you beasts of the forests, come and bewail my virginity; for my years have been cut off, and the time of my life has grown old in darkness" (*Bib. Ant.* 40.7). These elements also appear in the context of Seila's request to her father when told of her fate (*Bib. Ant.* 40.3). The address to nature here at the close of her lament frames the lament with references to nature; this and the motif of nature mourning both enhance the value of her life and death.

What is Pseudo-Philo trying to say through the figure that he has (almost entirely) created? A possible key to his interpretation may be found in how the words and the imagery he employs functioned in other texts at that time. We need not look very hard to find numerous examples of similar imagery used to describe the destruction of Jerusalem and/or the Temple.

The following are examples of some parallels between Seila's story and themes related to the destruction of Jerusalem and/or the Temple.

The Notion That God Decreed the Death

Much literature related to the destruction of Jerusalem emphasizes that God was ultimately responsible for its "death," rather than the obvious enemy, be it the Babylonians or Romans (Jer. 11:17; Bar. 2:20; Lam. 2:17; *BJ* 5.362–69; 6.401; 6.409–12; *LamR* 1.13.41; 2.2.5). God decreed Jerusalem's destruction because of divine anger against the people, particularly the leaders (Lam. 4:13; Bar. 4:7); God's anger was thus appeased by the destruction of the city (Lam. 2:4; 4:11; Bar. 2:19; *LamR* 4.22.25).

The Atoning Nature of the Destruction of Jerusalem

A corollary to the notion that God was responsible for Jerusalem's destruction is the notion that God poured out divine wrath upon the city and Temple rather than upon the people, and thus they were saved from annihilation.[58] Jerusalem and the Temple were innocent victims who bore the brunt of God's anger.[59] A prime example is found in *2 Apocalypse of Baruch*, which in message and tone parallels *Biblical Antiquities*:

> Have you not seen what has befallen Zion? Or do you think that the place [the Temple] has sinned and that it has been destroyed for this reason, or that the country[60] has done some crime and that it is delivered up for that reason? And do you not know that because of you who sinned the one who did not sin was destroyed, and that because of those who acted unrighteously, the one who has not gone astray has been delivered up to the enemies? (*2 Apoc. Bar.* 77:8–10).[61]

To be sure, the author portrays Seila as such an innocent victim; even God declares that she is wise and perceptive and implies that she is a saint. Yet, God has decreed that she must die because of her father's sin. His punishment is her death. *Biblical Antiquities* 40.6 possibly alludes to the atoning effect of her sacrifice: "Sheol has become my bridal chamber, though my people [dwell] on earth."

Jerusalem and the Temple Are Referred to as "Daughter"

Seila is Jephthah's daughter; likewise, Jerusalem and the Temple are, metaphorically speaking, referred to as daughters in Jewish texts. This imagery is especially prominent in the book of Lamentations. There, Jerusalem is described as the "virgin daughter of Zion" (Lam. 2:1, 13) or the "virgin daughter of Judah" (Lam. 1:15). The book of Baruch describes Jerusalem as weeping for its "only-begotten daughter" (Bar. 4:16).[62] Likewise, the Midrash refers to the Temple as "the virgin of Israel"[63] and to Jerusalem as a "virgin."[64] Israel is designated as "virgin daughter" in the *Assumption of Moses* 11:12.[65]

Jerusalem and the Temple Called "First" in the Midrash

Pseudo-Philo adds the word "first" to the biblical version of Jephthah's vow in describing whom he would offer in sacrifice and also specifies that Seila is "firstborn" (*Bib. Ant.* 39.11). The Midrash applies the same epithet to Jerusalem and the Temple:

> Here is another explanation of "This month shall be unto you the beginning (i.e., 'first') of months." God is in a way called "first," as it says, "I am the first, and I am the last" (Isa. 44:6). Zion is called "first," as it says, "Thou throne of glory, on high from the first, thou place of our sanctuary" (Jer. 17:12). . . . God who is called "the first" will come and build the Temple which is also called "first" (*ExodR* 15.1; see *Pesiq. R.* 51.3).

The Silence of Leadership

In *Biblical Antiquities,* the "wise men of the people" (the leaders) remain silent in the face of Seila's impending fate (*Bib. Ant.* 40.4), a characteristic of Israel's leadership in relation to the destruction of Jerusalem, whether in the biblical text or in postbiblical texts. Concerning the first destruction of Jerusalem, Lamentations 2:10 declares, "The elders of the Daughter of Zion sit on the ground in silence." Josephus (*BJ* 6.234) includes this motif in his description of the fall of Jerusalem in 70 C.E.: "The Jews, seeing this fire all about them,...stood as mute spectators only."

The Use of Marriage Imagery

Seila's lament is peppered throughout with marriage imagery. Similar imagery is frequently employed in both biblical and postbiblical literature to describe Jerusalem and/or Israel. The prophet Isaiah likens Jerusalem to a barren woman reunited with her husband and once again bearing numerous children (Isa. 54:1–8); the author of Revelation envisions "the new Jerusalem...prepared as a bride adorned for her husband" (Rev. 21:2). The Midrash compares the destruction of Jerusalem to an unconsummated marriage. According to *Lamentations Rabbah,* Jerusalem exchanged her bridal splendor for the rags of captivity and destruction: "So it is with Israel. So long as they obeyed the will of the Holy One, blessed be He, it is written, 'I clothed thee also with richly-woven work' (Ezek. 16:10).[66] ...But when they disregarded the will of the Holy One, blessed be He, He clothed them in exiles' garments (*bedadin*), as it is written, 'How does the city sit solitary—(*badad*)'" (*LamR* 1.1).[67] Note the similarity of imagery with *Biblical Antiquities* 40.6, which contrasts the beauty of Seila's clothing in her nobility with its deteriorated condition after her death. The author of *4 Ezra* draws an analogy between an unconsummated marriage and the death of an only son in reference to the destruction of Jerusalem, probably based on imagery drawn from Jeremiah 6:26 and Zechariah 12:10. For example, he is told that the death of the woman's "only son" as he "entered his wedding chamber" signifies "the destruction that befell Jerusalem" (*4 Ezra* 10:48).[68] Pseudo-Philo employs similar imagery to describe Seila, although he alone builds the metaphor around a feminine figure.[69]

The Lamentation

Some of the greatest lamentation literature in Judaism concerns the destruction of Jerusalem at the hand of the Babylonians in 587 B.C.E. In many cases, themes and imagery used to describe that catastrophic event are reused in laments of the second destruction in 70 C.E. These texts portray Jerusalem lamenting its own death (see Lam. 1:2, 4, 12; 2:9), as well as nature lamenting its death (see *2 Apoc. Bar.* 10:4–19).[70] Similarly, Seila's lament includes these elements.

It appears that Pseudo-Philo, by introducing specific motifs and imagery applied elsewhere to the destruction of Jerusalem or the Temple, presents Seila's death as in part a symbol for what the Jewish people had suffered in their recent past. He appropriates Seila's story as a paradigm of this national tragedy and adapts it to communicate a certain message to his contemporaries. We will look at the possible content of that message at the close of this chapter.

Seila's Death and Burial (*Bib. Ant.* 40.8–9)

The beginning of the account of Seila's death and burial follows the biblical text (Judg. 11:39–40). Seila returns to her father, and he does "everything he had vowed" (*Bib. Ant.* 40.8). But from that point, the author expands the story considerably. First, he specifies what the biblical storyteller could not, or would not, i.e., he states exactly what Jephthah did: " . . . offered the holocausts." A second, more significant, modification occurs in the continuation of the story, as a synoptic comparison indicates:

Judges 11:39–40	*Bib. Ant.* 40.8
So there arose an Israelite custom that for four days every year the daughters of Israel would go out to lament the daughter of Jephthah the Gileadite.	Then all[71] the virgins of Israel gathered together and buried the daughter of Jephthah and wept for her. And the children of Israel made a great lamentation and established in that month, on the fourteenth day of the month, that they should come together every year and weep for Jephthah's daughter, for four days.[72]

We see that the circle of mourners was much wider than that mentioned in Judges 11. Indeed, the mourning for Jephthah's daughter has assumed national proportions. This modification reveals the great significance Pseudo-Philo attached to her death, a significance that is explicable if her death is understood as a symbol for the destruction of Jerusalem.

According to my translation, the people of Israel established on the day of Seila's death, the fourteenth day of the month, that the nation would mourn her death four days every year. I would suggest that the month specified was the month of Nisan, the fourteenth day of which was the "festival of the offering of the firstborn"[73] and Passover Eve, when lambs were slaughtered in place of the firstborn of the people of God. Possibly, Pseudo-Philo connected Seila's death and Passover on the basis of the phrase *miyyamim yamimah* (year to year), found in both Judges 11:40 and Exodus 13:10,[74] thus providing a tangible link between the two events. Moreover, he indicates elsewhere that he attaches special significance to Passover (*Bib. Ant.* 30.16–17; 48.3; 50.2), which in some Jewish texts was linked with the Akedah.[75] Since Pseudo-Philo also links Seila with Isaac, he had a reasonable basis for associating Seila's death with Passover.

Another aspect of this analogy is *Biblical Antiquities*'s interpretation of Seila's death as in part a symbol of the destruction of Jerusalem, for, likewise, the Midrash associates the fall of Jerusalem with Passover: "'And he sated me with wormwood': with what He filled me on the first nights of Passover He sated me with on the night of the ninth of Ab (wormwood). The night of the week on which the first day of Passover occurs is always the same as that on which the night of the ninth of Ab falls" (*LamR* 3.15.5).[76]

The four days of mourning recall the four public fast days when Jews mourned the destruction of Jerusalem,[77] for the four days in *Biblical Antiquities* are not necessarily consecutive. These fast days were instituted after the first destruction of Jerusalem (Zech. 7:3, 5; 8:19) and continued to be observed after the second destruction of Jerusalem.

Finally, the author notes that Seila had a tomb that bore her name. This detail adds an element not even suggested by the biblical account, which presents the girl as nameless, remembered by a few nameless women. In *Biblical Antiquities,* by contrast, Seila becomes a national figure, properly honored in death, her memory kept alive by the whole people of Israel.

In *Biblical Antiquities,* we see that Jephthah's daughter emerges from obscurity and insignificance. Her tragic saga, rather than being passed over quickly and without comment, is the central element highlighted in the Jephthah cycle. Indeed, in *Biblical Antiquities,* Jephthah's story is Seila's story; the father quickly fades into the background as Pseudo-Philo focuses upon the daughter's death and explores various nuances of its meaning. He finds in her an important symbol, a symbol of the destruction of Jerusalem, whose "sacrifice" was decreed by God, yet ultimately for the good of the Jewish people. We will return to this after looking at Josephus's portrait of Jephthah's daughter.

Jephthah's Daughter in *Jewish Antiquities:* An Exemplary Daughter

The story of Jephthah's daughter is not a major focus of attention in *Jewish Antiquities.* Josephus devotes merely three paragraphs to the main narrative (*Ant.* 5.264–66) and part of another (*Ant.* 5.263) to the vow itself. His version consists entirely of narrative; the dialogue, so essential to the development of the biblical story, is eliminated.[78] Josephus adds little by way of description or narrative to the biblical version, although he reshapes—or rather refines—the portrait by allusions to similar stories in Greco-Roman literature. He also adds his own commentary, clearly censuring Jephthah's action.

Background: Jephthah and His Vow (*Ant.* 5.257–63)

Jephthah is presented in *Jewish Antiquities* as an outstanding military leader and statesman. As in the biblical account, he is an exiled commander of a band of mercenaries (*Ant.* 5.257–59) whom the Israelites approach about leading them in battle against the Ammonites (*Ant.* 5.258–60). Josephus adds that the Israelites had been enslaved for eighteen years (*Ant.* 5.263), which increases Jephthah's stature as a great liberator. Jephthah agrees to lead them, only upon their pledge to make him their permanent leader (*Ant.* 5.260). Then, he demonstrates his leadership abilities by "promptly taking charge of affairs" (*Ant.* 5.261) and entering into negotiations with the Ammonite king (*Ant.* 5.261–62).[79] When these break down,[80] however, Jephthah resorts to the military option and attacks the Ammonites, who are roundly defeated

(*Ant.* 5.263). The leader thus returns home triumphant, in great glory. It would have been a perfect victory, a perfect triumphal return, were it not marred by the shadow of the vow he made before the battle; for when he "made vows (in order to obtain) victory,"[81] he had promised "to offer up the first creature[82] that should meet him" (*Ant.* 5.263).

Josephus leads into the account of what transpired upon Jephthah's return home by setting up a contrast between the commander's mighty victory and the mighty defeat that awaited him: "But on returning home, he fell foul of a calamity far different from these fair achievements" (*Ant.* 5.264). The language here evokes the image of shipwreck, which, in turn, recalls the similar vow made by Idomeneus,[83] a heroic figure in Greek literature. This extrabiblical description sets the scene in a way that would heighten the drama and communicate more effectively to a Greco-Roman audience. They are cued to look for the inevitable appearance of a favored child, whose destiny was foreordained by his/her father's words, of which he/she was painfully unaware.

Thus, Josephus characterizes Jephthah as a mighty warrior and leader whose one tragic bane is his careless vow to sacrifice whatever would first meet him upon his return in victory. This corresponds very closely to the biblical account, the main difference being the coloring of the story by language and imagery to remind Josephus's Greco-Roman audience of similar stories in their own literature.

Jephthah's Daughter: Decision and Death (*Ant.* 5.264–66)

Josephus moves quickly into the crucial scene in which Jephthah's only daughter comes first to meet him. What heretofore had been merely a possibility has now become reality—it is she who must be offered in sacrifice. Josephus heightens the dramatic and tragic impact of the scene by adjoining descriptive phrases from various places in the biblical account: "And there was his daughter coming out to meet him (Judg. 11:34a), she was his only child (11:34b), she had never slept with a man (11:39)."

Jephthah responds to the disastrous turn of events more or less as he does in the biblical account, although Josephus expresses it in Greco-Roman style: "Wailing in anguish at the magnitude of the calamity, the father chid his daughter for her haste in meeting him; for he had dedicated her to God" (*Ant.* 5.265). He replaces the biblical "he tore his clothes," which would have had little meaning for his audience, by a phrase from Thucydides: "stunned at the magnitude of the calamity before him..." (*Thuc.* 3.113.3). As in Judges, Jephthah expresses his depth of caring for his only child in response to her being the first to meet him and also chides his daughter for meeting him.

The final phrase, "for he had dedicated her to God," stands in place of Jephthah's statement that he had made an irrevocable vow to God. Josephus again translates the biblical language and culture into terms understandable to his audience. In Greek literature, the story that most closely parallels that of Jephthah's daughter is the story of Iphigenia, who was devoted to Artemis in exchange for her father's victory over the Trojans,[84] although in this case, the goddess demanded her, whereas God did not demand Jephthah's daughter. In fact, Josephus emphasizes that God did not demand her (*Ant.* 5.266).

Jephthah does not declare that he cannot revoke the vow, as in the Bible. Josephus likely omitted this element because it was generally held—in both Jewish and Greco-Roman society—that one need not fulfill a vow that was hastily made or would result in harm to another.[85] Moreover, it is irrelevant whether or not Jephthah could revoke the vow for the crucial issue is his daughter's decision to submit to her father and to die for the good of her country.

It is enough for Jephthah's daughter to know that she is "dedicated to God." She knows what that entails and draws the conclusions. How she will respond is essential to the movement and meaning of the story. As in the saga of Iphigenia, she holds it within her power to shape the story so that her sacrifice "becomes not merely an act of bloody brutality inflicted by overwhelming force, but a choice of honor."[86] Josephus summarizes her response as follows: "But she without displeasure learnt her destiny,[87] that she must die in exchange for her father's victory and the liberation of her fellow-citizens" (*Ant.* 5.265).[88]

She must die in exchange for her father's victory (and glory) and for her country. Thus, her response highlights the duty to one's family and country; she responds as a good daughter should, particularly according to both Greek and Roman values. Helen Foley has demonstrated that in Greek drama, "good" women "align themselves with marriage, or . . . sacrifice themselves for the preservation of family, state or nation."[89] She adduces the example of Iphigenia, who chooses to die for Greece; as we have seen, Iphigenia's heroic response echoes that of Jephthah's daughter in *Jewish Antiquities.*

Besides attaching importance to the good of the state, Greco-Roman culture, as Jewish culture, also highly valued respect for and obedience to parents, particularly the patriarch of the family. In Roman society, the father had absolute power over the daughter, even the power of life and death.[90] Louis Feldman[91] discusses the importance of filial obedience in both Greek and Roman literature in relation to Isaac's response in Josephus's account of the Akedah. There, Isaac exclaims that he would deserve never to have been born at all were he to reject the decision of God and his father, and were this the resolution of his father alone, it would have been "impious to disobey" (*Ant.* 1.232). Although Jephthah's daughter's response is more abbreviated, it is not unlike Isaac's. She is concerned about her father's good and her country's good and willingly consents to give her life in accordance with his vow.

Finally, Jephthah's daughter's response to her destiny accords with the Stoic value of willing acceptance of one's fate. This is summarized by M. L. Clarke in *The Roman Mind:*

> The good man accepts his fate willingly.... In adversity, he gives to god not his obedience but his assent; he follows not because he must, but because he wishes to. Seneca quotes the lines in which Cleanthes had written of a joyful submission to destiny, adding his own epigrammatic summary, which expresses as well as can be expressed in a few words the Stoic idea of Fate: "Fate leads the willing follower, but drags the unwilling."[92]

Accordingly, Jephthah's daughter is portrayed as in every way a "model child," willingly submitting to her own destiny, to her father, and to her country as the highest good. This portrait does not differ in essence from that of the biblical version, but Josephus shapes it to appeal to his particular audience.

Josephus records in summary fashion Jephthah's daughter's request to go and "bewail her youth with her fellow citizens" and her father's granting of her request. This aspect of the story is clearly inconsequential to his portrait. He rather moves almost immediately to the subject of her death, which he describes more graphically than does the biblical narrator. Whereas in Judges the storyteller is "so confounded by the act"[93] that he "spares us the suspense and agony of the details,"[94] Josephus openly describes the gruesome deed: "He sacrificed his child as a burnt offering" (*Ant.* 5.266).

It is at this point that the stories of Jephthah's daughter and Iphigenia diverge, for it is nearly universally understood that in the case of Iphigenia, the goddess Artemis intervened to save her from actual death.[95] Although later interpreters have attempted to append the same happy ending to the story of Jephthah's daughter,[96] it has been "too little, too late"; there is no indication in the story itself or by its earliest interpreters that she was not actually sacrificed as a burnt offering. This is borne out by Josephus's commentary, recorded in the paragraph that follows his description of her death.

Commentary (*Ant.* 5.266)

Josephus closes his account with a commentary that introduces into the story the kind of declaration we would have wished to have found in the biblical story: "[It was] a sacrifice neither sanctioned by the law nor well-pleasing to God; for he [Jephthah] had not probed what might befall or in what aspect the deed would appear to them that heard of it" (*Ant.* 5.266).

In his commentary, Josephus clearly takes an apologetic posture. He is concerned to emphasize that the God of Israel in no wise approved of Jephthah's act, that it was illegal according to the Jewish scriptures, and that Jephthah was imprudent in making such a vow. Hidden between the lines is a response to the accusation that Jews practiced human sacrifice.[97] Perhaps the charge was supported by this story, for Josephus takes such pains to disavow that God had any part in its eventuation; and he also refers to "how the deed would appear" to those who heard about it.

In his commentary, he also contrasts the God of Israel with pagan gods, specifically Artemis, by an allusion in his statement that Jephthah's sacrifice was not "well-pleasing to God." Feldman[98] notes that in *Iphigenia in Aulis*, the chorus declares that Artemis "rejoices in human sacrifices." The God of Israel, by contrast, is not pleased with human sacrifice and nowhere prescribes it in the Torah. It is totally foreign to the nature of the Jewish God and as such is unequivocally rejected.

Josephus omits reference to the mourning (Judg. 11: 39–40), likely because it is not vital to his portrait of Jephthah's daughter. He has already made the two crucial statements—she is an exemplary daughter, and the God of Israel takes no pleasure in human sacrifice. Having made these, he quickly moves on to the rest of Jephthah's story. We may note that, despite his censure of Jephthah's conduct, he portrays this judge in the remainder of his story more or less as in the Bible. With the unspeakable deed behind him, Jephthah continues to serve as Israel's leader until his death six years later (*Ant.* 5.270).

Comparison of the Portraits of Jephthah's Daughter in *Biblical Antiquities* and *Jewish Antiquities*

Jephthah's daughter is portrayed very differently in these two documents, though both follow the basic outline of the biblical narrative. They agree on one notable point that is not present in the Hebrew or Greek versions, but is in the Vulgate (Latin)—that whatever should come first would be offered as a sacrifice. We also find a parallel between Jephthah's daughter's words "who could be sad in death, seeing the people freed?" (*Bib. Ant.* 40.2) and Jephthah's declaration that she must die "in return for . . . the liberation of her fellow-citizens" (*Ant.* 5.265).

Both Pseudo-Philo and Josephus portray Jephthah's daughter as a willing sacrifice, in agreement with the biblical account. But each incorporates this aspect into his portrait in his own way. Josephus, who gives the entire account a Greco-Roman coloring, makes Jephthah's daughter a model of exemplary character, expressed specifically in her willingness to set aside her individual welfare for the good of her family, people, and country. While this type of response is commended in any society, it emphasizes a characteristically Roman ideal.

Pseudo-Philo, in contrast, portrays Seila's willingness to sacrifice her life in Jewish terms, through developing the comparison between her offering and that of Isaac, as it came to be understood in the framework of the Akedah doctrine. He accomplishes this by both explicit analogy (*Bib. Ant.* 40.2) and implicit allusion. He declares that (1) God commands the sacrifice; (2) her sacrifice is efficacious for the good of the people; and (3) her death is precious before God always. Seila's association with the exemplary martyr of the Jewish people increases significantly the value of her life and death.

A major difference between the portrait in *Biblical Antiquities* and that in *Jewish Antiquities* is Pseudo-Philo's significant enhancement of Seila's character and role. Although Josephus does not portray Jephthah's daughter negatively, he does not give much attention to her story. He devotes to it a mere three paragraphs, which he relates primarily to make the statement that the God of Israel does not require or accept human sacrifice. The apologetic motivation likely reflects his intention to counter the anti-Semitic propaganda that Jews practiced human sacrifice.

Pseudo-Philo, in contrast, adds material not even suggested by the biblical text, such as God's declaration that Jephthah must sacrifice his firstborn and God's eulogy on Mount Stelac. He also inserts a lengthy lament in which both Seila and nature mourn her untimely death and lost life. His use of marriage imagery, although similar to that employed in Greco-Roman literature, along with his use of other imagery and language all indicate that he views Seila's death as symbolic of the destruction of Jerusalem and the Temple.

In both *Biblical Antiquities* and *Jewish Antiquities,* we find no suggestion that Jephthah's vow could have been revoked, in contrast to rabbinic dictums. Both authors present this differently, however, and use it for different purposes. For Josephus, it is simply irrelevant, because his point is that the daughter willingly submits to her father for his good and that of her people; if the vow were revocable, the example would lose its force and meaning.

In *Biblical Antiquities,* the vow is indeed irrevocable because it is God who vows that Seila must die and that the divine plan cannot be thwarted (*Bib. Ant.* 40.4). Moreover, precisely this last element is a point of difference between Josephus's and Pseudo-Philo's portraits. While Pseudo-Philo repeatedly asserts that God wills that Seila must die and implies that her death is an acceptable offering, Josephus roundly denies both: "a sacrifice neither sanctioned by the laws nor well-pleasing to God" (*Ant.* 5.266). Josephus's commentary accords more with the logical, expected response, while Pseudo-Philo seems to contradict the very essence of biblical religion. Because Pseudo-Philo portrays Seila as the feminine counterpart to Isaac and also because he views her death as in part a symbol of the destruction of Jerusalem, he brings the biblical narrative into accord with this analogy and presents God as having commanded her death (see Lam. 2:17). He also rewrites the final scene to present Seila as a national figure whose death is mourned by all Israel for four days every year.

Why did Pseudo-Philo invest Seila's death with such significance? Why did he portray her death as, in part, a symbol for the destruction of Jerusalem? Why did he portray her as the feminine counterpart to Isaac, particularly as portrayed in the Akedah? We must evaluate his particular characterization in relation to the context of the composition of *Biblical Antiquities,* which, I believe, was the destruction of Jerusalem. In his search to find meaning in this national disaster, Pseudo-Philo discovers in Jephthah's daughter a figure who offers an explanation. He begins with the biblical character who submits to her father's will, who gives her life willingly for the people, although innocent of guilt herself. He sees in her experience a counterpart to the Akedah and develops this feature of her character and role in order to lay a foundation for the second aspect of his portrait—her becoming a type or symbol of the destruction of Jerusalem. In her, the efficacious value of the Akedah and the tragic "sacrifice" of Jerusalem intersect; Jerusalem is a willing sacrifice, whose death is an acceptable offering before God and thus not in vain. The daughter is a mound of ashes, but the people are freed (*Bib. Ant.* 40.2); the daughter's bridal chamber is in Sheol, but the people dwell on earth (*Bib. Ant.* 40.6).

While both authors draw important lessons from Jephthah's daughter's story, Pseudo-Philo certainly honors her to a greater degree. All who read her story will know that "her death is precious before [God] always" and as such has value never accorded it elsewhere.

Notes

1. Hebrew: *dabar*. The text does not state that it was her father's *will* that she be offered in sacrifice.

2. The existence of numerous such stories in a wide variety of cultures testifies to the appropriateness of these themes for tragic literature. See Gaster, *Myth*, 430–32; Epstein-Halevi, *Parašiyyot*, 295–96; Apollodorus, *Epitome,* act 3, lines 21–22. The most famous of these is the story of Iphigenia, who was promised as a sacrifice by her father, Agamemnon. He did not fulfill his vow at the time, but later was constrained by misfortune in battle to make good on his vow. Although some versions of the story indicate that he actually sacrificed her, most imply that she was miraculously rescued before actually being put to death. It is said that she was carried off in a cloud by the goddess Artemis, whom she was forced to serve the rest of her life. See *Dictionary of Greek and Roman Biography and Mythology* (1849), s.v. "Iphigenia."

3. See Boling, *Judges*, 209–10; Milgrom, *Akedah*, 21.

4. See Trible, *Texts of Terror*, 101, 106.

5. Trible, *Texts of Terror*, 107; see *Ta'an.* 4a, where Jephthah is called "great," probably based on the link between him and Samuel in 1 Sam. 12:11.

6. Note also that he mentions Barak, with no reference to Deborah. Cf. 1 Sam. 12:11.

7. It is absent from the earliest extant interpretation, recorded in the book of *Jubilees* (17:15–18:19), and from Philo's interpretation (*De Abrahamo* 167–204), but is present in *Jewish Antiquities* (*Ant.* 1.222–36) and *Biblical Antiquities* (18.5; 32.3; and 40.2). For references to targumic and rabbinic interpretations, see Spiegel, *Last Trial*; Milgrom, *Akedah*; Davies and Chilton, "Aqedah"; Vermes, *Scripture and Tradition*, 191–218.

8. For examples, see Vermes, *Scripture and Tradition*, 205–6.

9. Some define the Akedah doctrine more narrowly. See Davies and Chilton ("Aqedah," 515), who define it only in terms of the "vicariously atoning sacrifice of Isaac, in which he is said to have shed his blood freely and/or to have been reduced to ashes." The dating of this doctrine continues to be debated. Davies and Chilton identify the doctrine only in terms of its second feature, which they claim was a rabbinic "invention, occasioned by the destruction of the Temple cult ... and pressed into service to combat the Christian claims of Passion-Atonement" (p. 516). They also categorically deny any trace of the Akedah doctrine in *Biblical Antiquities* (p. 515). R. J. Daly ("Soteriological Significance") argues for a pre-Christian date, as does Vermes, *Scripture and Tradition*, 193–227; see other works cited in Davies and Chilton, "Aqedah," 514. Although Davies and Chilton present a good case for a later dating of some of the traditions related to the Akedah, their definition is too narrow and leads them to dismiss on a priori grounds the references in *Biblical Antiquities* (see p. 528). We shall presently see that both features (willing sacrifice and expiatory value) are borrowed from the Akedah and worked into Pseudo-Philo's portrait of Jephthah's daughter.

10. Here is an example of Pseudo-Philo's concern with the issue of interpersonal relations within the community.

11. Judg. 11:12–28. Note, however, that Pseudo-Philo replaces the land dispute (associated with the Ammonite god Chemosh and the Israelite God) with an invective against the Ammonites' gods, which according to him are actually no gods at all. This alteration is another example of his polemic against idolatry.

12. Many translations read "whatever." The Hebrew text is ambiguous and indicates that either a human or animal is intended. See Boling, *Judges*, 208. G. Moore (*Critical and Exegetical Commentary*, 299) concludes that Jephthah clearly intended to offer a human sacrifice; Moore comments that in this context a vow to offer an animal would be "trivial to absurdity."

13. The word *primus* is not present in the Hebrew, Greek, or Aramaic versions, but is in the Vulgate and *Jewish Antiquities* (*Ant.* 5.263).

14. See also *Ta'an.* 4a: "Three [men] made haphazard requests ... Eliezer, the servant of Abraham; Saul, the son of Kish;

and Jephthah, the Gileadite.... Jephthah, the Gileadite, as it is written, 'Then it shall be, that whatsoever cometh forth out of the doors of my house' etc. It might have been an unclean thing."

15. See *LevR* 37.4: "Jephthah made a request in an improper manner.... But surely he could have had his vow disallowed by going to Phinehas? He thought: 'I am a king! Shall I go to Phinehas?' And Phinehas argued: 'I am a High Priest and the son of a High Priest! Shall I go to that ignoramus?' Between the two of them the poor maiden perished, and both of them incurred responsibility for her blood." The notion that Phinehas was then in Gilead and could have annulled Jephthah's vow stands behind the following talmudic declaration: "This is what the prophet had in mind when he said to Israel, 'Is there no balm in Gilead? Is there no physician there?' And it is further written, 'Which I commanded not, nor spake it, neither came it to my mind.'... 'Nor spake it'; this refers to the daughter of Jephthah" (*Ta'an.* 4a-b). See also *GenR* 60.3.

16. In *LevR* 37.4, God is portrayed as in some way responsible, but the Rabbis follow immediately with a discussion about how the vow could have been annulled.

17. Paul Winter ("*Monogenēs*") discusses nuances of meaning and occurrences in a variety of the literature in antiquity. He notes (p. 336) that in Hesiod, the term means "peerless, matchless, of singular excellence, unique, or the only one of his/her kind," while in the Hebrew Bible, it denotes both the "only one" and "priceless, irreplaceable,...highest possession" (p. 337). He likewise demonstrates that in the Bible there is a "free interchange of the terms *yaḥid, yedid,* and *bekor*" (p. 339). We may note that the LXX translates *yaḥid* in Genesis 22 as *agapētos* and *yeḥidah* in Judges 11 as *monogenēs*. Winter (p. 334) maintains that the term *monogenēs* denotes simply "the only one" (with no connotation of special relationship) in reference to Jephthah's daughter. But he adds that the Greek text behind the Old Latin reads *monogenēs* rather than *agapētos* in Genesis and notes the parallel in Judges. It appears that a certain prejudice against Jephthah's daughter—or at least in favor of Isaac—has entered into the translation and exegetical process; the term *monogenēs* denotes something special in relation to Isaac but not to her.

18. Note the similar language in *Jub.* 18:15, referring to Isaac: "And he [God] said, 'I swear by myself...because you

have done this thing and you have not denied your firstborn [var. only-begotten] son, whom you love, to me that I shall surely bless you'"; also *4 Ezra* 6:58, referring to Israel: "But we your people, whom you have called your first-born, only begotten, zealous for you, and most dear, have been given into their [the Gentiles'] hands." The same three terms appear here and in Pseudo-Philo's description of Jephthah's daughter.

19. Bar. 4:16. This reading is based on LXX A, which, as Winter ("*Monogenēs,*" 337) maintains, is the preferred reading, reflected also in the Latin: *a filiis unicam.*

20. See *Bib. Ant.* 49.8, where (in the story of Hannah) the audience is preinformed of the important events in the story.

21. Latin: *resolutus est,* to undo, melt.

22. Latin: *aperui os meum*; Hebrew: *paṣiti pi.* The Latin reflects the Hebrew verb *pataḥ,* which points to a wordplay between Jephthah's name (*yiftaḥ*) and action (*pataḥ*).

23. For example, Eluma, the mother of Samson (*Bib. Ant.* 42.1), and Sedecla, the witch of Endor (*Bib. Ant.* 64.3).

24. Cohn, "Apocryphal Work," 300. Nearly every commentator since has followed his lead. Perrot and Bogaert (in *Pseudo-Philon,* 2:189) offer the most extensive discussion of the etymologies, all based on the root *s'l.*

25. An interesting tradition is preserved in Methodius's *Symposium,* where, in a hymn that praises the martyr Thecla, he refers to Jephthah's daughter in similar terms: "The newly-killed one, his girl, Jephthah led as a sacrifice to God, her who knew no man, like a lamb led to the altar" (*Symposium* 11.78–80; quoted in Alexiou and Dronke, "Lament," 852).

26. Vermes, *Scripture and Tradition,* 202.

27. This indicates that he misunderstood the significance of her story in *Biblical Antiquities.* But see Davies and Chilton, "Aqedah," 527 n. 33.

28. He perhaps draws this conclusion from Seila's journey to the "wise men," which could be misunderstood as an attempt to have the vow annulled. But Seila's posture throughout the story is one of willing submission, lest her death be in vain.

29. Vermes, *Scripture and Tradition,* 199. But the contrast between the two fathers is clearly secondary. Surely, the greater purpose is to underline the correspondence between Isaac and Seila.

30. Ibid.

31. The notion of a death being "precious" or "acceptable" includes the aspect of the atoning value of the death, which became prominent in Jewish martyrology. The suffering of the righteous is thus valued because God is thereby moved to avenge those who suffer undeservedly for God. See Deut 32:43; *Asm. M.* 9; 2 Macc. 7:38; *4 Macc.* 17:22, among others. See also Licht, "Taxo."

32. Lattimore, *Story Patterns,* 49.

33. Ibid., 48.

34. Some have commented on the parallels between Jephthah's daughter and Iphigenia and have thus interpreted the biblical story as a variation on the fertility theme present in vegetation cult myths (which is the nature of the story of Iphigenia). But the biblical story is by no means universally interpreted this way. I. Frölich ("Historiographie," 394–401) undertakes to demonstrate the parallels between these legends and the presentation of Jephthah's daughter in *Biblical Antiquities,* specifically in the lament (*Bib. Ant.* 40.5–7). While there are admittedly some parallels in phraseology, I cannot agree that this is the primary meaning of the figure of Jephthah's daughter in *Biblical Antiquities,* especially given its socio-religious context.

35. For further discussion concerning the value of a "willing sacrifice" in rabbinic thought, see Lieberman, *Hellenism,* 158–59.

36. Some point to the two-month period in the biblical story as evidence that it reflects a vegetation cult myth. Its omission in *Biblical Antiquities* indicates that this theme plays no role in Pseudo-Philo's interpretation of the story.

37. For example, Prov. 18:7: "A fool's mouth is his undoing, and his lips are a snare to his soul." See also Sir. 23:8. Ps. 106:36–37 designates idolatry, expressed in child sacrifice, as a "snare."

38. Note also *ShShR* 2.8.2, which interprets "leaping upon the mountains, skipping upon the hills": "'Mountains' is a name for courts of justice, as it says, 'I will depart and go down upon the mountains' (Judg. 11:37)." The "courts of justice" would have been made up of the sages, or elders of the people; thus, the Midrash portrays the story similarly to *Biblical Antiquities.*

39. *Midrash Rabbah,* vol. 3: *Exodus Rabbah,* 139 n. 4.

40. There are several textual variants of the name of the mountain (Stelac, Stelach, Thelac, Telag, Schelach). It is gener-

ally agreed that the name reflects the Hebrew *šeleg* or Aramaic *telg'a,* meaning "snow." Mount Hermon is called *tur telg'a* in *Tg. Deut.* 3:9, and thus Mount Stelac is identified as Mount Hermon. For further references, see Perrot and Bogaert, in *Pseudo-Philon,* 2:190–91.

41. Nickelsburg, "Enoch," 581.

42. Ibid., 582.

43. *Bib. Ant.* 9.10; 18.4; 23.3, 7; 28.4; 42.2; 43.2; 53.3; 56.3; and implied in 58.3–4.

44. See *LamR* 2.14 on Lam. 2:10 ("The elders of the Daughter of Zion sit on the ground in silence"), where the Rabbis associate this verse with the issue of vows, though with a different meaning than here in *Biblical Antiquities.*

45. See *ExodR* 13.3: "When God warns a man once, twice, and even a third time, and he still does not repent, then does God close his heart against repentance so that He should exact vengeance from him for his sins. Thus it was with the wicked Pharaoh. Since God sent five times to him and he took no notice, God then said, 'Thou hast stiffened thy neck and hardened thy heart; well, I will add to this uncleanness'; hence 'For I have hardened his heart.'"

46. This a rabbinic statement, quoted in Feldman, "Prolegomenon," cxxiii.

47. See Davies and Chilton, "Aqedah," 535; Vermes, *Scripture and Tradition,* 208–11; Feldman, "Josephus' Version of the Binding of Isaac," 119.

48. By this I mean that there is no counterpart to the lament of Jephthah's daughter. Certainly, laments, as a literary form, are common in Greco-Roman literature. For a variety of examples, see Lattimore, *Themes.* See also Alexiou and Dronke, "Lament."

49. *OTP* reads: "That a father did not refuse the daughter whom he had sworn to sacrifice." The Latin reads: *ut pater non expuget filiam.* Perrot and Bogaert (in *Pseudo-Philon,* 2:191) comment about the difficulty in translating the verb and suggest the emendation *expectet* (to wait for; thus, "the father did not wait long for her"), with the explanation that she did not stay long on the mountain. The original verb *expugo/are,* which means "to wrest or subdue by force" or "to extort," is clearly more appropriate to the sense of the story. Also, the story centers upon Seila's willingness to submit to God's will and not

upon Jephthah's readiness to offer her. I have rendered the
Latin *devovit* more literally as "devoted," in accordance with
my interpretation of Seila's name. For reasons explained here
in my notes, the translation of the lament differs from Daniel
Harrington's translation in *OTP*.

50. The word "ruler" refers to God. See Cazeaux (in *Pseudo-
Philon*, 1:283), who also understands it as a reference to God.
Harrington (in *OTP*) translates the phrase: "so that a ruler
granted that his only-begotten daughter be promised for sacrifice," again focusing upon Jephthah's role. One meaning of
the Latin verb *audiat* is "to approve," as I have suggested it
be translated here. Accordingly, Seila affirms that because her
father did not force her to die, her ruler (God) will approve of
her, who was promised as a sacrifice.

51. *OTP* reads: "... while sitting in my women's chamber."
There are several variants in the Latin text. In Harrington's
critical text (*Pseudo-Philon*, vol. 1), they are listed as follows:
*sedens in genua mea (editio princeps), sedens in ingenuitate mea,
sedens in ingenuam meam*. Kisch notes the readings: *sedens in
virginitate mea* (Cheltenham Phillips 461) (followed by James:
"sitting in my virginity") and *secundum ingenuitatem meam* (Admont, Melk, Vienna, and Vatican MSS), choosing the latter:
"according to my nobility." Perrot and Bogaert and Harrington propose the text be emended to *in genicio meo*, based on the
parallelism with *nuptiarum mearum*, suggesting that *genico* is a
Latinized form of the Greek *gynaecum*. On this basis, they trans-
late the text "sitting in my women's chamber." We find similar
textual variants further in the text. While Harrington (followed
by Cazeaux and Perrot and Bogaert) emends the text in every
case to *in genico meo*, I prefer to treat each case individually
and thus opt for different readings in the three places. Here, I
prefer the reading "according to my nobility" for reasons that
will become clear as the lament is further analyzed.

52. The imagery here and above resembles that of Greek and
Latin epitaphs. For example, "The bridal couch was not scented
with saffron for you; they did not bring you to bed and to the
bride's chamber fragrant with desire" (quoted in Lattimore,
Themes, 193); see also Alexiou and Dronke, "Lament," 835.

53. The term *unigenitam*, which in *Bib. Ant.* 40.5 refers to
her relation to her father, is repeated here in relation to her
mother. The repetition points to its importance as a designation

of Seila. I have here rendered it "only-begotten" to highlight its special nuance, whereas *OTP* reads "only."

54. See Alexiou and Dronke, "Lament," 826, 839.

55. This is another very problematic phrase of the lament, due to the textual difficulties. The *editio princeps* reads: *et genuam meam*, and the Admont MS reads: *genua mea*. Cheltenham Phillips 461, Cheltenham Phillips 391, and Trèves read: *et genuisti eam super terram* (followed by James). Harrington and Perrot and Bogaert again emend the text to *et genicium meum super terram* ("on earth there is only my woman's chamber"), but the meaning of this is not at all clear. I suggest that the Latin *genus -us* (knee) (so the *editio princeps* and Admont MS) was confused with *genus -eris* (family, race, nation), and thus the text should read: *et genus meum super terram*, where *et* is either adversative or concessive. The point is that she has died, but her nation, or race, continues to exist.

56. See *Asm. M.* 11:12 for a similar description of a mother's care for a daughter preparing for marriage.

57. Again, here we have textual variants. The *editio princeps* reads: *in ingenuam meam* ("in my nobility"), referring to the aspect of being freeborn. Cheltenham Phillips 461, Cheltenham Phillips 391, and Trèves read: *ingenium meum*, which cannot be correct. Harrington and Perrot and Bogaert again emend the text to *in genicio meo*. James again reflects the reading: *in virginitate mea*. Here, I follow the *editio princeps* because of the parallel with 6a (above) and because it may be explained satisfactorily. Seila's fate is a symbol of the destruction of Jerusalem; "in my nobility" refers to her situation before her destruction or captivity.

58. See *LamR* 4.11.14; *Qat.* 31b.

59. To be sure, Jerusalem is not always portrayed as an innocent victim; often "her" sins are condemned.

60. Probably the Hebrew *ha'areṣ* stands behind this word; and thus Baruch is referring to "the Land," i.e., the Land of Israel.

61. See also *2 Apoc. Bar.* 20:2: "Therefore, I now took away Zion to visit the world in its own time more speedily"; *2 Apoc. Bar.* 32:2: "The building of Zion will be shaken in order that it will be rebuilt."

62. The Jerusalem/Zion imagery is not consistent in the literature. At times, it is pictured as a daughter, at times as a

mother. "Mother Zion" also appears as a broader, more cosmic concept, and her "daughter" as Jerusalem or the Temple.

63. See *Pesikta Rabbati* 29/30B (Eng. ed., 1:585), which depicts Amos as comforting Zion: "The Holy One, blessed be He, said through me: 'I will restore thy captivity and rebuild the Temple': 'On that day I will raise up the Tabernacle of David that is fallen' (Amos 9:11). Zion said: 'Keep your comfortings to yourself. Yesterday you said: "The virgin of Israel is fallen, she shall rise no more" (Amos 5:2). Now which am I to believe?' "

64. In the same discourse (ibid., 587), the prophecies of Jeremiah and Isaiah are contrasted: "Jeremiah prophesied pain, saying, 'How doth the city sit solitary!... How is she become a widow!' (Lam. 1:1). But Isaiah came and said, 'I see her as a virgin': 'As a young man espouseth a virgin, so shall thy sons espouse thee' " (Isa. 62:5).

65. "How, therefore, can I be [guardian] of this people, as a father is to his only son, or as a mother is to her virgin daughter [who] is being prepared to be given to a husband?"

66. Note the similarity to *Bib. Ant.* 40.6a: "For I have not been clothed in splendor according to my nobility."

67. See Bar. 5:1; *Ps. Sol.* 2:19–21. The Temple or tabernacle is likened to a bridal chamber in *LamR, Proem* 24; see also *Pesikta de Rab Kahana* 1.3; *Pesikta Rabbati* 33.

68. See also *LamR* 1.1.1; 4.11.14; Spiegel, *Last Trial,* 135.

69. To be sure, this imagery is related to feminine figures in classical literature and inscriptions, as demonstrated by Alexiou and Dronke. Pseudo-Philo was probably aware of Greek laments for girls who died before they were old enough to marry, for the language here closely parallels some of those epitaphs.

70. Feldman ("Prolegomenon," cxxiii) notes that Bogaert, though admitting similarities of style and content, plays down the parallels between Seila's lament and Jerusalem's lament over its destruction in *2 Apocalypse of Baruch.* Bogaert's position may be understood in light of his view that *Biblical Antiquities* was composed before 70 C.E.; that is, these texts could not be responding to the same situation. See further parallels in Ginzberg, *Legends,* 6:398 n. 39. (Note, however, that *mSot* 9:12 should be corrected to 9:2.)

71. This is an addition to the biblical text.

72. *OTP* reads: "...and established that in that month on the fourteenth day of the month they should come together every year and weep...for four days." The Latin text reads: "...*et constituerunt in eo mense XIIII die mensis ut convenientes per singulos annos plangerent...per dies quatuor.*" The word *ut* stands before *convenientes*, thus specifying that they established only "that they would come together each year and mourn four days," rather than specifying the time that they would mourn. I have translated the passage accordingly.

73. Ex. 13:1, 11–16. See Vermes, *Scripture and Tradition,* 214–15.

74. Ginzberg (*Legends*, 6:216 n. 9) suggests this possibility in his discussion of Pseudo-Philo's version of Hannah's story, where the biblical "yearly festival" is changed to "Passover."

75. See Vermes, *Scripture and Tradition,* 206ff.

76. See ibid., 214–17. The ninth of Ab was the day on which Jerusalem was destroyed both the first and second times.

77. See *Encyclopedia Judaica,* s.v. "Fasting and Fast Days"; Klein, *A Guide,* 242–51.

78. This tendency is consistent with the compositional techniques employed in *Jewish Antiquities.*

79. Josephus adds that they reproach Israel for the exodus from Egypt. In Judges, the primary issue is the land dispute between the two nations.

80. Josephus alters the story to portray Jephthah as a strong, decisive leader. Whereas Judg. 11:28 states that "the king paid no attention to Jephthah," in *Jewish Antiquities,* Jephthah dismisses the king's envoys and declares war against the Ammonites (*Ant.* 5.263).

81. The Loeb edition reads: "Then, after praying for victory, and promising to sacrifice...." The interchange between the verb "to pray" and "to vow" is in the Greek text, for *euchomai* denotes both. I have rendered it "make a vow" because of the correspondence to *nadar* in the Hebrew text (see LXX of Judg. 11:30), and also because there is another Greek verb which more specifically carries the connotation of "to pray" (*proseuchesthai*).

82. Greek: *prōton.* See Vulgate: *primus,* and *Bib. Ant.* 39.10–11. Note the parallel to the story of Idomeneus, who vowed to sacrifice to Neptune whatever would first meet him upon

his return after gaining victory over Troy. See *Apollodorus* (ed. Frazer), Appendix 12: "The Vow of Idomeneus."

83. The Greek verb *peripiptein* signifies "to fall foul of," or "to be dashed or wrecked against" (esp. ships), while *katorthousthai* means "to keep straight," as on a course. Thus, the image here is a ship moving ahead smoothly on a course and then becoming wrecked in a storm. One version of the story of Idomeneus has him caught in a storm at sea on his way home from Troy and thus vowing to Neptune to sacrifice whatever should first meet him should he return home in safety. The story goes that his son met him, but another version names his daughter as the first to meet him.

84. Actually, before Iphigenia was born, her father had vowed to sacrifice to Artemis the most beautiful thing the year would produce, but failed to keep his promise when Iphigenia was born. Only later, when Artemis, consulted in the midst of a national crisis, revealed that she would be propitiated only by Iphigenia's sacrifice, did Agamemnon keep his promise.

85. See *LevR* 37.4; *Ta'an.* 4a; Cicero, *Off.* 3.25.95; Lucretius, *De Rerum Natura* 1.84–104.

86. Lattimore, *Story Patterns,* 48.

87. The Greek verb *sumbainō,* translated here as "learned her destiny," denotes "to put together" or "to compute."

88. Note the similarity between this and *Bib. Ant.* 40.2, where Seila replies, "Who would be sad in death, seeing the people freed?"

89. Foley, "Conception," 142.

90. See Pomeroy, *Goddesses,* 150–54.

91. Feldman, "Josephus' Version of the Binding of Isaac," 118.

92. Clarke, *Roman Mind,* 118 (quoting Seneca, *Ep.* 96.1–2; 107.11); see also Seneca, *De. Prov.* 5.4ff.

93. Milgrom, *Akedah,* 21.

94. Trible, *Texts of Terror,* 105.

95. See Lattimore, *Story Patterns,* 40; *Dictionary of Greek and Roman Mythology* (1849), s.v. "Iphigenia."

96. Some have argued that Jephthah's daughter was cloistered for the remainder of her life and died unmarried, based on Iphigenia's story, which ends with her being carried away by Artemis to serve as her priestess. This idea was first suggested by Kimchi (twelfth century). G Moore (*Critical and Exegetical*

Commentary, 304) calls this "rationalistic subterfuge." Trible (*Texts of Terror*) does not take a position, but comments that "seclusion is living death" (p. 116 n. 59).

97. Feldman, "Hellenizations in Josephus' Versions of Esther," 150.

98. Feldman, "Josephus' Version of the Binding of Isaac," 126; idem, "Hellenizations in Josephus' Versions of Esther," 144.

3

Hannah

Hannah is an important, although secondary, figure in the Bible. In many ways, her role is traditional; she is a wife and mother, indeed the "mother of a hero."[1] Her conflict with her rival, her barrenness, and her intense longing to have a son are so common as to be stereotypic.[2] Yet, as we look more closely, we see a woman of great faith and piety who in her own right is gifted and valued. Nehama Ashkenasay summarizes the biblical portrait of Hannah: "The biblical narrator portrays her as a woman of great inner beauty who possessed manifold gifts, such as language abilities, far-sighted vision, and personal charm (indicated in her name, that is related, in Hebrew, to the noun *ḥen*, 'charm')."[3]

Hannah in *Biblical Antiquities:*
A Woman of Noble Character

Hannah becomes a highly prominent figure in *Biblical Antiquities,* as evidenced by the amount of material the author devotes to her story (*Bib. Ant.* 50–51) and how he reworks the biblical narrative to enhance her character. Although still the "mother of a hero" in this version of her story, she stands out as an exemplary figure apart from her relationship to her illustrious son. Nevertheless, her story remains closely linked with that of Samuel, and so we must first look briefly at aspects of his portrait, in order to understand and appreciate more fully Hannah's portrait.

Background: National Crisis and Promise

In chapter 49, the author sets the stage for Samuel's birth, creating an air of expectation through the motif of promise and fulfillment. Earlier, in chapter 48, he has informed us of the crisis of leadership within the community and resultant circumstances of the people: "They had no leader in those days, and each one did what was pleasing in his own eyes" (*Bib. Ant.* 48.5). Then he goes on to sketch the situation further: "And in that time the sons of Israel began to make a request from the Lord, and they said, 'Let all of us cast lots to see who it is who can rule us as Kenaz did. For perhaps we will find a man who may free us from our distress, because it is not appropriate for the people to be without a ruler'" (*Bib. Ant.* 49.1).

They seek a leader like Kenaz who could free them from their distress.[4] Kenaz, a figure created by Pseudo-Philo,[5] is a guardian of the covenant, a prophet, a visionary, and

a zealot. He is, as George W. E. Nickelsburg has summarized, "the first judge and a paragon of leadership."[6] The
people cast lots to determine the new leader, following
the pattern of choosing Kenaz (*Bib. Ant.* 25.2). But the
lots do not point to any leader, which the people interpret as a sign of God's rejection (*Bib. Ant.* 49.2). In this
way, Pseudo-Philo creates an atmosphere of distress and
desperation.

They again cast lots, this time tribe by tribe, but again
no tribe is indicated (v. 2), which they interpret as a further sign that "God has hated His people and His soul has
detested us" (v. 2). When they have abandoned hope, a
man named Nethez encourages them to repent and then
to pray again, this time casting lots by cities (v. 3). Thus,
Pseudo-Philo heightens suspense and builds expectations
about who the new leader will be.

When the lot falls upon Ramathaim,[7] there is a certain
resolution of tension. At last, God has responded; God
indeed has not abandoned the people. The people then
cast lots to determine the chosen leader (*Bib. Ant.* 49.5),
but when it falls upon Elkanah he refuses to become their
leader. There follows more dialogue with God about the
situation (*Bib. Ant.* 49.6–8), which Pseudo-Philo uses to
turn the focus of attention from Elkanah to Samuel: "His
son, who will be born from him, he will rule among you
and prophesy. And from this time on, a ruler will not
be lacking from you for many years" (*Bib. Ant.* 49.7). The
people respond: "Elkanah has ten sons,[8] and who of them
will rule or prophesy?" (*Bib. Ant.* 49.8). Their query introduces a messianic allusion or motif, borrowed from
the account of the anointing of David, when God sent
Samuel to anoint one of Jesse's sons as king and only later
indicated which son was to be anointed (1 Sam. 16:1).

God's reply provides the author with the opportunity
to introduce the crisis described in the biblical narrative
(Elkanah has two wives, one has children, the other is barren), together with the principal characters in the drama.
He mentions Peninnah by name but designates Hannah

as "the sterile woman whom I have given to him as a wife" (*Bib. Ant.* 49.8). He also gives away the ending of the story before it even unfolds, a technique that appears elsewhere in *Biblical Antiquities*.[9] God announces: "The one who is born from the sterile woman whom I have given to him as a wife will be a prophet before me. And I will love him as I have loved Isaac, and his name will be before me always" (*Bib. Ant.* 49.8). Samuel is juxtaposed with Isaac—both are beloved and both are born of sterile women. The specific language employed to describe Hannah closely parallels that of Philo of Alexandria in his own description of her:

> We might well expect then, that the barren woman, not meaning the childless, but the firm or solid [a play on words: *steiran-sterran*], who still abounds in power, who with endurance and courage perseveres to the finish in the contest, where the prize is the acquisition of the Best, should bring forth the Monad which is of equal value with the Seven; for her nature is that of a happy and goodly motherhood.[10]

What is significant about this correspondence in exegetical traditions is that in Philo's commentaries, Hannah is described by language that is also associated with Wisdom. In this commentary on 1 Samuel 2:5, Philo declares that Hannah brought forth a child identified with the number seven (a symbol for Wisdom); elsewhere (*Deus* 2), he calls Hannah "the gift of the wisdom of God." We will see that Pseudo-Philo incorporates these and other aspects of Philo's description of Hannah.[11] According to him, she indeed "with endurance and courage perseveres to the finish in the contest"; she brings forth Wisdom's child and is herself a figure of Wisdom. Thus, this reference to Hannah as "the sterile woman" probably is very deliberate; it is Pseudo-Philo's first hint at features of the particular portrait he will shape in the lines that follow.

In summary, chapter 49 (which is unique to *Biblical*

Antiquities) introduces the primary concern of the people of Israel after Phinehas's death—Who would be their leader? It is dramatically highlighted by the literary device of the casting of lots, leading to God's announcement that a great leader would soon be born, and that miraculously, for he would be born from "the sterile woman."

This section functions to place the birth of Samuel in a larger context; he is the answer to the whole nation's prayer for a leader, not just to Hannah's prayer for a son. It is not one woman's story, but one nation's story. Only later will the woman's story take on a significance of its own. To this point, the spotlight has focused upon Elkanah,[12] the other leaders, and the promised son. Hannah has been introduced, but not by name. We are told that she is one of two wives and that, though barren, she will be God's instrument in fulfilling the promise to the nation by giving birth to a son. Chapters 50–51 relate the dramatic story of the unfolding of the promise. From this point, Elkanah more or less fades into the background, as the spotlight turns upon Hannah.

Personal Crisis and Resolution

In both the Bible and *Biblical Antiquities*, the material related to Hannah's story divides naturally into two major types—narrative and poetry. But apart from this basic similarity and the fundamental plot, the correspondence between the two texts is minimal. Although Pseudo-Philo begins with the biblical account and quotes sporadically from 1 Samuel, on the whole, he reworks the material to introduce and/or highlight those aspects that he wishes to emphasize in order to create his own particular portrait of Hannah. We will see that he greatly develops the interaction between Hannah and Peninnah and Hannah and Eli, as well as Hannah's nurturing of Samuel.

Pseudo-Philo begins his description of Hannah and Peninnah with a nearly exact citation of 1 Samuel 1:2:

1 Samuel 1:2	*Bib. Ant.* 50.1
He had two wives; the name of the one was Hannah, and the name of the other Peninnah. Peninnah had children, but Hannah had no children.	And Elkanah had two wives. The name of one was Hannah, and the name of the other was Peninnah. And because Peninnah had children and Hannah did not, Peninnah taunted her.

From that point, however, he moves into a discussion of the rivalry between Hannah and Peninnah; he does this by modifying the biblical phrases to produce a cause-effect relationship. This alteration subtly shifts the emphasis from the fact of Hannah's barrenness to the effect of her barrenness—she is taunted by her rival. The biblical account withholds this information until later in the story (1 Sam. 1:6), when relating the events that took place yearly.

Pseudo-Philo models the motif of the taunting of a barren wife by a fertile second wife after the story of Sarah and Hagar and also draws upon the story of the rivalry between Leah and Rachel. Both Leah and Peninnah are fertile rival wives who do not find the love and acceptance from their husbands that children should supposedly bring. In the case of Peninnah, her bitterness and jealousy are uncontained; they spill over into a constant flood of denigration and ridicule of Hannah.

The author indicates his intention to underscore Peninnah's taunting of Hannah by expanding the terse biblical references to a yearly occurrence (1 Sam. 1:6–7) into a daily ordeal Hannah endured (*Bib. Ant.* 50.2–5). The motif of taunting is pivotal because it injects a new theme—vindication of the righteous—into the story, with Hannah representing the righteous. Pseudo-Philo presents this theme in structurally parallel double contexts—the motif is played out daily at home (unique to *Biblical Antiquities*) and at Shiloh (as in the Bible). The motif is developed around a tripartite pattern: (1) Peninnah's taunt, (2) Hannah's response, and (3) a statement about Hannah's character. This pattern will serve as an outline for the following discussion.

Section 1 (Bib. Ant. 50.1–2a)

Peninnah's Taunt (Bib. Ant. *50.1*). The text reads: "What does it profit you that Elkanah your husband loves you, for you are a dry tree? And I know that he will love me, because he delights in the sight of my sons standing around him like a plantation of olive trees." Besides the obvious parallels to the circumstances of Sarah and Hagar and Rachel and Leah, the author draws upon other biblical allusions, such as imagery from Isaiah and the Psalms. Isaiah 56:3 states, "And do not let the eunuch say, 'I am just a dry tree.'" Perhaps his allusion to this "dry tree" points out the hopelessness of Hannah's condition,[13] or possibly he alludes to Hannah's "dryness" to suggest the imagery of nursing, which he will later develop significantly (*Bib. Ant.* 51.2).

A third possibility is suggested by the continuation of the message in Isaiah: "I will give [to the eunuchs] . . . a monument and a name better than sons and daughters" (Isa. 56:5). This text declares that a "monument and a name"—not physical progeny—are the rewards for piety.[14] In *Biblical Antiquities,* Hannah later declares that the ability to bear children is not an indicator of righteousness or value: "Neither she who has many sons is rich nor she who has few is poor, but whoever abounds in the will of God is rich" (*Bib. Ant.* 50.5). In this response, Hannah challenges the kind of "theology" expressed in Psalm 128, to which Peninnah had alluded in her taunt (see *Bib. Ant.* 50:1): "Happy is everyone who fears the Lord, who walks in his ways. You shall eat the fruit of the labor of your hands; you shall be happy, and it shall go well with you. Your wife will be like a fruitful vine within your house; your children will be like olive shoots around your table" (Ps. 128:1–3).

Peninnah implies that Hannah is barren because she does not "fear the Lord" or "walk in His ways" (Ps. 128:1).[15] Pseudo-Philo explicitly contradicts this notion, however, by twice affirming Hannah's piety using the same terms found in Psalm 128: (1) "Hannah had been fearing God from her youth" (*Bib. Ant.* 50.2). (2) Hannah states, "I have walked before you from the day of my youth" (*Bib. Ant.* 50.4). We see that Hannah is not barren because of sin, but because God has ordained it, in order to work a greater miracle among the people of Israel: "But Eli the priest did not want to tell her [Hannah] that a prophet had been foreordained to be born from her" (*Bib. Ant.* 50.8).

A similar challenge to Peninnah's inference is found in a postbiblical Jewish text, the Wisdom of Solomon, which may provide a link between the passages in Isaiah and *Biblical Antiquities.*[16] In his comments upon Isaiah 56:5, the author refers to both "the barren woman" and "the eunuch":

> For blessed is the barren woman who is undefiled, who has not entered into a sinful union; she will have fruit when God examines souls. Blessed also is the eunuch whose hands have done no lawless deed, and who has not devised wicked things against the Lord; for special favor will be shown him for his faithfulness, and a place of great delight in the temple of the Lord.... Better than this is childlessness with virtue, for in the memory of virtue is immortality, because it is known both by God and by mortals (Wisd. Sol. 3:13–14; 4:1).

Hannah's Reaction (Bib. Ant. *50.2*). The text simply states that "Hannah was saddened very much."

A Statement about Hannah's Character (Bib. Ant. *50.2*). "But she had been fearing God from her youth." This simple and pointed statement about her biblical piety, added by Pseudo-Philo to the biblical account, serves to clarify that Hannah's barrenness is not due to sinfulness.

Section 2 *(Bib. Ant. 50.2–3)*

In this section, although the setting is the "holy day of Passover," the same elements occur in the same order. Elkanah goes up to sacrifice while the women stay home. Apparently, he returns to find Hannah miserably sad and depressed because of Peninnah's taunting. He encourages her and persuades her to eat, after which she goes to pray at Shiloh.

Pseudo-Philo's alteration of the context from a yearly family sacrifice to the feast of Passover indicates that he attaches some meaning to this point. Ginzberg suggests that the designation is based on the hermeneutical principle of analogy (Heb.: *gezerah shawah*), by which the phrase "from year to year" (Heb.: *miyyamim yamimah*) in 1 Samuel 1:4 is associated with and interpreted by the same phrase in Exodus 13:10, where it refers to Passover.[17]

Peninnah's Taunt (Bib. Ant. *50.2b*). The text reads:

> A wife is not really loved even if her husband loves her or her beauty. Let Hannah not boast in her appearance; but she who boasts, let her boast when she sees her offspring before her. And when among women the fruit of her womb is not so, love will be in vain. For what did it profit Rachel that Jacob loved her? And unless the fruit of her womb had been given to him, his love would have been in vain.

Peninnah continues to dwell upon Hannah's childlessness and her own fecundity. She has ten sons (v. 3), but though she would have us believe that her ability to bear children has brought a sense of self-worth, her behavior indicates that it has not given her the putative joy and esteem that she so forcefully acclaims.

Hannah's Response (Bib. Ant. *50.3*). Here, Pseudo-Philo more or less follows the biblical text, with one significant variation, which will be discussed in the next section:

1 Samuel 1:7–8	*Bib. Ant.* 50.3
She [Peninnah] used to provoke her. Therefore Hannah wept.... Her husband Elkanah said to her, "Hannah, why do you weep? Why do you not eat? Why is your heart sad? Am I not more to you than ten sons?"	And when Hannah heard these words, her soul grew faint and poured out tears. And her husband saw her and said, "Why are you sad? And why do you not eat? And why does your heart fall within you? Are not your ways of behaving better than the ten sons of Peninnah?"

Hannah was so sad that she wept and would not eat, even on "the holy day of Passover," when, according to tradition, Jews were to be joyful and to eat the Passover sacrifice.

A Statement of Hannah's Character (Bib. Ant. *50.3*). Elkanah praises Hannah in a very interesting way. Pseudo-Philo changes the focus of the biblical question from Hannah's love for him to Hannah's character. Her "ways of behaving [are] better than the ten sons of Peninnah." We find a near parallel to this in the story of Ruth, when Naomi's friends declare: "For your daughter-in-law, who loves you, who is more to you than seven sons, has borne him" (Ruth 4:15). Ruth trusted in God absolutely and showed covenant faithfulness (Heb.: *hesed*) without hope of material reward, although the reward eventually came (Ruth 1:8; 3:10). Elkanah thus praises Hannah's character by associating her with Ruth, and his allusion to Ruth's story also turns our thoughts ahead to the birth of the promised leader.

In summary, Pseudo-Philo emphasizes by repetition that Hannah was not barren because of sinfulness. We will see that Samuel's eventual birth provides, among other things, a vindication of Hannah's righteousness. This theme of vindication stands alongside the affirmation that progeny is not the ultimate expression of God's blessing. The two tendencies are somewhat contradictory—Hannah intensely desires a son, that is, to be vindicated; yet she later will affirm that "neither she who has many sons is rich nor she who has few is poor, but whoever abounds in the will of God is rich" (*Bib. Ant.*

50.5). She exhibits a profound trust in God; although she has "not been heard in her prayer" (50.5), she faithfully continues to pray.

The version of Hannah's prayer in *Biblical Antiquities* differs considerably from the biblical version:

1 Samuel 1:11	*Bib. Ant.* 50.4
O Lord of hosts, if only you will look on the misery of your servant, and remember me, and not forget your servant, but will give to your servant a male child, then I will set him before you as a nazirite until the day of his death.[18]	Did you not, Lord, search out the heart of all generations before you formed the world? Now what womb is born opened or dies closed unless you wish it?[19] And now let my prayer ascend before you today lest I go down from here empty, because you know my heart, how I have walked before you from the day of my youth.

In 1 Samuel 1:11, her prayer takes the form of a vow, while Pseudo-Philo replaces the vow with: (1) a declaration about God's foreknowledge and sovereignty over childbirth in general and over Hannah's situation in particular; (2) Hannah's claim that she has walked before God from the day of her youth; and (3) her petition. He also indicates important concerns by inserting a section of inner dialogue, by which Hannah reveals more of her circumstances and her response:

> And Hannah did not want to pray out loud as all people do. For then she thought, saying, "Perhaps I am not worthy to be heard, and Peninnah will then be even more eager to taunt me as she does daily when she says, 'Where is your God in whom you trust?' But I know that neither she who has many sons is rich nor she who has few is poor, but whoever abounds in the will of God is rich. For who may know what I have prayed for? If they know that I am not heard in my prayer, they will blaspheme" (*Bib. Ant.* 50.5).

He repeats the point that Peninnah taunts Hannah daily and reemphasizes it by having Hannah quote from Psalm

42:3 in reference to Peninnah's taunting. In this lamentory psalm, the psalmist describes the daily taunting he endures (vv. 3 and 10) and then prays, in the accompanying psalm, that God would vindicate him in the face of his enemies (Ps. 43:1). In Hannah's story, Eli later tells Hannah that through Samuel's birth, her "womb has been vindicated"[20] (*Bib. Ant.* 51.2), perhaps indicating that Pseudo-Philo has duplicated the pattern of lament and divine response found in these two psalms.

A corollary to the theme of taunting is Hannah's concern that God not be blasphemed. Hannah's barrenness reflects on God. She has faithfully observed the Torah, yet God seemingly has not kept the covenantal promises. This causes Peninnah to conclude that God has abandoned Hannah and to hold this up to her daily; she taunts Hannah not only because she is childless, but also because God has not answered her prayer. Pseudo-Philo brings out this point in another way by his allusion to Psalm 42:3, 10, which injects a new feature into the story. The psalmist is downcast not so much because of his circumstances, but because his enemies constantly taunt him that God has abandoned him. His circumstances cause his enemies to ridicule God.[21] The allusion to Psalms 42–43 indicates that Pseudo-Philo interprets the rivalry between Hannah and Peninnah as a dramatization of the message of these psalms. Hannah and Peninnah become types of the righteous and wicked, respectively.[22] Hannah represents the people of Israel (more specifically, righteous Israel), whom it appears God has abandoned. She embodies the message to "hope in God, for [you] will again praise him, [your] help and [your] God" (Ps. 42:5, 11; 43:5).

The Omission of Hannah's Vow

The author completely omits the vow made by Hannah as she prays for a son. Because this is such a central feature of the biblical narrative (1 Sam. 1:11), we must ask why he has chosen to omit it. The most obvious explanation is simply that there is no need for it, since the son has already been promised to the people (*Bib. Ant.* 49.7–8). The answer to Hannah's prayer is one and the same with the answer to the people's prayers, as the priest Eli later declares to Hannah: "You have not asked alone, but the people have prayed for this. This is not your request alone, but it was promised previously to the tribes" (*Bib. Ant.* 51.2).

The omission of the vow seemingly heightens the miraculous nature of Samuel's birth and role and diminishes the human aspect. The anguish of a barren woman and her wrestling with God are exchanged for a predestinarian promise to an entire nation. We should note, however, that Hannah herself is not aware of the promise. In retelling Hannah's conversation with Eli, Pseudo-Philo informs us that Eli "did not want to tell her that a prophet had been foreordained to be born from her" (*Bib. Ant.* 50.7); only later, when Samuel is dedicated, does Eli tell her of the significance of Samuel's birth (*Bib. Ant.* 51.2).

Hannah and Eli (Bib. Ant. 50.6–8)

The exchange between Hannah and the aged priest at Shiloh more or less corresponds to the biblical story, in which Eli mistakenly assumes that Hannah is drunk and rebukes her, quoting directly from 1 Samuel 1:14: "Put away your wine." Pseudo-Philo maintains the focus upon Peninnah's taunting by expanding the biblical conversation to include a reference to this issue: "And she said, 'Is my prayer so heard that I am called a drunken woman? Now I have drunk the cup of my weeping.' And Eli the priest said to her, 'Tell me why you are being taunted'" (*Bib. Ant.* 50.7). Eli raises the issue even though Hannah has not mentioned being taunted. His request certainly does not flow naturally from the conversation in the text but seems intrusive, which points to the author's intentional effort to keep this issue at the fore in his version of Hannah's story.

Hannah responds by reviewing her story, emphasizing the fact of her barrenness and that "God has shut up [her] womb"; Eli then assures her that her "prayer has been heard" (*Bib. Ant.* 50.7). He does not, however, furnish any other details about how he knows this or how it will come to pass. The scene closes with Hannah returning home, "consoled of her sorrow," although telling "no one what she had prayed" (*Bib. Ant.* 50.8).

Why did Eli "not want to tell her that a prophet had been foreordained to be born from her" (*Bib. Ant.* 50.8)? Perhaps it would lessen the didactic force and impact of her own struggle of faith as she continued to trust God in the midst of adverse circumstances. Because Pseudo-Philo holds up Hannah as a model of piety to be emulated by those of his own day, her example would be rendered meaningless were she to know at this point that her prayer would be answered.

Resolution: The Promise Fulfilled
(*Bib. Ant.* 51.1–2)

The Birth and Dedication of Samuel
(Bib. Ant. 51.1)

These scenes more or less follow the biblical outline— Hannah conceives, bears a son, names him Samuel, and keeps him at home until he is two years old, at which time she dedicates him to God at Shiloh (1 Sam. 1:20–28). But Pseudo-Philo modifies the details of the story considerably, again to present it in his own way. For example, in contrast to the biblical account, at the dedication ceremony the spotlight remains on Hannah:

1 Samuel 1:23–28 | *Bib. Ant.* 51.1

[23]So the woman remained and nursed her son, until she weaned him. [24]When she had weaned him, she took him up with her, along with a three-year-old bull, an ephah of flour, and a skin of wine. She brought him to the house of the Lord at Shiloh.... [25]Then they slaughtered the bull, and they brought the child to Eli. [26]And she said, "...I am the woman who was standing here...praying to the Lord. [27]For this child I prayed; and the Lord has granted me the petition that I made to him. [28]Therefore I have lent him to the Lord; as long as he lives, he is given to the Lord."

And Hannah remained there and nursed the infant until he was two years old. And when she had weaned him, she went up with him and brought gifts in her hands. And the child was very handsome, and the Lord was with him. And Hannah placed the boy before Eli and said to him, "This is the desire I desired, and this is the request I have asked."

Two principal features of the biblical story are omitted—reference to Elkanah and to sacrifice (v. 25). We have already noted the author's lack of interest in cultic matters, which accounts for the second omission. With regard to Elkanah, he replaces the conversation between Elkanah and Hannah with the summary phrase "and Hannah remained there." In 1 Samuel, Hannah is the sole subject of verses 23b–24 and 26–28; the subject abruptly changes to a plural in verse 25 by introducing Elkanah into the scene, though the reference seems intrusive at this point. Pseudo-Philo's version, with no reference to sacrifice or to Elkanah, certainly flows much more naturally. The Greek version, the Septuagint, emphasizes Elkanah's role to the exclusion of Hannah's.[23]

In light of the biblical versions, the version in *Biblical Antiquities*, which presents Hannah as solely responsible for her son, is all the more striking. Hannah is portrayed as an independent, responsible person, capable of carrying out decisions she has made. To be sure, this corresponds in part to the biblical portrait; but there Elkanah is nearly always in the picture in some way (Hebrew Bible), or nearly exclusively responsible (Greek Bible).

Eli's Response (Bib. Ant. 51.2)

Pseudo-Philo creates a speech in which Eli discloses the full import of Samuel's birth. The priest replies to Hannah's declaration that the boy who stands before him is the answer to her prayer by highlighting both the community's role in this event and its broader significance. In the process, Hannah's character and role take on a new dimension. Eli replies: "You have not asked alone, but the people have prayed for this. This is not your request alone, but it was promised previously to the tribes. And through this boy your womb has been vindicated[24] so that you might set up prophecy[25] for the people[26] and set up the milk of your breasts as a fountain for the twelve tribes" (*Bib. Ant.* 51.2). Eli acknowledges the significance of Samuel's birth for Hannah and reveals to her its significance for the entire nation. Hannah's prayer for a son has intersected with Israel's prayer for a leader; the answer to both prayers is Samuel. Similarly, Hannah's vindication has as its corollary Israel's vindication; Samuel's birth is proof that God has not rejected them or abandoned them (*Bib. Ant.* 49.2–3, 8).

While Eli validates the importance of Hannah's prayer and God's granting her personal petition, he also declares that she plays a highly significant, indeed vital, national role, which is twofold: "You might set up prophecy for the people and set up the milk of your breasts as a fountain for the twelve tribes." The general reference to nursing derives from the biblical version of the story (1 Sam. 1:23), but the specific imagery comes from a variety of sources, most of which are figurative.[27] Pseudo-Philo's use of this imagery signals a movement into the metaphorical realm, with Hannah becoming a type (a figure), particularly a type of Wisdom.

A variety of postbiblical Jewish texts associate Wisdom with nursing or mothers in general. The following are examples: (1) Sirach 15:2–3: "She [Wisdom] will come to meet him like a mother, . . . feed him with the bread of

learning, and give him the water of wisdom to drink."
(2) Sirach 51:17: "And she [Wisdom] became for me a
nurse."[28] (3) Wisdom of Solomon 7:22a: "For Wisdom,
the fashioner of all things, taught me." (The word translated "fashioner" is likely *'aman,* which closely resembles
'iman, "mother.")[29] (4) Philo (*Ebr.* 31): Wisdom is "the
mother and nurse of the All."[30] (5) *4 Ezra* 8:4: "Then
drink your fill of understanding, O my soul, and drink
wisdom, O my heart." (In this context [see vv. 10–12],
Ezra later declares that God commands the breasts to give
milk.) (6) *Odes of Solomon* 8:14: "Christ speaks: 'And my
own breasts I prepared for them, that they might drink
my holy milk and live by it.'"[31]

Imagery in *2 Apocalypse of Baruch* also closely parallels
that of *Biblical Antiquities*. In response to the complaint
that "the shepherds of Israel have perished,... the lamps
which gave light are extinguished, and the fountains from
which we used to drink have withheld their streams,"
Baruch replies: "Shepherds and lamps and fountains
came from the Law and when we go away, the Law will
abide. If you, therefore, look upon the Law and are intent upon Wisdom, then the lamp will not be wanting and
the shepherd will not give way and the fountain will not
dry up" (*2 Apoc. Bar.* 77:15–16).

In *Biblical Antiquities,* both the Torah and light are embodied in the person of Samuel (*Bib. Ant.* 51.4, 7). Torah
(parallel to Wisdom) is also embodied in the person of
Hannah (51.4), who is the source of the fountain for the
twelve tribes. Samuel is Wisdom's child; he drinks the
"milk of Wisdom," and through him, Wisdom's "milk"
(the Torah) will nourish "the twelve tribes" of Israel.
Hence, Hannah, rather than functioning as a secondary
figure, becomes very much a primary figure in this document, while Samuel, as the mediator of Wisdom, becomes
somewhat less prominent.

The imagery of a nursing mother also recalls the
mother goddess figures, particularly Isis (often represented nursing her infant son Horus), who was worshiped

in many parts of the Greco-Roman world.[32] Indeed, the Egyptian goddess of wet-nursing was believed to be a manifestation of Isis.[33] Moreover, many historians of religion recognize that the figure of Isis nursing her infant son was Christianized by the early church and soon became a significant prototype of the representation of Mary and her son Jesus. This transferral developed within Syrian Christianity[34] and is a particular expression of the feminine aspect of Syrian religion in general. Here in *Biblical Antiquities,* very interestingly, we are presented with a Jewish "Madonna and child," mediated though the figure of Wisdom.

Martin Hengel suggests that the hypostasis of Wisdom in Jewish thought "represents a transformation of the Semitic mother goddess."[35] Pseudo-Philo's incorporation of such imagery in his retelling of the story reflects a certain Hellenistic tendency and may point to a non-Palestinian provenance, although, to be sure, Palestinian Judaism had its share of such influence.

Hannah's Response (*Bib. Ant.* 51.3-6)

Hannah's response takes the form of a hymn,[36] but unlike its biblical counterpart (1 Sam. 2:1), it is not a prayer. It more closely resembles a Wisdom psalm (in the tradition of Psalm 49 or Psalm 78), which recounts God's mighty acts in Israel's history. In form it closely parallels the Hymn of Deborah in *Biblical Antiquities* (*Bib. Ant.* 32). Its structure does not correspond to that of the biblical Song of Hannah, though references to it are interspersed throughout, along with other biblical and postbiblical phraseology and allusions. Pseudo-Philo created the hymn to communicate the significance of the fulfillment of God's promise, both to Hannah and to Israel.

To facilitate discussion, I have divided the hymn into

sections according to similarity of themes or natural breaks in the text, commenting upon each unit individually.

Biblical Antiquities 51.3–4c

> Come to my voice,[37] all you nations, and pay attention to my speech, all you kingdoms, because my mouth has been opened that I should speak and my lips have been commanded to sing a hymn to the Lord.[38] Drip, my breasts, and tell your testimonies, because you have been commanded to give milk.[39] For he who is milked from you will be raised up,[40] and the people will be enlightened by his words, and he will show to the nations the statutes, and his horn will be exalted very high.[41] And so I will speak my words openly, because from me will arise the ordinance of the Lord, and all men will find the truth.

The Wisdom motif, including nursing imagery, is carried over from the narrative into the hymn. Hannah's words echo those of Wisdom in Proverbs 8:1, 4, 6: "Does not Wisdom call, and does not understanding raise her voice?... To you, O people, I call, and my cry is to all that live.... Hear, for I will speak noble things, and from my lips will come what is right."

In this section, the author again draws an analogy between words and milk. Hannah declares that her mouth has been commanded to speak and then commands her breasts to "drip... and tell your testimonies." Note the correspondence between words and milk; Hannah's breasts speak as they give milk.

Pseudo-Philo does not hesitate to portray a woman as speaking a message worthy to be heard. Hannah speaks "openly" as a true prophetess.[42] Her message accentuates the role of her son and the mighty works of God in the past and future (vv. 5–6), as well as the significance of her own role in the fulfillment of God's purposes for Israel and the world: "From me will arise the ordinance of the Lord, and all men will find the truth" (v. 4).

Biblical Antiquities 51:4d–5

Do not hurry to say great things or to bring forth from your mouth lofty words, but delight in glorifying (God). For when the light from which wisdom is to be born will go forth,[43] not those who possess many things will be said to be rich, nor those who have borne in abundance will be called mother. For the sterile one has been satisfied in childbearing,[44] but she who had many children has been emptied. Because the Lord kills in judgment, and brings to life in mercy. For them who are wicked in this world he kills, and he brings the just to life when he wishes. Now the wicked he will shut up in darkness, but he will save his light for the just.[45] And when the wicked have died, then they will perish. And when the just go to sleep, then they will be freed. Now so will every judgment endure, until he who restrains will be revealed.

This section corresponds very closely to its biblical counterpart (1 Sam. 2:1–10), in both general structure and wording. Its primary themes are the reversal of fortune between the righteous and wicked and the future of both. Hannah begins with her own experience (*Bib. Ant.* 51.4) and then moves to the larger category of the righteous and wicked, the eschatological element reflecting later interpretations of 1 Samuel 2:6–9.[46] This movement from the personal aspect of God's vindication to its broader significance corresponds to Pseudo-Philo's portrayal of events in the narrative portion of the document (e.g., *Bib. Ant.* 51.2–3).

In the section relating to Hannah personally (51.4), the interplay between the imagery of wealth, progeny, and fullness (satisfaction), on one hand, and poverty, barrenness, and emptiness, on the other hand, corresponds to

the biblical text (1 Sam. 2:5). God has now vindicated
Hannah, and the reversal is complete, because Peninnah
"has been emptied" of her children. What had been her
boast has been taken from her. This notion that Peninnah's children have been taken from her is not suggested
by either the biblical story or Pseudo-Philo's version of
the story, although it possibly reflects a traditional interpretation of 1 Samuel 2:5: "She who was barren has borne
seven children, but she who has had many children pines
away." The allusion to death leads quite naturally into
the subject of the future lot of the righteous and wicked
(*Bib. Ant.* 51.5).

Biblical Antiquities 51:6a–e

Speak, speak, Hannah, no longer be silent. Sing a
hymn, daughter of Batuel,[47] about the miracles that
God has performed with you. Who is Hannah that a
prophet is born from her? Or who is the daughter of
Batuel that she should bear the light to the peoples?

Hannah's repeated exhortation to speak openly about the
miracles God has wrought through her contrasts with her
posture before Samuel's birth, when she was silent. She
is liberated from her silence because she has been vindicated and because of what God has done for Israel
through her. She has played a crucial role in this great
miracle, which is the gift of the long-awaited leader to
nourish and enlighten the people.

Biblical Antiquities 51.6f–o

Rise up, you also, Elkanah, and gird your loins.[48] Sing
a hymn about the wonders of the Lord. Because Asaph
prophesied in the wilderness about your son, saying,
"Moses and Aaron were among his priests, and Samuel
was there among them."[49] Behold the word has been
fulfilled, and the prophecy has come to pass. And

these words will endure until they give the horn to his anointed one and power be present at the throne of his king.

This entire section, excluding the last two lines, has no parallel in 1 Samuel. It functions to emphasize the importance of Samuel as the promised leader whose leadership will continue until the inauguration of the reign of God's "anointed one." In Samuel, Israel finally has proper leadership and thus will enjoy God's blessing once again. Here is yet another example of the author's tendency to highlight Israel's leadership.

Hannah herself plays a striking role. She is a worship leader, leading even her husband in worship. She also interprets scripture to him and discerns the meaning of Samuel's birth. In this, she resembles Deborah, who discerns God's will and takes the lead over Barak, even in the worship celebration following the battle (*Bib. Ant.* 32.18). In both cases, the men, whom we expect to take the lead, are eclipsed by the many-talented women with whom they are associated.

Biblical Antiquities 51.6p-q

The text states: "And let my son stay here and serve until he be made a light for this nation." Although the essence of this declaration corresponds to the biblical dedication episode (1 Sam. 1:28), the language recalls one of Isaiah's servant songs (Isa. 49:1, 6): "The Lord called me before I was born, while I was in my mother's womb he named me [cf. *Bib. Ant.* 51.1]. . . . He [the Lord] says, 'It is too light a thing that you should be my servant to raise up the tribes of Jacob and to restore the survivors of Israel; I will give you as a light to the nations, that my salvation may reach to the end of the earth.'" In contrast to Isaiah, however, *Biblical Antiquities* specifies that Samuel will be a light for "this nation," that is, for Israel. This obviously deliberate change brings the declaration into line with

Eli's announcement concerning Samuel (*Bib. Ant.* 51.2), although elsewhere the prophet is ascribed a more universal role (*Bib. Ant.* 51.4). On this subject, the treatise seemingly retains an inconsistent stance.

Pseudo-Philo's portrayal of Hannah as a decisive, responsible, autonomous woman is striking. Hannah dedicates her son to the Lord and prophesies concerning his ministry. In contrast to 1 Samuel, Elkanah is not involved at all; it is her desire, her act, her son. Although this portrait is indeed rooted in the biblical account, Pseudo-Philo further develops it in this direction, as evidenced by his omission of the conversation communicating Elkanah's approval of his wife's decision (1 Sam. 1:23). This development is in part an aspect of his characterization of Hannah as a Wisdom figure, for Wisdom stands on her own and is not subordinate to any male figure.

Epilogue:
The People Dedicate Samuel (*Bib. Ant.* 51.7)

This episode is wholly created by Pseudo-Philo. He first states that Hannah and Elkanah[50] go home "with gladness, rejoicing and exulting in heart over all the glory that God had worked in them," and then adds a second dedication:

> But the people came down to Shiloh together . . . and they came to Eli the priest and brought to him Samuel. And they stood Samuel before the Lord, anointed him, and said, "Let the prophet live among the people, and may he be a light to this nation for a long time" (*Bib. Ant.* 51.7b).

This double dedication likely derives from 1 Samuel 3:20, which states that "all Israel . . . knew that Samuel was a trustworthy prophet of the Lord," and follows the pattern of Saul's anointing as king, that is, private anointing followed by a public ceremony and celebration (1 Sam. 10). It functions to demonstrate that the prophecy about the promised leader has been fulfilled in Samuel—both his parents and the nation attest to its fulfillment, expressed in respective ceremonies.

Hannah in *Jewish Antiquities:* A Woman of Inferior Character

Hannah is portrayed rather negatively in *Jewish Antiquities,* in contrast with the biblical portrayal. Her character and role are significantly downgraded and her abilities ignored. She is not a poetess, and even her traditional maternal roles—naming and nurturing—are either shared with men or given over entirely to them. At the same time, Elkanah's role in *Jewish Antiquities* is significantly upgraded. He appears in scenes where he is absent in the biblical versions and plays a more prominent role in others. Indeed, he casts his shadow over nearly every scene. What is primarily a woman's story in the Bible becomes much more a man's story in this document.

Josephus reveals his valuation of Hannah's character first of all by the way he leads into her story. He treats the whole saga as an aside, a momentary digression, in his account of the demise of the priesthood under Eli: "But here I would first recount the story of the prophet and then proceed to speak of the fate of Eli's sons and the disaster that befell the whole people of the Hebrews" (*Ant.* 5.341).

Although Josephus must introduce Samuel because of the prophet's later role, he attaches no real significance to Samuel's birth and background. Accordingly, he devalues and weakens Hannah's character and role.

Elkanah's Barren Wife (*Ant.* 5.341–45)

This section, with some variation, parallels the biblical versions (I include the Greek Bible):

1 Sam. 1:1–2 (Heb.)	(Greek)	*Ant.* 5.342
There was a certain man of Ramathaim, a Zuphite from the hill country of Ephraim, whose name was Elkanah....[51] He had two wives; the name of the one was Hannah, and the name of the other Peninnah. Peninnah had children, but Hannah had no children.	There was a certain man from Armathaim Sipha from the mountains of Ephraim, and his name was Elkanah. ...This one had two wives; the name of the first was Anna, and the name of the second was Phennana. And Phennana had children, but Anna did not have children.	Alkanes, a Levite of the middle class, a man dwelling among the people of the tribe[52] of Ephraim and an inhabitant of the city of Armatha,[53] married two wives, Anna and Phenanna. By the latter he had children, but the other, though childless, remained beloved of her husband.

We find here several variations from the biblical versions. Josephus introduces Elkanah immediately; the spotlight focuses upon him from the very beginning—and will remain on him through the final scene of the story. He is identified as a Levite, a designation that, although not present in 1 Samuel 1, is biblical (1 Chron. 6:27). He is "of the middle class." Ginzberg suggests that this is a "haggadic interpretation of the Hebrew phrase 'between the heights' (*haramathaim*)."[54]

Josephus tells us that Hannah is "beloved of her husband" earlier in the story than the biblical narrator implies this (1 Sam. 1:5). He also does not repeat the names of the women the second time, designating them merely as "the latter" (Peninnah) and "the other" (Hannah). Additionally, he highlights Elkanah as the father, rather than the circumstances of the women; he tells us that Elkanah had children by Peninnah and none by Hannah, instead of the biblical detail that "Peninnah had children, but Hannah had no children."

Josephus's description of the family sacrifice at Shiloh varies from that of the biblical storyteller on two significant points. First, he omits the adverbial phrase "year after year"; according to him, the procedure he describes occurs only at this time. The omission is significant because it is an essential element in the shaping of the biblical scene. The fact that these events occurred year after year serves to create an atmosphere of disappointment and despair and to evoke the range of emotions that accompany such a desperate situation. Thus, Josephus does not take pains to present Hannah's story in a way that would lead his audience to understand or appreciate her intense suffering.

Second, he omits the details that Peninnah taunted Hannah because of her barrenness, as the following indicates:

1 Samuel 1:4–7	*Ant.* 5.343
He would give portions to his wife Peninnah and to all her sons and daughters; but to Hannah he gave a double portion, because he loved her, though the Lord had closed her womb. Her rival used to provoke her severely, to irritate her, because the Lord had closed her womb. So it went on year after year; as often as she went up to the house of the Lord, she used to provoke her. Therefore Hannah wept and would not eat.	When he was distributing portions of meat to his wives and children, Anna, beholding the children of the other wife seated around their mother, burst into tears and bewailed her barrenness and lonesome lot.

According to the biblical account, Peninnah regularly provoked Hannah to the point that Hannah was so upset that she was unable to eat. Josephus's omission of this element transforms Hannah from a rational human being, who responds as would anyone to such constant, cruel harassment, into a silly, frantic woman, who has no control over her emotions and actions. According to Josephus, it is merely the sight of Peninnah and her children that causes Hannah to lose control: "Anna, beholding the children of the other wife seated around their mother, burst into tears."

This portrayal of a woman as weak, overly emotional,

and lightheaded concurs with Josephus's attitudes expressed elsewhere (*Ant.* 4.219; 13.417; *BJ* 7.399). Accordingly, he removes the element that would justify Hannah's
behavior and portrays her as he himself views women or
in a way that would appeal to his audience. We may note
that this degree of negativity is unparalleled in all of the
literature related to Hannah.

Josephus omits the scene in which Elkanah questions
Hannah about her despondency and refusal to eat, summarizing it by the narrative comment, "and her grief
proving stronger than her husband's consolation.... "
He rather moves directly into a description of Hannah's
prayer: "She went off to the tabernacle, to beseech God
to grant her offspring and to make her a mother, promising that her firstborn should be consecrated to the service
of God and that his manner of life should be unlike that
of ordinary men" (*Ant.* 5.344). Here, he more or less follows the biblical account, although he summarizes and
interprets it for a non-Jewish audience.[55]

There are some subtle variations in Josephus's version
of Hannah's prayer, though the general structure corresponds to the biblical account. Hannah beseeches God to
(1) grant her offspring and (2) make her a mother. She
does not specifically request a male child, only that she
become a mother. Simply becoming a mother is her all-
consuming passion. Josephus gives further expression to
this view in the following scene in which Eli confronts
Hannah (*Ant.* 5.345). Because Hannah "lingers a long
time over her prayers," the old priest mistakenly concludes that she is drunk and commands her to leave.
Josephus clearly follows the Greek Bible, for the Hebrew
text states that Eli merely orders Hannah to stop drinking
at the sanctuary. Hannah replies that "she had drunk but
water"[56] and "that it was for grief at the lack of children
that she was making supplication to God."

Again, Josephus fails to mention that Peninnah taunted
her relentlessly. To be sure, even according to the biblical
version, Hannah desires to have a child. But the story is

presented in such a way that we are not completely certain which is the greater source of irritation, anxiety, and unhappiness for Hannah—her barrenness or Peninnah's taunting. Hannah's reply to Eli in 1 Samuel is nonspecific: "I have been pouring out my soul before the Lord.... I have been speaking out of my great anxiety and vexation all this time" (1 Sam. 1:15–16). Hence, we see that Josephus interprets the biblical account according to his own views of women—or at least chooses to highlight what accords with those views.

Eli's final message to Hannah differs from that in the biblical versions:

1 Samuel 1:17	(Greek)	*Ant.* 5.345
Eli answered, "Go in peace; the God of Israel grant that petition you have made to him."	And Heli answered and said to her, "Go in peace; the God of Israel give you all your petition which you have asked of him."	He exhorted her to be of good cheer, announcing that God would grant her children.

Josephus replaces the nonspecific blessing with a specific statement that God would grant Hannah children. By this, he reinforces his characterization of her as a woman obsessed with having children. Although this petition is certainly implied in the Bible, it is specified in *Jewish Antiquities.*

Elkanah's Wife Becomes a Mother (*Ant.* 5.346–47)

Josephus considerably abbreviates the story of Samuel's birth: "Repairing thus in good hope to her husband, she took her food with gladness, and on their return to their native place she began to conceive; and an infant was born to them, whom they called Samuel, as one might say, 'asked of God.' They came therefore again to offer sacrifices for the birth of the child and brought their tithes[57] also" (*Ant.* 5.346).

Josephus omits Hannah's response to Eli and has Hannah return immediately to her husband "in good hope." The Hebrew Bible does not mention Hannah's husband but merely states that "the woman went to her quarters and ate [something], and her countenance was sad no longer" (1 Sam. 1:18). The Greek Bible, however, does refer to Hannah's return to Elkanah: "And the woman went her way, and entered into her lodging, and ate with her husband, and drank, and her countenance was no more sad." Here, as elsewhere, Josephus's version corresponds to the Greek.

Although a clear textual tradition stands behind the reference to Hannah's husband, Josephus's rephrasing of the text so that she "repair[s] . . . to her husband" again reflects his attitudes toward women. He presents Hannah as under her husband's authority and supervision. The entire episode is framed by her relationship to her husband; she leaves her husband to go to the sanctuary to pray, and she returns to her husband immediately thereafter. Indeed, nearly throughout the story, she remains under the shadow of Elkanah. And where he is not directly involved, Eli plays the authoritarian role.

We encounter this tendency to portray Hannah as under Elkanah's authority also in the birth announcement and naming of Samuel: "And an infant was born to them, whom they called Samuel." The Bible (1 Sam. 1:20) names Hannah as the subject: "Hannah . . . bore a son. She named him Samuel." Josephus's rewording of the text, limiting Hannah's role and enhancing Elkanah's, further reflects his views about male and female roles.

Josephus moves immediately from Samuel's birth to his dedication: "They came therefore again to offer sacrifices for the birth of the child and brought their tithes also. And the woman, mindful of the vow which she had made concerning the child, delivered him to Eli, dedicating him to God to become a prophet. So his locks were left to grow and his drink was water" (*Ant.* 5.347).

Josephus seems to say that Samuel was immediately

dedicated to God and left at the tabernacle. He omits the intervening scenes in which Hannah remains at home with Samuel while the others go to Shiloh and then nurses him until he is weaned (1 Sam. 1:21–23). It is not clear what Josephus means by his statement that the sacrifices offered were "for the birth of the child." If he is referring to the purification offerings prescribed in Leviticus 12, then he clearly contradicts the biblical versions, which state that Hannah did not go to Shiloh before Samuel was weaned. Additionally, this would imply that Samuel was dedicated at forty days. Indeed, the flow of the narrative most naturally indicates that he was dedicated at a very early age. But perhaps these sacrifices were thanksgiving sacrifices, which because they were votive offerings could have been offered at any time,[58] and thus we may not infer any time frame from the narrative.

At any rate, Josephus omits any reference to Hannah's very important role as the "nurturer" of Samuel. He employs the verb *trephō,* connoting both "to bring up" and "to nourish," to describe Samuel's upbringing in the sanctuary. As I have noted, he does not specify when Samuel was brought to the sanctuary and omits scenes that refer to Hannah's nursing him. Whether he indeed presents Samuel as having been nurtured in the sanctuary or omits this important feature of the story merely out of lack of concern or interest, the effect remains the same—a further deemphasis of Hannah's role in Samuel's life.

Josephus closes the story with the comment that "Although[59] Samuel lived and was nurtured in the sanctuary, Elkanah had by Anna yet other sons and three daughters." The biblical text behind this is 1 Samuel 2:21: "And the Lord took note of Hannah; she conceived and bore three sons and two daughters. And the boy Samuel grew up in the presence of the Lord." Josephus not only introduces Elkanah into the story where it is not necessary for any logical reason, he even subordinates the statement about Samuel to the notice about Elkanah's ability to father children. Thus, Hannah's story is in reality Elkanah's story; it begins and ends with the spotlight on the father.

Comparison of the Portraits of Hannah in *Biblical Antiquities* and *Jewish Antiquities*

Pseudo-Philo and Josephus diverge significantly in their portrayals of Hannah, agreeing only on the very basic plot and characters of the biblical narrative. Each author presents a portrait very different from that of the Bible in regard to Hannah's story itself and to her character and role.

Josephus does not give much attention to Hannah's story; it is merely an aside in the saga of the demise of the priesthood under Eli's leadership. He abbreviates the account considerably, primarily by omitting the Song of Hannah. Although omissions of hymns are common in *Jewish Antiquities,* by this editorial decision he removes from Hannah two important roles she fills in the Bible, *Biblical Antiquities,* and rabbinic literature—poetess and prophetess. Pseudo-Philo, in contrast, gives major attention to Hannah's story, leading into it with prophecies containing messianic overtones, and greatly expanding both the narrative and the hymn.

Josephus diminishes Hannah's role significantly; indeed, he presents Hannah's story as Elkanah's story. He includes the father in a role usually designated to the mother in the Bible (naming the child), and throughout the story, Hannah remains under his shadow. Josephus even rewrites the notice that Hannah had other children (1 Sam. 2:21) to declare instead that Elkanah had other children by Hannah.

By contrast, in *Biblical Antiquities,* Elkanah plays a secondary role. Although the story begins with him, the focus quickly turns upon Hannah, where it remains throughout. He appears again only twice, once to testify to Hannah's noble character and again in the Hymn of Hannah, where Hannah exhorts him to join in the hymn and teaches him scripture.

Another role portrayed differently in the two documents is that of nurturer. According to 1 Samuel 1:22–23, Hannah nurses Samuel until he is weaned. *Jewish Antiquities* does not mention Hannah nursing him but implies that he was brought to the sanctuary at an early age and nurtured there. By contrast, Pseudo-Philo develops the nursing role into a major element, whereby Hannah becomes a figure of Wisdom whose milk nourishes not only Samuel, but all Israel. Thus, what Josephus chooses to omit, Pseudo-Philo chooses to focus upon and amplify.

We find also a major contrast between the authors' portrayals of Hannah's character. Josephus presents her as a frantic female who is crazy to have a child. He rewrites the story, removing the notice that Peninnah regularly taunted Hannah, and the effect of that is that he portrays Hannah as becoming distraught with grief merely at the sight of Peninnah's children gathered around their mother. Pseudo-Philo, in contrast, develops the taunting into a key element. He utilizes it as a means of illustrating the noble character of Hannah. He rewrites the story so that Peninnah's yearly taunting (1 Sam. 1:6–7) becomes even more frequent, indeed a daily ordeal that Hannah must endure. Though this interpretation appears also in rabbinic literature, he develops it in a unique way. He situates it in a much larger context, by incorporating language from Psalms 42–43, where the psalmist laments the plight of a righteous person who is daily taunted by the wicked, and calls upon God for vindication. He thus associates Psalms 42–43 with Hannah's circumstance—Hannah represents the righteous psalmist, while Peninnah represents the wicked enemy(ies).

Thus, the drama between Hannah and Peninnah typifies the drama between the righteous and the wicked, between Israel and its enemies. Hannah's steadfast trust in God in the midst of her seemingly hopeless circumstances is truly exemplary, and her eventual vindication exemplifies the surety of Israel's vindication in the face of those who taunt it with the same question, "Where is your God?"

Josephus's portrayal of Hannah is shaped by two factors—his audience and (more so) his stated views regarding women. On the one hand, he seeks to heighten the dramatic element of his story, in conformity to Greek literary conventions. On the other hand, his portrayal accords with his description of women as weak and in need of male supervision. Hannah must be under Elkanah's authority because she is not capable of functioning apart from him. Indeed, this portrait clearly reveals Josephus's negative attitudes toward women, primarily because the characteristics and actions he attributes to Hannah are incidental to the story; he has no other discernible motive for portraying Hannah as he does. For this reason, Josephus's treatment of her story contributes greatly to a further understanding of his attitudes toward women and husband/wife relationships. His choice of material to include and exclude, as well as his particular alterations, all for the sake of bringing the story into conformity with his views, reveal his own biases and presuppositions. His portrayal of Hannah is a literary expression of his stated position that "the woman . . . is in all things inferior to the man" and should be in submission to men (*CAp* 2.201).

Pseudo-Philo's portrayal stands apart from that of Josephus—and all other known interpreters. He significantly enhances both Hannah's character and role, and her story becomes paradigmatic of the Israelites' story. Her crisis is their crisis, her longings are their longings, her fulfillment is their fulfillment. While Hannah's association with the broader concerns of the Jewish people derives from the biblical account, this relationship is expanded considerably in *Biblical Antiquities*.

As in the case of Josephus, we may ask whether Pseudo-

Philo's editorial work is intentional or incidental—that is, whether it results simply because he views women this positively. Although, to be sure, he views women positively, it seems that he portrays Hannah in this way primarily because of the example he wishes to draw from her life. His modifications of the story all serve to present Hannah as a model of piety and faithfulness on a personal level, as well as a model of Israel as she moves from barrenness to vindication, when she becomes the source of Wisdom for the nations. By example, Hannah speaks even when she is silent and even before Samuel is born. The message that shines through her experience is one of hope—the promise of fecundity (in all its nuance of meaning) and eventual vindication, and the value of trust in God and doing God's will. Also, as a Wisdom figure, she offers the promise that Wisdom will indeed give birth to a new leader, who will provide the leadership the people have prayed and longed for, who will enlighten the nation—and even all people.

Notes

1. Athalya Brenner (*Israelite Woman*, 92–105) employs the phrase and discusses various aspects of this role.

2. Other examples are Sarah and Hagar (Gen. 16), Rebecca (Gen. 25), Rachel and Leah (Gen. 29–30), and Samson's mother (Judg. 13).

3. Ashkenasay, *Eve's Journey*, 82.

4. Latin: *qui liberet nos de nos pressura nostra*. *Pressura* reflects the Hebrew *ṣorerēnu*, whose root can denote either "pressure" or "enemy." The root is also found in *ṣarah* (rival wife), which describes Peninnah in 1 Sam. 1:6.

5. See Judg. 3:9, 11. Josephus mentions his name (*Ant.* 5.182–84) but does not develop the character.

6. Nickelsburg, "Good and Bad Leaders," 54. He adds that "Kenaz takes office at a time when Israel's existence is in serious jeopardy."

7. Other manuscripts read *Arimathem* (*editio princeps*) or *Arimathes* (Codex Regius Parisinus); cf. LXX: *Armathaim*. This is the first point at which there is a connection with the biblical narrative (1 Sam. 1:1).

8. The number ten is based on Elkanah's question: "Am I not more to you than ten sons?" (1 Sam. 1:8).

9. For example, *Bib. Ant.* 9.7–8; 30.2.

10. Philo, *Deus* 13–15 (quoted by Winston [*Wisdom of Solomon*, 131], who remarks about its similarity to Wisd. Sol. 4:1).

11. This is not to say that *Biblical Antiquities* is dependent literarily upon Philo. It is possible that this particular exegetical tradition was widely known at that time. Also, though Pseudo-Philo may incorporate some of these traditions, he uses them

very differently; in his book we find no trace of the allegorical interpretations of Philo.

12. The Midrash emphasizes Elkanah's role. See Ginzberg, *Legends*, 4:57–58. Ashkenasay (*Eve's Journey*, 13) comments that this is an example of the rabbinic "attempt to bring the biblical story into conformity with prevalent sexist attitudes." Pseudo-Philo's focus on Elkanah does not reflect a similar tendency, for he is soon completely eclipsed by Hannah.

13. A eunuch is permanently unable to beget children. It could suggest that Hannah is past the age of childbearing.

14. The promise is for those eunuchs who "keep my Sabbaths, choose what pleases me, and hold fast to my covenant" (Isa. 56:4).

15. David Winston (*Wisdom of Solomon*, 131) adduces evidence that later interpreters put this accusation on the lips of Hagar, in taunting Sarah. See *1 En.* 98.5.

16. Winston (*Wisdom of Solomon*, 59) conjectures that the Wisdom of Solomon "was likely composed ca. 37–41 C.E."; thus, the work could have served as a link between these two texts.

17. Ginzberg, *Legends*, 6:216: "The . . . Midrash (Aggadat Bereshit 19, 60) takes the 'memorable day' (1 Sam. 1:4) to refer to the day of Passover which is spoken of in the preceding verse as *miyyamim yamimah*, in accordance with the use of that phrase in Exod. 13:10. The same view is shared by Pseudo-Philo 48.3; 50.2, which reads *Die bono paschae*. . . ."

18. Some Rabbis questioned whether Samuel was indeed a Nazarite (see *mNazir* 5). The problem was rooted in the biblical statement that Samuel killed Agag (1 Sam. 15:33), which would have defiled him.

19. See Gen. 30:2.

20. Harrington translates the Latin *iustificata est* as "justified." But if the Greek verb behind this is *dikaioō* and the Hebrew *ṣdq*, it may also be translated "vindicate." I have chosen this rendering because it suits the theme of vindication of the righteous in Hannah's story. Note also the parallel in Luke 7:35: "Wisdom is vindicated by her children." In the context of Eli's declaration in *Biblical Antiquities*, Hannah clearly takes on the character and role of Wisdom (*Bib. Ant.* 51.3), as also in her hymn that follows (51.3–4). See below for further details.

21. See Deut. 32:26–27.

22. A similar phenomenon occurs elsewhere in *Biblical Antiquities*. When David meets Goliath on the battlefield, he places their own rivalry, representative of Israel and its enemy, into the broader context of the rivalry between their two mothers, Ruth (David) and Orpah (Goliath): "Were not the two women, from whom you and I were born, sisters? And your mother was Orpah, and my mother Ruth. And Orpah chose for herself the gods of the Philistines and went after them, but Ruth chose for herself the ways of the Most Powerful and walked in them" (*Bib. Ant.* 61.6).

23. 32LXX^B states that "they brought him before the Lord, and his father [Heb.: they] slew his offering . . . and he brought near the child and slew the calf."

24. See n. 20, above.

25. Here, I follow the *editio princeps*, as do James and Hartom. Harrington opts for the Admont reading, "advantage." See Feldman, "Prolegomenon," cxxxi.

26. Harrington (*OTP*, 365) comments that the reference is to Israel because of the parallelism with "the twelve tribes." But Feldman ("Prolegomenon," cxxxi) argues that it is plural, as Hebrew *goyyim*, and refers to Israel's broader ministry as "a light to the nations" (Isa. 49:6). Harrington's view is more convincing.

27. Note, for example, the imagery applied to Jerusalem (Mother Zion) in Isa. 66:10–11: "Rejoice with Jerusalem, and be glad for her, all you who love her; rejoice with her in joy, all you who mourn over her—that you may nurse and be satisfied from her consoling breast; that you may drink deeply with delight from her glorious bosom." A biblical source that refers literally to nursing is Sarah's exclamation upon giving birth to Isaac (Gen. 21:7): "Who would ever have said to Abraham that Sarah would nurse children?" Note that Pseudo-Philo explicitly links Samuel with Isaac (*Bib. Ant.* 49.8). On p. 193 of his commentary on the Wisdom of Solomon, David Winston summarizes an allegory in which Philo of Alexandria explicitly likens Sarah, who was barren, to Wisdom.

28. This is the translation of Winston, *Wisdom of Solomon*, 192.

29. Suggested by Winston, *Wisdom of Solomon*, 176.

30. This comes from Philo's commentary on Prov. 8:22. Win-

ston (*Wisdom of Solomon*, 177) remarks that Philo follows the terminology of Plato's *Timaeus* 49A–50D.

31. See also *Odes of Sol.* 30:2: "And come all you thirsty and take a drink, and rest beside the fountain of the Lord." Also see 19:1–4: "A cup of milk was offered to me, and I drank it in the sweetness of the Lord's kindness. The Son is the cup, and the Father is he who was milked; and the Holy Spirit [N.B. a parallel to Wisdom] is she who milked him; because his breasts were full, and it was undesirable that his milk should be released without purpose. The Holy Spirit opened her bosom, and mixed the milk of the two breasts of the Father."

32. See Witt, *Isis*; see also Pomeroy, *Goddesses*, 217–26. Lieberman (*Hellenism*, 136–37) refers to *t'Aboda Zara* 5.1, which lists as an idol "the image of a woman nursing her child," and to the commentary in *b'Abodah Zara* 43a, which states that "a woman nursing [a child] represents Eve who suckled the whole world." Archaeological excavations reveal that Isis was worshiped in Greco-Roman Palestine, even in Jerusalem. See Hengel, *Judaism and Hellenism*, 1:158.

33. This is noted by J. Collins in his comments on the Hellenistic Jewish work *Artapanus* (*OTP* 2:898 n. e).

34. See Joseph Plumpe, *Mater Ecclesia*, 124: "It is of course entirely possible and probable that in Asia Minor at about the half-way mark of the second century the *Mater Ecclesia* was received, fully developed, from the great center of Eastern Christianization, Antioch, through the gates of Syria. In the apocryphal *Epistola Apostolorum* ... the Lord quotes to the apostles a prophecy that is not found in the Old Testament canon: 'Behold, out of Syria will I begin to call together a new Jerusalem, and Sion will I subdue to me, and it shall be taken, and the place which is childless shall be called the son and daughter of my Father, and my Bride.' "

35. Hengel, *Judaism and Hellenism*, 1:154.

36. My discussion of the Hymn of Hannah will focus primarily upon Pseudo-Philo's portrait of Hannah; it is not within the scope of this study to discuss in detail all of the ideas in the hymn or its biblical counterpart and/or interpretations of it.

37. This is the reading of the *editio princeps* (*Venite in voce mea*). The Admont MS reads: *Venite in voce magna*. The first is the better reading because it maintains the parallelism with "Pay attention to my speech."

38. See Isaiah's directive to the "barren woman" to sing a hymn (Isa. 54:1). Also see *Odes of Sol.* 8:4: "You who were in silence, speak, for your mouth has been opened." D. E. Aune ("Odes of Solomon," 446) comments that this "appears to be an injunction to congregational prophecy." If that be the case with the ode, the close parallel in *Biblical Antiquities* suggests that the Hymn of Hannah was sung in a communal worship context. Note also that in this same ode, Christ describes himself in terms of the milk he gives from his breasts (v. 14): "My own breasts I prepared for them, that they might drink my holy milk and live by it."

39. See *4 Ezra* 8:10–11: "You have commanded that from the members themselves (that is, from the breasts) milk should be supplied, which is the fruit of the breasts, so that what has been fashioned may be nourished for a time."

40. The expression "raised up" carries messianic overtones. Perhaps Pseudo-Philo alludes to the prophet "like Moses" whom God had promised to "raise up" for Israel (Deut. 18:15, 18).

41. In 1 Sam. 2:1, Hannah speaks about her horn; Pseudo-Philo changes it to "his horn," thus altering it from an expression of praise into a prophecy about Samuel's greatness as a leader.

42. The Rabbis accorded her this role also (*S. 'Olam Rab.* 20, 21; *Meg.* 14a). See *Tg. Neb. 1 Sam.* 2:1, which specifies that Hannah spoke her hymn by the Holy Spirit.

43. See Wisd. Sol. 7:29, where Wisdom is compared with light: "She [Wisdom] is more beautiful than the sun, and excels every constellation of the stars. Compared with the light she is found to be superior."

44. The Hebrew Bible (1 Sam. 2:5c) states: *'aqarah yaledah šiv'ah*. It is commonly translated "the barren woman has borne seven children," understanding *šiv'ah* as the number seven. Pseudo-Philo renders it as a verb (satisfied) and *yaledah* as a noun (childbearing). He could have based this on the reversal theme (Hannah before was "empty" and now she is "satisfied"), or perhaps he hesitated to attribute to Hannah "seven" children, when the Bible states that she had only five more children (1 Sam. 2:21). Indeed, he omits any reference to other children. On Philo of Alexandria's interpretation of *šiv'ah* as Seven, signifying Wisdom and Rest, see *Deus* 3.

45. See *2 Apoc. Bar.* 48:50: "For surely, as you [the righteous] endured much labor in the short time in which you live in this passing world, so you will receive great light in that world which has no end."

46. This element is especially prominent in the Targum, which we noted also in relation to the Targum of the Hymn of Deborah.

47. Philo mentions this name in relation to Wisdom (*Fug.* 50): "And it is wisdom's name that holy oracles proclaim by 'Bethuel,' a name meaning in our speech 'Daughter of God'" (quoted in Winston, *Wisdom of Solomon,* 193–94).

48. This recalls Deborah's exhortation to Barak (Judg. 5:12, and in *Bib. Ant.* 31.1), where it denotes getting to a task. But note also *T. Job* 46–50, where Job's daughters gird their loins (with magical cords) and are given a heavenly language with which to sing hymns and prophesy. This feature, present also in *Bib. Ant.* 51.3a, could suggest a communal worship context. See n. 38, above.

49. Ps. 99:6. The linking of Elkanah and Asaph in these lines is not unique, for they are also associated in the Midrash. See Ginzberg, *Legends,* 6:215 n. 1.

50. The LXX and Lucianic manuscripts also have a plural verb, while the Hebrew Bible and Targum specify that Elkanah went home.

51. At this point, the biblical versions list Elkanah's genealogy. Josephus generally omits such material.

52. This is my translation. The Loeb edition reads "from the tribe of Ephraim," which is impossible if Elkanah is a Levite.

53. This name appears in several forms: Ramathan (Codex Regius Parisinus, Codex Oxoniensis, Codex Marcianus), Aramathan, Aramath (Lat.).

54. Ginzberg, *Legends,* 6:215 n. 4.

55. Josephus interprets Hannah's vow to dedicate her firstborn as a Nazarite for an audience unfamiliar with Jewish practice. He simply states that "his manner of life would be unlike ordinary men." Later, however (5.347), he explains more fully: "[The woman] dedicated him to God to become a prophet, so his locks were left to grow and his drink was water."

56. Josephus rewords Hannah's assertion that she had drunk no wine or beer (1 Sam. 1:15). The mention of water hints at

the story of Samson, whose mother was commanded—among other things—not to drink wine or strong drink, because her child was to be a Nazarite (Judg. 13:7, 13–14).

57. The word "tithes" is found in the Greek version of 1 Sam. 1:21. Perhaps it entered into the text due to the close connection in Leviticus 27 between commandments dealing with things dedicated to God, the dedication of the firstborn, and the commandments related to tithes.

58. See Leviticus 7. It could also have been an offering "for special vows" or a "freewill offering" (Num. 15:1–12).

59. This is my translation; the force of the *men...de* construction is concessive.

4

The Witch of Endor

The witch[1] of Endor is an intriguing figure. On the one hand, her profession is condemned by prophet, priest, and king;[2] on the other hand, her abilities are respected and her services solicited in time of crisis, and this without polemical commentary within the biblical text.[3] While recognizing the validity of her profession, biblical authors rejected it as a legitimate means of determining the will of God. It is striking, however, that despite negative attitudes in the Bible toward necromancy, the witch of Endor is portrayed as a woman of "courage,...competence, and compassion."[4]

The Witch of Endor
in *Biblical Antiquities:*
A Veteran Magician

Pseudo-Philo treats the story of the king of Israel's encounter with the witch of Endor somewhat differently than does the biblical narrator, though the general
structure of the story remains the same. He expands some
sections and omits others, such as the sequel in which the
woman persuades Saul to break his fast by eating the food
she has prepared. He introduces details not found in the
biblical story, some of which suggest motives for actions
or further describe the events and characters. Most notably, he describes the witch as a Gentile "magician," the
"daughter of the Midianite diviner who led Israel astray."
Such details serve to present a very different portrait
from that in the Bible.

Background: Saul Seeks Guidance (*Bib. Ant.* 64.1–3)

The episode of Saul's visit to the witch of Endor begins as
in the biblical text, with the notice of the death of Samuel.
The first phrase of the account in *Biblical Antiquities*
corresponds to 1 Samuel 28:3, with a few minor variations. While the biblical text, after giving notice about
Samuel's death (1 Sam. 28:1), goes on to say that "Saul
had expelled the mediums and wizards from the land,"
Pseudo-Philo presents this element in another way, by inserting a section of inner dialogue by which Saul reveals
his motivation for his action: "Then Saul thought and
said, 'Because I am to expel the wizards[5] from the land of
Israel, they will be mindful[6] of me after my departure'"
(*Bib. Ant.* 64.1).
The biblical text links the death of Samuel with Saul's

expelling the mediums (1 Sam. 28:3), but Pseudo-Philo brings out this relationship more clearly. He also highlights Saul's desire to do something spectacular so he would be remembered as was Samuel. This addition recalls a biblical episode in which Saul sets up a monument for himself at Carmel (1 Sam. 15:12) in order to ensure that he will be remembered.

Pseudo-Philo then reinforces his own comments about Saul's motivation; he does this by adding God's commentary that Saul took this action "to make a name for himself" (*Bib. Ant.* 64.1).[7] Moreover, this element serves to associate the king with the builders of the tower of Babel (*Bib. Ant.* 6.1–2), which in this document is the premier symbol of idolatry and apostasy.[8] For Pseudo-Philo, Saul's resorting to divination by a necromancer reveals his true character and as well as his apostasy from the worship of the true God. He further emphasizes the spiritual bankruptcy of Saul's leadership by adding the notice that Saul will seek "to obtain divination from [the wizards], because he has no prophets." His placing the pronouncement that Saul would ultimately resort to necromancy at the beginning of the story further reflects the deterministic tendency of *Biblical Antiquities.*[9]

Although Pseudo-Philo follows the structure of the biblical text in turning next to the subject of the Philistines' challenge to Saul's forces, his version deviates considerably and becomes virtually a new story. He emphasizes Israel's vulnerability without a prophet to intercede for it and thus explicitly links the Philistine incursion with the warrior David's exile and Samuel's death, attributing the incursion to a lack of proper leadership:

And then the Philistines[10] said . . . , "Behold, Samuel the prophet is dead, and who prays for Israel? And David, who fought on their behalf, is Saul's enemy, and he is not with them. And now let us rise up and go and fight and attack them and avenge the blood of our fathers." And the Philistines gathered together and came for battle (*Bib. Ant.* 64.2).

The author then returns the spotlight to Saul, as in the biblical account, but with a significant difference:

1 Samuel 28:5–6	*Bib. Ant.* 64.3
When Saul saw the army of the Philistines, he was afraid, and his heart trembled greatly. When Saul inquired of the Lord, the Lord did not answer him, not by dreams or by Urim, or by prophets.	When Saul saw that Samuel was dead and David was not with him, his hands grew faint, and he inquired of the Lord, but He did not listen to him. And he sought out prophets, and none appeared to him.

The major alteration is that while in the Bible Saul is afraid when he sees the Philistines, in *Biblical Antiquities* he is afraid when he sees that Samuel is dead and David is gone. The variation shifts the emphasis to Israel's vulnerability without "good leaders" (a common theme in the document) by implying that if Samuel and David were with Israel, Saul would not be afraid. Again, without proper leadership, Israel is vulnerable to its enemies.

Saul's frustrated attempts at legitimate divination more or less accord with 1 Samuel 28:6. In his desperation for guidance, Saul finally turns to a necromancer. Here, too, we find evidence of Pseudo-Philo's editorial work:

1 Samuel 28:7	*Bib. Ant.* 64.3
Then Saul said to his servants, "Seek out for me a woman who is a medium, so that I may go to her and inquire of her." His servants said to him, "There is a medium at Endor."	And Saul said to the people, "Let us seek out some medium and inquire of him what I should plan out." And the people answered him, "Behold, now there is a woman, Sedecla by name, and she is the daughter of the Midianite diviner[11] who led Israel astray with sorceries, and behold she dwells in Endor."

The variations are numerous. First, Saul asks the people to help him find a medium and also to join him in inquiring through him/her. This reflects Pseudo-Philo's tendency regarding good and bad leaders—bad leaders lead the people astray, affecting the entire nation; good leaders do the opposite. Second, Saul does not specify that this medium be a woman (contra 1 Sam. 28:7); the term is masculine, indicating that in Pseudo-Philo's view, women were not the only (or the primary) practitioners of illegitimate religion.[12] Third, the author makes two extrabiblical statements concerning the witch herself: (1) He gives her a name (Sedecla). As we have seen, the naming of unnamed biblical characters occurs elsewhere in this work (see *Bib. Ant.* 40.1; 42.1). (2) He describes her as a Gentile. Though the Bible does not specify her ethnic identity, we may logically assume that she was an Israelite. By contrast, *Biblical Antiquities* describes her as "the daughter of the Midianite diviner," presumably Aod the Magician (*Bib. Ant.* 34). She is thus identified with one of Israel's archenemies (see also *Bib. Ant.* 18.13; 61.1).

Sedecla Is Engaged by Saul (*Bib. Ant.* 64.4)

In the opening portion of the narrative relating these events, the variations from the Bible are minor: "And Saul put on his worst[13] clothes and went off to her, he and two men with him, by night and said to her, 'Raise up Samuel for me'" (*Bib. Ant.* 64.4). Samuel is named from the start rather than upon further questioning by the witch, as in 1 Samuel 28:11.

Sedecla's response is in part abbreviated and in part expanded in *Biblical Antiquities*. The author omits the woman's rehearsal of Saul's actions in expelling the necromancers and her accusation that she is being tricked (1 Sam. 28:9) and communicates the essential response: "I fear Saul." As in the Bible, Saul assures her that she will not be harmed. But Saul's response is expanded:

And Saul said to himself, "When I was king in Israel,[14] even if the Gentiles did not see me, they knew nevertheless that I was Saul." And Saul asked the woman, saying, "Have you ever seen Saul?" She said, "I have seen him often." Saul went outside and wept[15] and said, "Behold, now I know that my appearance has been changed, and the glory of my kingdom has passed from me."

Pseudo-Philo employs the motif of Sedecla's nonrecognition of Saul to make a point about the complete bankruptcy of Saul's kingdom. The spirit, which had changed his appearance (see *Bib. Ant.* 20.2; 27.10), is no longer upon him (*Bib. Ant.* 60.1), and she is not able to recognize him. Biblical basis for the notion that the spirit's presence changed Saul's appearance may be traced to 1 Samuel 10:6.[16]

Samuel Is Raised Up (*Bib. Ant.* 64.5–7)

Pseudo-Philo treats the element of the woman's recognition of Saul differently than does the biblical storyteller. According to 1 Samuel 28:12, she sees Samuel and immediately recognizes Saul. We are not told how simply seeing Samuel causes her to recognize Saul. An exegetical tradition preserved in several manuscripts of the Greek Bible names Saul as the one she saw, which is even more puzzling. Pseudo-Philo conflates the two traditions, thereby explaining that seeing the two together led her to recognize Saul, although he still does not tell us exactly how this happened: "And when the woman saw Samuel rising up and she saw Saul with him, she shouted and said, 'Behold you are Saul, and why have you deceived me?' " (*Bib. Ant.* 64.5).

After Saul assures her that she need not fear, Sedecla proceeds to describe what she sees, prefacing her account with an addition to the biblical story: "Behold, forty years have passed since I began raising up the dead for the Philistines, but such a sight as this has never been seen

before, nor will it be seen afterward" (*Bib. Ant.* 64.5).
This addition serves to heighten the dramatic intensity
of the experience and thus the solemnity and authority of Samuel's message. But Pseudo-Philo makes four
other statements incidentally through Sedecla's words:
(1) He makes it very clear that what has occurred is
unique. (2) He implies that Sedecla was not truly able to
raise the dead (although she claims to be a veteran), for
she responds with astonishment when Samuel appears.
(3) Sedecla works for the Philistines, which further associates her with Gentiles and Israel's enemies. (4) Sedecla
has been practicing her art for forty years,[17] a time period
that is surely stereotypic.

Saul then asks Sedecla a second time to relate what she
has seen, although he phrases the question slightly differently: "What is his appearance?" The repeated question
serves to maintain the focus upon Samuel's appearance
and thus his robe, the key element upon which the
message of the encounter turns.

Whereas in 1 Samuel 28:13 the witch says, "I see a divine being [Heb.: *'elohim*] coming up out of the ground,"
in *Biblical Antiquities* she replies, "You are asking me about
divine beings."[18] The Latin word rendered "divine beings" (*diis*) is a literal translation of the Hebrew, which
though commonly meaning "God" or "gods," in this case
obviously refers to Samuel. In *Biblical Antiquities,* the
word is plural either because it is based on a plural noun
in Hebrew or because the witch describes not only Samuel
but also the "two angels leading him" (*Bib. Ant.* 64.6).

Sedecla then states that the spirit does not have "the appearance of a man,"[19] reinforcing the previous statement
that she is describing a "divine being." Her description
differs from that of the Bible. Whereas the biblical text
(1 Sam. 28:14) tells us that Samuel is an "old man[20]
...wrapped in a robe,"[21] *Biblical Antiquities* (64.6) states
that "he is clothed in a white robe with a mantle placed
over it," adding that two angels are leading him.[22] The
author focuses upon Samuel's mantle, for it is the mantle

that causes Saul to become distraught. It reminds him of the incident following the battle against the Amalekites, when he was confronted by Samuel for his failure to carry out the *herem* (dedication to God by total annihilation) against the defeated enemy (1 Sam. 15). At that time, after Samuel had announced Saul's loss of the kingdom (15:26) and turned to go, Saul "caught hold of the hem of his robe, and it tore" (15:27). The prophet then used this as an object lesson: "The Lord has torn the kingdom of Israel from you this very day" (15:28).

Perhaps the sight of the mantle led Saul also to recall Samuel's words uttered immediately before the incident involving the prophet's mantle: "For rebellion is no less a sin than divination" (1 Sam. 15:23). At that point, Saul had not actually engaged in divination (by illegitimate means), only rebellion. But it was that rebellion that ultimately led to his conjuring up Samuel and that ultimately sealed his doom. Pseudo-Philo indicates that he links these two incidents by having Samuel tell Saul, "You have now sinned a second time in neglecting God" (*Bib. Ant.* 64.7).

Saul's response to Sedecla's description differs considerably from the biblical account:

1 Samuel 28:14	*Bib. Ant.* 64.6
So Saul knew that it was Samuel, and he bowed with his face to the ground, and did obeisance.	And Saul remembered the mantle[23] that Samuel tore when he was alive, and he struck his hand on the ground and pounded it.

In the second part of the response, the only element common to both versions is "the ground." We see that Pseudo-Philo continues to portray Saul more negatively than does the Bible, altering Saul's expression of awe and worship to one of distress and anger.

In *Biblical Antiquities* Samuel begins his message to Saul with the same question he asks him in the biblical text: "Why have you disturbed me by bringing me up?" (1 Sam. 28:15). Rather than answering Saul's request, he follows with several other statements concerning afterlife and Sedecla's necromantic abilities:

> And so do not boast, king, nor you, woman; for you [pl. *vos*] have not brought me forth, but that order that God spoke to me while I was still alive, that I should come and tell you that you have sinned now a second time in neglecting God. Therefore, after I rendered up my soul my bones have been disturbed so that I who am dead should tell you what I heard while I was alive. Now therefore tomorrow you and your sons will be with me when the people have been delivered into the hands of the Philistines; and because your insides were eaten up with jealousy, what is yours will be taken from you (*Bib. Ant.* 64.7b–8).

The first part of Samuel's message basically corresponds to that in 1 Samuel 28, though it is greatly abbreviated. The second part is an addition, reflecting the rabbinic doctrine of reciprocal punishment, which appears elsewhere in *Biblical Antiquities*.[24] Moreover, through the prophet's message, Pseudo-Philo clearly states that neither Sedecla nor Saul has raised up Samuel; no one should mistake his appearance as indicative of her ability to raise the dead, at least not such a righteous man as Samuel.[25]

Saul's response differs considerably from the biblical version, omitting one element and adding another:

1 Samuel 28:20	*Bib. Ant.* 64.9
Immediately Saul fell full length on the ground, filled with fear because of the words of Samuel; and there was no strength in him, for he had eaten nothing all day and all night.	And Saul heard the words of Samuel and grew faint and said, "Behold I am going to die with my sons; perhaps my destruction will be an atonement for my wickedness." And Saul rose up and went away from there.

For some clear reasons (see below), Pseudo-Philo omits reference to Saul's fast before the seance. However, he adds the king's final words, "perhaps my destruction will be an atonement for my wickedness," a statement that introduces a notion parallel to the rabbinic doctrine that premature death atones for sins.[26]

The end of the biblical story relates the servants' and witch's attempt to persuade Saul to eat something (1 Sam. 28:21–23) and her subsequent preparation of a meal for him and his servants (vv. 24–25). Pseudo-Philo omits these scenes, probably because they present the witch in a humane light, which does not accord with his presentation of her. If she indeed is related to the magician who led Israel astray and has herself been working for Israel's enemies for forty years, how could she at the same time be hospitable and kind? Whatever Pseudo-Philo's reasons, the omission eliminates a positive feature of her portrait and thus renders it more negative in his version than in the Bible.

The Witch of Endor in *Jewish Antiquities:* Paragon of Virtue

The portrayal of the witch of Endor in *Jewish Antiquities* is one of the most striking in all of Josephus's works. Indeed, she is his most positively portrayed female character even though she is neither a matriarch nor a traditional prophetess, but a woman whose profession is unremittingly condemned throughout biblical literature. Josephus devotes a full sixteen paragraphs (*Ant.* 6.327–42) to the story of Saul's visit to the necromancer, three of which (6.340–42) constitute a panegyric on the witch herself. In that rather lengthy addition to the biblical account, he praises her excellent character and holds her up as an example for all to emulate. Moreover, throughout the entire story, Josephus says nothing even remotely negative about her. All of this renders his version more intriguing than any other treatment of her story.

Saul Seeks Guidance (*Ant.* 6.327–31)

Josephus omits mention of Samuel's death[27] and moves immediately from the notice about the Philistines coming for battle against Saul's forces (*Ant.* 6.325–26) into a discussion about Saul's expulsion of the diviners (*manteis*), necromancers,[28] and other such practitioners.[29] He explicitly excludes prophets from this list ("except the prophets"), probably because Josephus's Greco-Roman audience would have considered a prophet in the same category as the other diviners, or because divination through them was legitimate in ancient Israel. Or perhaps he mentions them separately because further in the story he tells us that Saul consulted the prophets (*Ant.* 6.329), which would be strange if prophets had been expelled with the other diviners.

In discussing Saul's quest for counsel about the battle, Josephus follows the biblical account closely, although adding a few details and omitting even fewer. He specifies where the Philistine army camped and adds that Saul was afraid of the Philistines because of the superior size and capability of their army. He expands somewhat the section relating Saul's unsuccessful attempt at divining God's will before the battle, omitting reference to dreams (although he refers to them later [*Ant.* 6.334]) and Urim (which would have been meaningless to his non-Jewish audience), and focuses solely on divination through prophets. He also specifies the subject of the inquiry ("the battle and its outcome"), which is merely implied in the biblical account.

Another addition to the biblical story serves both to heighten the dramatic impact and to evoke sympathy for

Saul: "But, as no response came from God, Saul was yet more afraid and his heart failed him, foreseeing inevitable disaster since the Deity was no longer at his side" (*Ant.* 6.329). Saul is indeed a tragic figure—abandoned by God and mad with fear.

As in the biblical account, Saul then gives the order to find a woman who makes inquiry through spirits of the dead.[30] Josephus, however, expands this by further describing her profession: "Search out . . . a woman among the necromancers and those who call up the spirits of the dead, that so he might learn how matters would turn out for him. For this sort of necromancer raises up the spirits of the dead and through them foretells the future to those who inquire of them" (*Ant.* 6.329). Josephus uses the standard Greek term for necromancer and describes the woman as one of a class of professionals "who call up the spirits of the dead," thus indicating that there was more than one type of necromancer. The same is also suggested by a phrase in the following sentence: "For this sort of necromancer. . . . " In this regard, sources indicate that there were two types of necromancers—those who raised the dead to divine the future and those who did so to influence it.

Josephus's presentation of Saul's preparations for visiting the witch differs from the biblical version:

Samuel 28:8	*Ant.* 6.330
So Saul disguised himself and put on other clothes and went there, he and two men with him. They came to the woman by night.	Saul, without the knowledge of any in the camp, stripping off his royal robes and accompanied by two servants whom he knew to be quite trustworthy, came to Dor to this woman.

Josephus's account is more detailed. He tells us that no one knew about Saul's excursion, except two "trustworthy" servants; moreover, he focuses upon what Saul took off rather than what he put on to disguise himself. He repeats the name of the witch's city, and omits the detail that they went at night. According to extrabiblical texts, necromantic inquiries took place either in the day or at night.[31]

The section relating the witch's response contains an interesting addition to the biblical version: "The woman, however, objected, saying that she would not defy the king, who had expelled that class of diviners; nor was it fair on his part, who had suffered no wrong from her, to lay this snare to catch her in forbidden acts and cause her to be punished" (*Ant.* 6.331).

Josephus expands the witch's reply in a way that makes her response exemplary. First, her statement that she would not defy (*kataphronēsein*) the king expresses a Roman ideal.[32] Moreover, we may detect here an expression of Josephus's stated position that Jews should not defy Caesar (the Romans); for he believed that such authority was ordained by God and that the Jews were better off under Roman sovereignty and protection.[33] By having the witch respond in this way—instead of merely fearing for her life (1 Sam. 28:9)—Josephus presents her as a model of exemplary behavior.

Second, Josephus presents the witch as having been treated unjustly, although completely innocent of any wrongdoing against her king. This is significant because he will return to this motif and build upon it further in the story. He introduces it at the first encounter between the witch and Saul, and it serves to set the stage for his overall presentation of her as a woman of noble character.

Saul's assurance to the witch that she would not be harmed differs from the biblical version in form (in *Jewish Antiquities,* it is in narrative form) and in content. Although Saul refers to his promise, he more or less replaces it with three statements of assurance: (1) no one would know of it; (2) he would tell no one; and (3) she would be in no danger. The third statement alone corresponds to the biblical promise: "As the Lord lives, you will not be punished for this" (1 Sam. 28:10). Although omitting the oath, Josephus communicates its emphatic force by repeating the promise three times. With this, Saul succeeds in convincing the witch and then proceeds to request that she bring up the soul (*psuchē*) of Samuel.

Samuel Is Raised Up (*Ant.* 6.332–36)

This section is expanded by additions that heighten the dramatic effect and answer certain questions raised because of gaps in the biblical story.

The scene in which the woman recognizes Saul differs considerably from the Bible:

1 Samuel 28:12	*Ant.* 6.332
When the woman saw Samuel, she cried out with a loud voice; and the woman said to Saul, "Why have you deceived me? You are Saul!"	The woman, ignorant who Samuel was, summoned him from Hades. And when he appeared, the woman, beholding a venerable and godlike man, was overcome and, in her terror at the apparition, cried, "Are you not King Saul?" (for Samuel revealed who he was).

Josephus provides a smoother transition between Saul's request and Samuel's appearance. While the Bible omits reference to the witch's actually calling up Samuel, Josephus states that she "summoned him from Hades." In his description of Samuel, Josephus also provides details we would like to know: What was the spirit like? Why did the witch cry out when she saw Samuel inasmuch as she was a professional who surely was accustomed to seeing ghostly apparitions? How did the witch recognize Samuel?

Josephus describes the spirit of Samuel in terms meaningful to a Greco-Roman audience. Samuel is an *andra semnon* (august, honorable, holy man) *kai theoprepē* (befitting a god).[34] The former likely derives from 1 Samuel 28:13, which describes Samuel as *'elohim,* a god or divine being; Josephus later refers specifically to this description (*Ant.* 6.333). The sight of this "divine man" filled the witch with terror. Josephus heightens the intensity of the already highly dramatic incident by adding a vivid explanatory phrase: "[the woman] ... was overcome and, in her terror at the apparition, cried ... " (*Ant.* 6.332).

Finally, Josephus explains how the witch knew who Saul was: She saw Samuel, and he "revealed who he [Saul] was." This explanation is less fantastic than that of the Rabbis, who propose that a spirit rises headfirst if it has been called up by a king, whereas otherwise it rises feetfirst.[35]

The witch's exclamation upon recognizing Saul is phrased differently than in 1 Samuel 28:12. Whereas there she first asks, "Why have you deceived me?" and then shouts, "You are Saul!" in *Jewish Antiquities*, she omits the first question and turns the statement into a question: "Are you not King Saul?" These are the only words the witch speaks directly in the entire account. Possibly Josephus has her speak here to heighten the dramatic effect.[36]

Saul immediately confirms his identity and then asks the witch why she is so frightened (*Ant.* 5.333). His query replaces the biblical exhortation not to fear punishment and subsequent inquiry as to what she sees (1 Sam. 28:13). This alteration, coupled with the witch's reply that she "saw someone arise in form like God," transfers the source of the witch's fear from punishment to the apparition itself. This shift is consistent with Josephus's presentation of the story, for he also eliminated reference to her fear of Saul at an earlier point. The continued focus on Samuel's spirit not only maintains the dramatic momentum, but also serves to enhance Samuel's character and role.

The witch relates that she "saw someone arise in form like God." Here Josephus translates the Hebrew *'elohim* (1 Sam. 28:13) according to its primary meaning as *theous* (God). But he seems to have been uncomfortable with referring to even so illustrious a prophet as Samuel as "a god," and thus modifies the word by adding *morphēn* (form), so that it describes Samuel's appearance.

Saul's request for further description of the apparition corresponds to the biblical account, though in *Jewish Antiquities* he specifies what he wishes to know: "the appearance, the dress, and the age of the man" (*Ant.* 6.333). In her response, the witch describes three aspects of his appearance: (1) he is "of advanced age"; (2) he is "of distinguished aspect"; and (3) he is "clad in a priestly mantle."[37] Josephus implies that Saul cannot see Samuel (see 1 Sam. 28:14), for he specifies that it is these points of description that lead the king to realize it is indeed Samuel who stands before him (*Ant.* 6.334). Also, Saul responds as he does in the Bible: "Falling to the ground, [the king] saluted him and made obeisance."

Josephus leads into the scene in which Saul converses with Samuel (*Ant.* 6.334) much in the same way as the biblical writer. Samuel asks why Saul has "disturbed him and caused him to be brought up"; and Saul explains his situation and dilemma caused by his inability to obtain an oracle, "whether through prophets or dreams." Saul concludes his plea on a positive note, which is an addition: "You will provide for me."[38]

Samuel replies that he cannot give Saul any information since "God has abandoned" him (*Ant.* 6.335), and then reiterates what he has told him already—David will be king in his place, and he will "lose both [his] sovereignty and [his] life" (*Ant.* 6.336) because of his disobedience at the time of the war against the Amalekites. He adds that Saul and his sons will fall in battle, but specifies only that Saul would be with him the next day.[39] Saul responds by falling to the ground and lying "inert as a corpse." The comparison of Saul's posture to a corpse points dramatically to his impending fate, and Josephus's reshaping of Samuel's speech so his final words announce that Saul would be with him the next day renders the simile even more poignant. Saul is as good as dead.

The Witch Ministers to Saul (*Ant.* 6.338–39)

Up to this point, Josephus has retold the biblical story rather faithfully. There are no glaring omissions, and the changes he has made serve to explain (or interpret in Greco-Roman terms), fill in gaps, or heighten the dramatic effect of the various scenes in the story. He digresses from this pattern, however, in his portrayal of the witch. While on the whole her character and role correspond to those she has in the Bible, at one point we have seen that Josephus adds an element that enhances her character. When Saul (incognito) requests that she raise up a spirit for him, the witch refuses, asserting that she "would not defy the king." Thus, Josephus has modified the story to shape her character into one worthy of emulation.

In the present scenes, this tendency continues and gains momentum until it culminates in Josephus's eulogy of the witch (*Ant.* 6.340–42). While the basic story derives from the Bible (1 Sam. 28:21–25), Josephus freely expands it, resulting in an enhancement of the witch's character. Hence, the following sections contain some of the most interesting material in Josephus's account of the story, indeed in his entire account of biblical history.

The scene begins, as in the Bible, with the witch attempting to persuade Saul to eat something, though Josephus expands and rewords the witch's appeal:

1 Samuel 28:21	*Ant.* 6.338
She said to him, "Your servant has listened to you; I have taken my life in my hand, and have listened to what you have said to me. Now therefore, you also listen to your servant; let me set a morsel of bread before you."	The woman constrained[40] him to partake of food, asking this favor of him in return for that hazardous act of divination, which though not lawful for her to perform through fear of him so long as she had not recognized him, she had nevertheless undertaken to carry out. She entreated him to let her set a table with food before him.

Josephus presents the witch's request in terms of a favor that Saul should do for her in return for what she has done for him. To be sure, this corresponds to the basic sense of the biblical text, but Josephus's way of wording the request highlights that particular aspect above what we infer from the biblical text.

Two different words of exhortation appear in this section—"constrain" and "entreat" (*parekalē*). Josephus will employ two other exhortatory words in this same section (*Ant.* 6.338)—*ebiasato* (insist) and *sunepeisen* (persuade together). His use of such a variety of synonyms increases the force of the witch's attempts to persuade him. It communicates that she used every argument she could think of to encourage him to eat. This, too, ultimately enhances her character, for she is so magnanimous and compassionate that she is unable to rest until she has seen that another's needs are properly taken care of.

Another indication that Josephus indeed aims to highlight the witch's role in persuading Saul to eat is the fact that he changes the story to lessen the part played by Saul's servants while increasing her role. Upon Saul's steadfast refusal to eat, the Bible states, "But his men joined the woman in urging him, and he listened to them" (1 Sam. 28:23). It is thus the servants who ultimately persuade him to eat; although the pronoun "them" could include the woman, the sense of the text is that the servants persuaded him. By contrast, *Jewish Antiquities* emphasizes her role: "She insisted and helped to persuade him." Even though Josephus tells us that "she helped to persuade him," he does not even refer to the servants at this point. If we were not familiar with the biblical story, we would not know whom she helped until later in the story (*Ant.* 6.339).

Josephus's editorial work is very pronounced in the following section, which describes the woman's gift to Saul: "Though she owned but one calf, which she had brought up and had taken trouble to care for and feed beneath her roof, for she was a laboring woman and had to be content with this as her sole possession, she slaughtered it, prepared the meat and set it before his servants and himself. And Saul that night returned to his camp" (*Ant.* 6.339). He transforms the Bible's simple reference to a "fatted calf" that the witch had "at home" (1 Sam. 28:24) into a description of her one and only personal possession, even companion, that she herself had raised "beneath her roof." He focuses upon the calf and expands the description to heighten the meaning and value of the witch's action and to evoke certain emotions within his audience. He aims to inspire admiration for—and imitation of—her character and conduct.

His interpretation could have been at least suggested by the biblical phrase "*la'iššah* [to the woman (there was)] *'egel marbeq* [a fatted calf] *babbayit* [at home]" (reading the last phrase as "in the house"), but it is unlikely that the biblical storyteller intended that we understand the text in this way.[41] Quite possibly, Josephus drew his description from another biblical source entirely, for it bears a striking resemblance to what we read in Nathan's parable of the poor man and the ewe: "The poor man had nothing except one little ewe lamb, which he had bought. He brought it up, and it grew up with him and with his children; it used to eat of his meager fare, and drink from his cup, and lie in his bosom, and it was like a daughter to him" (2 Sam. 12:3).

Nathan goes on to tell of the slaughter of this ewe to provide a meal for a traveler who had come (v. 4). To be sure, the point of the two stories is very different, but they hold several elements in common. Josephus knew well the dramatic impact of this poignant story and its power to evoke emotion and response. He thus has woven some of its basic elements into his portrait of the witch in order to highlight the magnitude of her gift to Saul.[42]

The matter of her feeding Saul constitutes an essential element in Josephus's portrayal of the witch. He focuses upon this deed and further develops it because he sees in the witch's actions an exemplary character trait that he desires that his audience emulate (parenetic value) and, as we shall presently see, that also presents the Jews in a positive light to non-Jews (apologetic value). What he has expressed here more or less implicitly through narrative, he will express explicitly in the section that follows; there he devotes a full three paragraphs to a panegyric on the noble character of the witch of Endor.

Eulogy of the Witch of Endor (*Ant.* 6.340–42)

This section is in its entirety created by Josephus and as such is of paramount importance in assessing his own portrait of the witch. Here, she is lauded for her generosity, compassion, and lack of vindictiveness. Moreover, she is held up as an example of what pleases God and disposes God to grant blessings to humankind. In other words, she is a practitioner of true religion. To be sure, Josephus does not commend her profession, although he in no wise condemns it; it is indeed striking that he could portray one of such an ignoble profession, according to Jewish valuations, as being of such noble character.

The eulogy begins with a statement of the overriding quality of character that Josephus commends, her generosity:

Here it is but right to commend the generosity [*philotimias*] of this woman who, though she had been prevented by the king from practicing an art which would have made it easier and more comfortable for her at home, and though she had never seen Saul before, yet bore him no resentment for having condemned her profession nor turned him away as a stranger and as one with whom she had never been acquainted; but instead she gave him sympathy and consolation, exhorted him to do that which he regarded with great unwillingness and offered him with open friendliness the one thing which in her poverty she possessed. And this she did, not in return for any benefit received, nor in quest of any favor to come—for she knew that he was about to die—, whereas men are by nature wont either to emulate those who have bestowed some kindness upon them or to be beforehand in flattering those from whom they may possibly receive some benefit (*Ant.* 6.340–41).

The witch is first of all not vindictive; she could have refused to help Saul because he had taken away her means of support in forbidding her to practice her profession. Her lack of vindictiveness is an expression of a classical ideal—*clementia* (kindness, mercy, compassion), a virtue particularly emphasized by Seneca, who sought to temper the harsher forms of Stoicism practiced by some. M. L. Clarke summarizes Seneca's teaching in this regard:

The Stoics, he says in one of his works, are thought to be hard, but in fact none are really kinder and more devoted to mankind than they. Though the wise man will not feel pity, he will show clemency, which, Seneca explains, differs from pity as religion differs from superstition. He will help others, not from emotion, but because of the bond that unites mankind, and of all virtues none is more becoming to a man than clemency.[43]

The witch is also hospitable, more specifically, hospitable to a stranger. Josephus makes this point by emphasizing that she did not know Saul. The introduction of this element provides a clue as to at least one of Josephus's motives in portraying the witch as he does—she serves as an example of Jewish hospitality to strangers, in response to anti-Semitic accusations to the contrary. Feldman points out the apologetic character of *Jewish Antiquities* vis-à-vis such accusations that the Jews were hostile to strangers and generally hated other peoples:

Among the qualities prized by the ancients there is almost none more important than to be a good host and
to be a good guest. It is thus not surprising that a major epithet of Zeus is *ksenios*, implying that he is the
protector of the right of hospitality.... To the Greeks
a major test of civilization was the manner in which
a *ksenos* [stranger] was dealt with; and since in the
Greco-Roman world the Stoics, in particular, stressed
the brotherhood of mankind, this charge against the
Jews was especially serious.[44]

Thus, for apologetic reasons, Josephus highlights those
qualities of character in the witch—who is a Jewess (at
least nothing indicates that she is not)—that conform
to Greco-Roman ideals. As we will see, he also seeks to
encourage imitation of these qualities (*Ant.* 6.342).

The witch also shows Saul "sympathy and consolation"
and encourages (*etrepsato*) him to do what is best for
himself. Ultimately, she offers him with zealous kindness
(*ektenōs kai philophronōs*) her only possession.[45] These qualities and actions are also Stoic ideals, which fall under the
general rubric of *humanitas*. In an essay on *humanitas*,
Clarke defines this ideal according to a variety of Stoic
philosophers, noting that it is based on the notion that
a common bond unites human beings and should govern one's relationships. According to Cicero, *humanitas*
expressed itself in "kindliness, helpfulness, and consideration for others,"[46] as well as "sympathy and tolerance."[47]
Josephus portrays the witch as exemplary of these traits.

Josephus concludes his portrait with an exhortation: "It
is well, then, to take this woman for an example and show
kindness to all who are in need, and to regard nothing
as nobler than this or more befitting the human race or
more likely to make God gracious and ready to bestow
upon us his blessings" (*Ant.* 6.342).[48] Here, he echoes the
exhortation of Seneca, his contemporary, concerning the
Stoics: "No school is more kindly and gentle, none more
full of love to man and more concerned for the common

good..." (*Clem.* 2.5.3). "No one of all the virtues is more seemly (befitting) for a man, since none is more human" (*Clem.* 1.3.3).

Josephus concludes the exhortation—and the entire eulogy—with a promise that God will be favorably disposed (*eumenē*) and will "bestow blessings" on those who follow the witch's example. The ultimate reward for a life well lived is the care and guidance of God, which is an expression of God's providence (*pronoia*). The Stoic principle of *pronoia*[49] is, in Harold Attridge's opinion, "the fundamental theological theme of the *Antiquities*.... [For Josephus] history is a record of divine providence at work rewarding the good and punishing the wicked."[50]

Comparison of the Portraits of the Witch of Endor in *Biblical Antiquities* and *Jewish Antiquities*

As in the portrait of Hannah, the portrait of the witch of Endor in the two documents contrasts sharply. What is striking, however, is that here it is Josephus who portrays the character very positively, while Pseudo-Philo depicts her more negatively than the biblical storyteller or Josephus.

For example, Pseudo-Philo portrays the witch (Sedecla) as a Gentile magician, and, moreover, as "the daughter of the Midianite diviner who led Israel astray." He also depicts her as having been raising the dead for the Philistines for forty years, although he also clearly declares that God, and not Sedecla, has raised up Samuel. These details are unique to *Biblical Antiquities* and thus reveal Pseudo-Philo's particular perspective on her character. He rounds out his portrait by omitting the final scene (1 Sam. 28:21–25), in which the woman persuades Saul to eat and provides for his needs. Obviously, he excludes this episode because it does not suit his overall negative portrayal of her character. We may understand Pseudo-Philo's portrait of the witch as an expression of his opposition to idolatry and other such practices. Also, his association of idolatry with Gentiles is consistent with general attitudes toward Gentiles on the part of Jews of his own day. For example, a Hebrew synonym for "Gentile" is "idolator."

Josephus, in contrast, portrays the witch of Endor more positively than all the other female characters in this study, and the positive aspects of her character and actions on the whole conform to Roman ideals, particularly *clementia* and *humanitas*. He expands her story significantly and changes several details to present her in this very positive light. For example, the witch refuses to raise up Samuel not because she fears for her life, but because it would not be right to defy one's king. Similarly, she does not merely kill for Saul a fatted calf, but she kills her one beloved calf, her only source of income. This detail is added—rather, transferred from the parable of the poor man and the ewe (2 Sam. 12:1–14)—not only to heighten the dramatic effect, but also to portray her as the epitome of hospitality and generosity. In a lengthy epilogue, Josephus explicitly eulogizes her for these characteristics and commends her example as one to be emulated by all who seek to practice true religion and be blessed by God.

We have offered a reasonable explanation for Pseudo-Philo's negative portrait of the witch of Endor. But how do we explain Josephus's overwhelmingly positive portrait? How does she become the outstanding woman of noble character in all of Josephus's works? As with *Biblical Antiquities*, the answer lies in his audience and his purpose. He was writing for an audience for which the occult was fashionable, who would have seen no incongruity in a necromancer being of such exemplary character.

Additionally, Josephus's apologetic objective led him

to recognize in the witch's example an opportunity that he could not leave unexploited. She is a Jewess whose character and conduct accord with the highest of Greco-Roman ideals; hence, in this case, his overriding purposes have outweighed his generally negative personal opinions regarding women. Likewise, although with the opposite result, Pseudo-Philo's apologetic concerns have outweighed his generally positive disposition toward women.

Notes

1. Technically speaking, she is not a witch; for a witch practices black magic, that is, attempts to influence the future rather than just divine it. The witch of Endor is more properly a medium or a necromancer (one who divines by means of the dead). In 1 Sam. 28:7–8, she is called a *ba'alat 'ob,* which denotes either one who owns and operates a necromantic pit, or one who controls a spirit. The word in question is *'ob,* which is not used consistently in the Bible. See Smelik, "Witch of Endor."

2. Deut. 18:9–15; Lev. 19:31; 20:6, 27; 2 Kings 23:24; Isa. 8:19.

3. Saul is condemned for consulting a medium in the late biblical book of 1 Chronicles (10:13–14).

4. Brenner, *Israelite Woman,* 73.

5. The Latin term is *maleficos,* which is a general word for evildoer. Morton Smith (*Jesus the Magician,* 33) notes that *malefico* is "another term for magician."

6. There is a textual variant here also. The *editio princeps* reads: *memor mei erunt* (presumably Israel), and one of the Admont MSS reads: *memor mei erit* (presumably God). In either case, Saul's motive is selfish. I have chosen the first reading because of the context, which speaks about Israel's "remembering of" Samuel upon his death.

7. Pseudo-Philo portrays Saul as completely evil. Thus, he twists even this seemingly good act into evil by attributing it to an evil motive. Such polarizing of personalities, presenting them as either thoroughly evil or thoroughly good, is common in midrashic literature. See, for example, the portrayal of Balaam, as discussed in Vermes, *Scripture and Tradition,* 126–77.

Feldman ("Prolegomenon," cxlii) attributes Pseudo-Philo's remarks to a need to explain why Saul consulted a medium when he himself had expelled them.

8. Frederick Murphy ("Retelling the Bible," 282) refers to the present passage in his discussion of this important issue in *Biblical Antiquities*.

9. For example, *Bib. Ant.* 30.2; 39.11; 49.8.

10. *Biblical Antiquities* consistently (except for *Bib. Ant.* 4.7) designates the Philistines as *Allophili*. This is a direct transliteration of the Greek *Allophuloi,* meaning "other race" or "other nation."

11. There are three variant readings here. The *editio princeps* reads *filia Debicum* (or *Debin dianitae*); Phillips reads *Debin Madianite*; many manuscripts read *Adod Madianite*. Perrot and Bogaert (in *Pseudo-Philon*, 2:240) suggest that we read *filia debicum* (or *Debin*) as *filia divini* and follow James in emending *Adod* to *Aod* (see *Bib. Ant.* 34).

12. See the pronouncement by Ludwig Blau in his article on necromancy (*The Jewish Encyclopedia* [1912], s.v. "Necromancy"): "Necromancy, like idolatry and magic in general, was practiced chiefly by women." Some would deny that magic and necromancy are expressions of "illegitimate religion." It is, however, not within the scope of this study to deal with this subject; at least all could agree that from Pseudo-Philo's perspective, these were expressions of illegitimate religion.

13. 1 Sam. 28:8 states that "Saul disguised himself and put on other clothes."

14. Curiously, Saul remarks, "When I was king in Israel." The Latin *regnabam* is clearly imperfect. Perhaps Pseudo-Philo words it this way because David has already been anointed king (1 Sam. 16), or because Saul has already acknowledged: "The glory of my kingdom has passed from me" (*Bib. Ant.* 64.4).

15. Matt. 26:75/Luke 22:62, where Peter responds similarly to the fulfillment of Jesus' prophecy concerning him.

16. For other examples of the power of the Spirit, or inspiration, to change one's appearance, see Philo, *Mos.* 2.272; idem, *Virt.* 217; idem, *Ebr.* 146–47; Plutarch, *De. Def. Or.* 432D.

17. Hartom (in *Hasefarim*, 49) connects this statement with 1 Sam. 28:13: *'elohim ra'iti 'olim min ha'areṣ,* as if she says that she has seen many spirits rising up from the ground, that is, she has practiced necromancy for a long time.

18. The Greek Bible renders *'elohim* literally as *theous* (gods), while the Aramaic reads *mala'ca' deyahweh* (the angel of the Lord). James translates it "the gods," and Cazeaux renders it *des dieux*. See Smelik, "Witch of Endor," 168.

19. Note the similar description in Dan. 3:25.

20. The Greek Bible reads *orthinon* ("standing upright or straight") for Hebrew *zaqen*. Ginzberg (*Legends*, 4:70; 6:236 n. 75) suggests that the translators read *zaqef* rather than *zaqen*, which gave rise to the belief that a spirit rises with its head downward unless it is summoned by a king. See also Lieberman, *Hellenism*, 238–39; *LevR* 26:7; *bSanh.* 65b.

21. Ginzberg (*Legends*, 6:237 n. 77) refers to the notion that the dead rise at the judgment in their burial garments. Saul Lieberman ("Some Aspects," 510–11) gives further examples from both rabbinic and Roman literature.

22. This motif is common in early Jewish and Christian literature and serves to emphasize Samuel's importance. See Josephus's version of Moses' death (*Ant.* 4.236), according to which Joshua and Eleazar accompany Moses to Mount Nebo when he is about to die. See also the ascension of Jesus (Acts 1:10–11), as well as the *Gospel of Peter* 10:39ff., which depicts two angels leading Jesus out of the tomb at the resurrection, and various New Testament resurrection accounts that speak of angels at the tomb.

23. 1 Sam. 15:27 states that Saul tore the mantle. See 1 Kings 11:29–32.

24. For example, *Bib. Ant.* 31.5; 44.10; 53.10; see also Winston, *Wisdom of Solomon*, 232–33.

25. See Ginzberg, *Legends*, 6:237 n. 77.

26. See Perrot and Bogaert, in *Pseudo-Philon*, 2:244–45; Feldman, "Prolegomenon," cxliv. Perhaps we should understand the Latin term behind "destruction" (*ruina*) as literally referring to the mutilation of Saul's body after the battle (1 Sam. 31:8–13), which would reflect another rabbinic doctrine, that degradation of a corpse effects atonement. See Lieberman, "Some Aspects," 506–8.

27. Josephus does give notice of Samuel's death in 5.292, which corresponds to 1 Sam. 25:1. That the second reference is repetitive may explain why he omits it here.

28. Greek: *eggastrimuthous*, literally "ventriloquists." This is the most common term used for necromancer in Greek versions

of the Bible. It was believed that the necromancer appeared to raise the dead by throwing his/her voice to sound like a spirit.

29. The term *technē* appears again in 5.340. Morton Smith ("Occult in Josephus," 241) discusses Josephus's use of the term *manteis*, suggesting that the historian had personal experience with the *technē* of an exorcist (*Ant.* 8.45ff.) and was proud that such skills were "the heritage of the Jewish people."

30. He agrees with the Bible in specifying a woman. In antiquity, military personnel commonly resorted to divination before a battle. See Lucan, *Parisalia* 6.400.

31. Hoffner ("Second Millennium Antecedents," 393) maintains that these rituals were performed at night, but *Tan. B.* 3.82 specifies that the ritual must be performed during the day. See also *tBaba Meṣi'a* 107b.

32. Roman society placed great value upon submission to the authority of the state and performing one's duty as a good citizen. Although many Stoics preferred a mixed constitution (democracy, kingship, and aristocracy), modeled after Spartan society, they advocated monarchy as the best of the simple forms of government, primarily because they believed it to be the most natural. See Griffin, *Seneca*, 202–10; see also Clarke, *Roman Mind*, 36, 103, 109, 112.

33. Horst Moehring ("Joseph ben Matthia," 896–901) cites references to this position in Josephus's works. He notes that for Josephus, "the Roman empire possesses cosmic character and constitutes part of God's design for that particular period in history" (p. 898). "The Jews owe their freedom to live by their ancestral laws to the Romans who on several occasions have defended this freedom when it was endangered by local [Jewish] authorities. . . . It would be criminal madness ever again to endanger the peaceful relations between Rome and the Jews" (pp. 896–97).

34. The term *prepōn* was used by the Stoics to refer to "conduct consistent with man's nature, that is, with the qualities in which man differs from the animals, the possession of reason and the moral sense" (Clarke, *Roman Mind*, 37). Hence, the modifier *theos* specifies the connotation of that which is consistent with God's (or god's) nature. On the "divine man" in Greco-Roman culture, see Smith, "Occult in Josephus," 239; and idem, *Jesus the Magician*, 19.

35. See n. 20, above.

36. Betsy Amaru ("Portraits," 145 n. 5) summarizes Willem van Unnik's observation that Josephus characteristically paraphrases dialogue and that he draws attention to points of emphasis by employing direct speech.

37. Josephus qualifies the word "mantle" with the adjective "priestly." Marcus explains in a footnote: "Josephus adds the word 'priestly' because *me'il* is the word used regularly in later Hebrew of the priest's robe."

38. There is a textual variant of the verb. The *editio princeps* and Latin texts read: *pronoēsamenon* (Aorist part.), while Marcus elects the reading *pronoēsomenon* (pres. part.). Whiston, following the *editio princeps*, translates the phrase: "Who always tookest care of me"; Marcus translates it with a future sense, which best suits the context.

39. The Hebrew Bible does not mention Saul and his sons falling in battle, but states that they (all) will be with Samuel the next day (1 Sam. 28:19). In contrast, the Greek Bible omits reference to anyone being with Samuel: "tomorrow you and your sons will fall." Thus, Josephus conflates the two readings, but changes the Hebrew Bible's reference to Saul and his sons to simply Saul, for reasons that are not clear.

40. The Greek verb, *sunēnagkazō*, is a strong word, meaning "to exhort or compel by force."

41. The anarthrous construction does not imply "only one," but refers to one of a group. Possibly she had only one fatted calf. *Babbayit* simply means "at home."

42. That Josephus omits reference to the bread (1 Sam. 28:24) further indicates the centrality of the calf motif.

43. Clarke, *Roman Mind*, 129. See Seneca, *Clem.* 2.5–6.

44. Feldman, "Hellenizations in Josephus' Versions of Esther," 140–41.

45. David Winston ("Philo's Ethical Theory," 391–400) highlights the significance of *philanthrōpia* in the writings of Philo, as well as parallels with Stoic thought. In comparison with *Ant.* 6.342, it is interesting that Philo states that one who practices *philanthrōpia* imitates God (p. 398). See also Wisd. Sol. 1:6; 7:23.

46. Clarke, *Roman Mind*, 135.

47. Ibid., 137.

48. Such exhortations commonly appear in *Jewish Antiquities*, and indeed are consonant with one of Josephus's stated

purposes in composing his work (*Ant.* 1.14). See Attridge, "Josephus," 213, 217, 224–25.

49. See Clarke, *Roman Mind,* 116; Feldman, "Flavius Josephus Revisited," 797.

50. Attridge, "Josephus," 218. Feldman ("Introduction," 44) notes that Josephus "uses the favorite word for providence, *pronoia,* no fewer than 121 times in the *Antiquities* and 39 times in his other works."

5

Summary of the Portrayal of Women in *Biblical Antiquities* and *Jewish Antiquities*

I have presented here eight portraits of biblical women, four according to each author, which provide ample material to evaluate the overall portrayal of women in *Biblical Antiquities* and *Jewish Antiquities*. Clearly, each author alters the biblical stories to present particular traits or events, and these alterations indicate most conspicuously the author's own agenda in telling the story. In the preceding chapters, I have analyzed inductively the various portraits in depth individually and comparatively to determine points of similarity and dissimilarity between the perspectives of Pseudo-Philo and Josephus. We are now ready to assess each author's portrayal of women in the respective documents.

The general picture that emerges from our analysis is: (1) Pseudo-Philo and Josephus diverge considerably in their portrayal of the same figures, from the biblical stories and extrabiblical traditions, and from each other; and (2) on the whole, Pseudo-Philo portrays women more positively than does Josephus. In three portraits—Deborah, Jephthah's daughter, and Hannah—Pseudo-Philo transforms the biblical character into a major figure in Israel's history by attributing to her roles and character traits not present in the biblical narratives; in two cases (Deborah and Jephthah's daughter), he enhances the portrait to render her a counterpart to a significant male biblical figure.

Thus, Deborah—a prophetess and judge in the biblical account—becomes in *Biblical Antiquities* an apocalyptic visionary, a ruler over Israel, and a preacher in the Deuteronomic tradition. Indeed, her prophetic roles (guiding, protecting, interceding for the people) are enhanced to the point that she becomes the feminine counterpart to Moses as he is portrayed in biblical and postbiblical tradition. Similarly, Jephthah's daughter, as an exemplary martyr whose sacrifice is acceptable to God, becomes the feminine counterpart to Isaac as he came to be portrayed in the Akedah doctrine. Hannah also emerges as an important figure in her own right; she becomes an exemplary character, a model of faith and piety in the face of desperate circumstances and mocking infidels.

Moreover, each of these women takes on a symbolic or typological character in *Biblical Antiquities*. Deborah appears as a Wisdom figure, sent by God to enlighten the Israelites, to guide them and give them rest. As such, she represents the gift of Wisdom, granted to Israel's leadership after national repentance and prayer for restoration. She is the means whereby Israel would be liberated from its enemies and protected from further attack. As a mother figure, Deborah typifies the feminine qualities of compassion, protection, and nurturing. The sacrifice of Jephthah's daughter becomes in part a symbol of the "willing sacrifice" of Jerusalem, demanded by God. and acceptable to God, offering a message of hope that Jerusalem's "sacrifice" will guarantee Israel's continued existence. Hannah's plight typifies the struggle between the righteous and wicked, as well as the vindication of

Wisdom in the life of Israel. Her motherly role of nursing becomes a metaphor of Wisdom, or Torah, nurturing
her children. Thus, Pseudo-Philo significantly develops
the portraits of both Deborah and Hannah to present
them as outstanding Wisdom figures, a phenomenon that
reflects the special prominence given to Wisdom in his
work.

We must emphasize, however, that even though these
characters take on a metaphorical aspect, they do not lose
their flesh-and-blood reality, as, for example, they do in
Philo of Alexandria's allegorical interpretations. This is
a fundamental distinction because Philo portrays women
positively only as they represent greater spiritual realities
and not as real human beings who are female.

Of the four figures, the author portrays negatively only
the witch of Endor. He casts her as a Gentile magician
who has worked for Israel's enemies for forty years but
who has no power over Samuel. By and large, however,
this portrait is shaped by his opposition to idolatry rather
than negative attitudes toward women. In his story of the
witch of Endor, he directs his polemical commentary—in
the form of additions to and omissions from the biblical
story—not specifically against women but against magic
and idolatry in general.

Josephus, in contrast, is less consistent in his portraits
of the women. While two portraits (Deborah and Hannah) are considerably more negative than their biblical
counterparts, one (Jephthah's daughter) does not differ
significantly, and one (the witch of Endor) is actually more
positive. The witch of Endor stands out as his most interesting character because the overwhelmingly positive
portrait deviates so radically from what we would expect
concerning a witch in biblical religion—and concerning
a woman in *Jewish Antiquities*.

Josephus portrays Deborah, Jephthah's daughter, and
Hannah less positively than does Pseudo-Philo. Both Deborah and Hannah conform to Josephus's own stated opinions regarding women or to accepted roles for women

in Greco-Roman society, including Palestine; it is to that society that *Jewish Antiquities* is addressed. Deborah is denied leadership roles outside of the prophetic (spiritual) realm; Hannah is weak-minded, overly emotional, and subordinate to the males in the story. Jephthah's daughter exemplifies a model daughter and affords Josephus the opportunity to demonstrate emphatically that the God of the Jews "does not take pleasure in human sacrifice." Such parenetic and apologetic tendencies also led Josephus to develop the witch of Endor into the epitome of hospitality and generosity, as well as submission to authority, which are likewise Roman ideals. We may add that Deborah, too, serves as an example of the veracity of Jewish prophets and thus attests to God's *pronoia,* which is a particularly Stoic doctrinal tenet. Moreover, both Deborah and Hannah are portrayed more negatively in *Jewish Antiquities,* simply to bring their portraits into conformity with Josephus's stated opinions concerning women. He betrays no other motive, whether parenetic or apologetic, for intentionally denying Deborah the leadership roles she fills in the biblical account or for portraying Hannah as weak-minded and subordinate to males.

Our understanding and evaluation of Josephus's position regarding women are facilitated by his own autobiographical references and explicitly stated opinions within his works themselves, as well as relatively accurate knowledge of the date and audience of *Jewish Antiquities.* We know that he wrote to present Judaism in a positive light to a largely pagan Greco-Roman audience and to exhort Jews living in that environment to continue to follow their ancient way of life as prescribed in their scriptures. It is important to note that he did not write *Jewish Antiquities* either to or from a specific religious community, although it is possible that his views reflected those of some group(s) of Jews, whether in Palestine or the Diaspora.

In the case of *Biblical Antiquities,* discerning the author's motives in his editorial work—choosing which characters to spotlight and rewriting their stories—is rendered more difficult by the nearly complete paucity of such explicit references within the work. We simply do not know with certainty when or where or by whom the document was composed, although the author provides some hints. His repeated emphasis upon God's covenant with Israel and ultimate fulfillment of covenantal promises, despite Israel's present circumstances, points to a composition after the destruction of Jerusalem. Also, language, motifs, and issues treated in *Biblical Antiquities* parallel those in texts that are clearly datable to the period following the destruction, *2 Apocalypse of Baruch* and *4 Ezra*, for example.

As to the provenance of *Biblical Antiquities,* we can be quite certain that it was written for a Jewish audience and probably a Hellenistic Jewish audience. As to a more specific identification, we find no compelling reason to look to Egypt (although the author occasionally incorporates traditions similar to those found in the Wisdom of Solomon or Philo of Alexandria's works) or even to Judean Palestine. Certain elements of the document do correspond, however, to those present in exegetical traditions indigenous to northern Palestine or, more probably, Syria. These include special prominence given to women and use of feminine imagery, incorporation of some elements of Wisdom and goddess traditions, and literary parallels to texts identifiable as Syrian in provenance, that is, *2 Apocalypse of Baruch*, the *Odes of Solomon*, the Gospel of Matthew, the Johannine literature, and the epistles of Ignatius.

It appears that *Biblical Antiquities* is a product of a particular religious community, or circle of communities. This is probably the only record we have of this community; we possess no treatise offering direct information about its character or history. The text does speak indirectly, however, offering us hints of these features. Specifically as it relates to women, three aspects stand out: (1) the centrality of Wisdom theology; (2) the pneumatic, or charismatic, character of the community; and (3) the leadership role played by women in the religious life of the community.

The role of Wisdom theology, which represents the work of God in feminine terms, is significant in *Biblical Antiquities*. The author deliberately chooses to introduce Wisdom elements into biblical narrative and to develop both male and female biblical characters according to Wisdom traditions. For example, Moses and Samuel are presented as Wisdom figures as well as Deborah and Hannah. Certainly, Pseudo-Philo could have chosen to develop these figures in masculine terms, through Logos theology as does Philo of Alexandria. The fact that he has chosen instead to highlight the feminine element reflects the value this approach held within his own community.

Likewise, the role of the Holy Spirit is central in *Biblical Antiquities*, which is actually a corollary to the prominence of Wisdom theology. The religious experience represented in the document is charismatic in nature, as the Spirit speaks prophetically through the biblical characters, inspiring messages from God and hymns of praise that recount the mighty works of God. Occasionally, this takes on mystical and apocalyptic character, and men and women biblical figures have visionary experiences that communicate information from God about end-time events. As is often the case in such charismatic religious environments, it is probable that women played a leadership role in the community that produced *Biblical Antiquities*. Where those with prophetic gifts are held in high esteem and women as well as men express these gifts, then women serve as leaders. Although we have little, if any, knowledge of such charismatic groups within Judaism, various Christian groups throughout history have given expression to this religious experience. A primary example is the Montanists (second half of the second century), who were led by two prophetesses—and who were condemned as heretics, partially because of their questionable Christology that described Christ in feminine terms and held that the age of the Spirit had superseded the age of Christ.

Admittedly, our knowledge of what role women played practically in Pseudo-Philo's community is limited to what we can infer from this single document. It is difficult to imagine, though, that a group that produced such a text would have marginalized women or relegated them to inferior positions simply on the basis of gender. The fact that Pseudo-Philo portrays women as he does within the framework of the biblical narrative— the sacred story—reflects his concern to authenticate and render authoritative his particular views of women. *Biblical Antiquities* is not presented as merely a treatise on prophetesses and women leaders. When Deborah preaches a covenantal sermon and takes the lead in the apocalyptic battle, it is presented as divine revelation. When Hannah takes center stage in the narrative and then leads the worshiping community (even explaining scripture to her husband), it is presented as divine revelation. When Jephthah's daughter, firstborn and beloved, willingly offers herself in a sacrifice that is demanded by God and that is "precious before [God] always," it is presented as divine revelation. Hence, Pseudo-Philo's community appears to have recognized the special gifts and callings of "women of God" as well as men of God. It is a community that speaks through the stories and characters of *Biblical Antiquities*. Hence, it is a community in which women knew and taught scripture; communicated freely God's messages of comfort, hope, reproof, and exhortation; led in worship and the singing of hymns; and interceded before God for the community.

Undoubtedly, *Biblical Antiquities* opens a previously hidden window into the life of women in early Judaism. The fresh air that blows through this window is a welcomed, refreshing change from the stifling atmosphere that surrounds the stories of many women in antiquity; the message that blows upon those breezes breaks the silence of women whose voices must no longer fail to be heard. Clearly, this unusual ancient document provides a new and significant perspective, one that must not be neglected in the study of women "in the varieties of Judaism,"[1] and women in antiquity in general.

---

1. Kraemer, "Women in the Religions," 131.

Bibliography

Alexiou, M., and P. Dronke. "The Lament of Jephthah's Daughter." *Studi Medievali*, 3rd ser., 12/2 (1971): 819–63.

Allegro, J. M. "The Wiles of the Wicked Woman: A Sapiential Work from Qumran's Fourth Cave." *Palestine Exploration Quarterly* 96 (1964): 53–55.

Alonso-Schökel, Luis. "Narrative Structures in the Book of Judith." Paper presented at the Center for Hermeneutical Studies in Hellenistic and Modern Culture, colloquy 11, Berkeley, Calif., Graduate Theological Union, 1975.

Alter, Robert. *The Art of Biblical Narrative*. New York: Basic Books, 1981.

Amandry, P. "La divination en Grece: état actuel de quelques problemes." In *La divination en Mesopotamie ancienne et dans les régions voisins*, 171–78. Paris: Presses Universitaires de France, 1966.

Amaru, Betsy Halpern. "Portraits of Biblical Women in Josephus' Antiquities." *Journal of Jewish Studies* 39 (1988): 143–70.

The Apocrypha and Pseudepigrapha of the Old Testament. Edited by R. H. Charles. 2 vols. Oxford: Clarendon Press, 1913.

Apollodorus. *Epitome*. Translated by James George Frazer. Loeb Classical Library. London: William Heinemann, 1963.

Archer, Leonie J. "The Role of Jewish Women in the Religion, Ritual, and Cult of Graeco-Roman Palestine." In *Images of Women in Antiquity*, edited by Averil Cameron and Amelie Kuhrt, 273–87. Detroit: Wayne State University Press, 1983.

Arnold, E. V. *Roman Stoicism*. New York: Humanities Press, 1958.

Ashkenasay, Nehama. *Eve's Journey: Feminine Images in Hebraic Literary Tradition*. Philadelphia: University of Pennsylvania Press, 1986.

Attridge, Harold. *The Interpretation of Biblical History in the "Antiquitates Judaicae" of Flavius Josephus.* Harvard Dissertation Series, 7. Missoula, Mont.: Scholars Press, 1976.

————. "Josephus." In *Jewish Writings of the Second Temple Period: Apocrypha, Pseudepigrapha, Qumran Sectarian Writings, Philo, Josephus,* edited by Michael E. Stone, 210–25. Assen: Van Gorcum, 1984.

Aune, D. E. "The Odes of Solomon and Early Christian Prophecy." *New Testament Studies* 28 (1982): 435–60.

Bailey, James L. "Josephus' Portrayal of the Matriarchs." In *Josephus, Judaism, and Christianity,* edited by Louis H. Feldman and Gohei Hata, 154–79. Detroit: Wayne State University Press, 1987.

Beggiani, Seely J. *Early Syriac Theology.* Lanham, Md.: University Press of America, 1983.

Bernstein, Moshe J. "Josephus as a Biblical Exegete: The Ruth Narrative." Ph.D. diss., Yeshiva University, 1980.

Betz, Otto. "Miracles in the Writings of Flavius Josephus." In *Josephus, Judaism, and Christianity,* edited by Louis H. Feldman and Gohei Hata, 212–35. Detroit: Wayne State University Press, 1987.

Biale, Rachel. *Women and Jewish Law: An Exploration of Women's Issues in Halackic Sources.* New York: Schocken Books, 1984.

Bird, Phyllis. "Images of Women in the Old Testament." In *Religion and Sexism: Images of Women in the Jewish and Christian Traditions,* edited by Rosemary Radford Ruether, 41–88. New York: Simon and Schuster, 1974.

Bloch, Renée. "Midrash." In *Approaches to Ancient Judaism: Theory and Practice,* edited by William Scott Green, 29–50. Brown Judaic Studies, 1. Missoula, Mont.: Scholars Press, 1978.

Boling, Robert C., trans. *Judges: Introduction, Translation, and Commentary.* Anchor Bible, 6. Garden City, N.Y.: Doubleday, 1979.

Braun, Martin. *History and Romance in Graeco-Oriental Literature.* Oxford: Basil Blackwell, 1938.

Brenner, Athalya. *The Israelite Woman: Social Role and Literary Type in Biblical Narrative.* Sheffield, Eng.: JSOT Press, 1985.

Chalier, Catherine. *Les matriarchs: Sarah, Rebecca, Rachel et Lea.* Paris: Éditions du Cerf, 1986.

Charlesworth, James H. "A History of Pseudepigrapha Research." In *Aufstieg und Niedergang der römischen Welt II.*

Vol. 19:1, *Religion (Judentum: Allegemeines; Palastinisches Judentum)*, edited by Wolfgang Haase, 77–81. New York: de Gruyter, 1979.

———. "The Odes of Solomon—Not Gnostic." *Catholic Bible Quarterly* 31 (1969): 357–69.

———. "Qumran, John, and the Odes of Solomon." In *John and Qumran*, edited by James H. Charlesworth, 107–36. London: Geoffrey Chapman, 1972.

Cicero. *Cicero: On Moral Obligation*. Translated by John Higginbotham. Loeb Classical Library. London: Faber and Faber, 1967.

Clarke, M. L. *The Roman Mind: Studies in the History of Thought from Cicero to Marcus Aurelius*. New York: W. W. Norton, 1968.

Cohen, Naomi. "Josephus and Scripture: Is Josephus' Treatment of the Scriptural Narrative Similar Throughout the *Antiquities* I–XI?" *Jewish Quarterly Review* 54 (1963): 311–32.

Cohn, Leopold. "An Apocryphal Work Ascribed to Philo of Alexandria." *Jewish Quarterly Review*, old ser., 10 (1898): 277–332.

Collins, J. J. "Testaments." In *Jewish Writings of the Second Temple Period: Apocrypha, Pseudepigrapha, Qumran Sectarian Writings, Philo, Josephus*, edited by Michael E. Stone, 325–55. Assen: Van Gorcum, 1984.

Condon, Thomas M. "Gender Roles and Female Status in the Book of Judges." Master's thesis, Graduate Theological Union, 1986.

Conzelmann, Hans. "The Mother of Wisdom." In *The Future of Our Religious Past: Essays in Honor of Rudolph Bultmann*, edited by James M. Robinson. Translated by Charles E. Carlston and Robert P. Scharlemann, 230–43. New York: Harper and Row, 1971.

Craigie, P. C. "Deborah and Anat: A Study of Poetic Imagery (Judges 5)." *Zeitschrift für die Alttestamentliche Wissenschaft* 90 (1978): 374–81.

Craven, Toni. *Artistry and Faith in the Book of Judith*. Society of Biblical Literature Series, 70. Chico, Calif.: Scholars Press, 1983.

Cross, Frank Moore. "The Evolution of a Theory of Local Texts." In *Qumran and the History of the Biblical Text*, edited by F. M. Cross and S. Talmon, 306–20. Cambridge, Mass., and London: Harvard University Press, 1975.

Daly, R. J. "The Soteriological Significance of the Sacrifice of Isaac." *Catholic Bible Quarterly* 39 (1977): 45–75.

Daube, David. "Rabbinic Methods of Interpretation and Hellenistic Rhetoric." *Hebrew Union College Annual* 22 (1949): 239–64.

Davies, P. R., and B. D. Chilton. "The Aqedah: A Revised Tradition History." *Catholic Bible Quarterly* 40 (1978): 514–46.

Downey, Glanville. *A History of Antioch in Syria from Seleucus to the Arab Conquest.* Princeton, N.J.: Princeton University Press, 1961.

Endres, John C. *Biblical Interpretation in the Book of Jubilees.* Catholic Bible Quarterly Monograph Series, 18. Washington, D.C.: Catholic Biblical Association of America, 1987.

Epstein-Halevi, Elimelech. *Parašiyyot Ba'aggadah Be'or Meqorot Yevaniim.* Haifa: University of Haifa, n.d.

Exum, J. Cheryl. "'Mother in Israel': A Familiar Figure Reconsidered." In *Feminist Interpretation of the Bible,* edited by Letty M. Russell, 73–85. Philadelphia: Westminster Press, 1985.

Feldman, Louis H. "Flavius Josephus Revisited: The Man and His Writings, and His Significance." In *Aufstieg und Niedergang der römischen Welt II.* Vol. 21:1, *Religion (Hellenistisches Judentum in römischer Zeit: Philon und Josephus),* edited by Wolfgang Haase, 763–805. New York: de Gruyter, 1984.

———. "Hellenizations in Josephus' *Jewish Antiquities:* The Portrait of Abraham." In *Josephus, Judaism, and Christianity,* edited by Louis H. Feldman and Gohei Hata, 145–46. Detroit: Wayne State University Press, 1987.

———. "Hellenizations in Josephus' Portrayal of Man's Decline." In *Religions in Antiquity: Essays in Memory of Erwin Ramsell Goodenough,* edited by Jacob Neusner, 336–53. Studies in the History of Religions, 14. Leiden: E. J. Brill, 1968.

———. "Hellenizations in Josephus' Versions of Esther." *Transactions and Proceedings, American Philological Association* 101 (1970): 143–70.

———. "Introduction." In *Josephus, Judaism, and Christianity,* edited by Louis H. Feldman and Gohei Hata, 23–67. Detroit: Wayne State University Press, 1987.

———. *Josephus: A Supplementary Bibliography.* New York: Garland Press, 1986.

———. *Josephus and Modern Scholarship: 1937–80.* Berlin: de Gruyter, 1984.

———. "Josephus' Commentary on Genesis." *Jewish Quarterly Review* 72 (1981): 121–31.

———. "Josephus' Portrait of Deborah." In *Hellenica et Judaica: Hommage à Valentin Nikiprowetzky,* edited by A. Caquot, M. Hadas-Lebel, and J. Riaud, 115–28. Paris: Éditions Peeters, 1986.

———. "Josephus' Portrait of Saul." *Hebrew Union College Annual* 53 (1982): 45–99.

———. "Josephus' Version of the Binding of Isaac." *Society of Biblical Literature Seminar Papers* (1982), edited by Kent Harold Richards, 113–28.

———. "Prolegomenon." In *The Biblical Antiquities of Philo.* Translated by M. R. James. 1917. Reprint. New York: Ktav Publishing House, 1971.

———. "Prophets and Prophecy in Josephus." *Society of Biblical Literature Seminar Papers* (1988), edited by David J. Lull, 424–41.

Fiorenza, Elisabeth Schüssler. *Bread Not Stone: Introduction to Feminist Interpretation of Scripture.* Boston: Beacon Press, 1985.

———. "The Will to Choose or Reject: Continuing Our Critical Work." In *Feminist Interpretation of the Bible,* edited by Letty M. Russell, 125–36. Philadelphia: Westminster Press, 1985.

———. "Wisdom Mythology and the Christological Hymns of the New Testament." In *Aspects of Wisdom in Judaism and Early Christianity,* edited by Robert L. Wilken, 17–41. Notre Dame, Ind.: University of Notre Dame Press, 1975.

Fischer, Clare. "Women and Religion: A Select Bibliography from the ATLA Database." 3rd ed. American Theological Library Association, October 1983. Unpublished.

Foley, Helen P. "The Conception of Women in Athenian Drama." In *Reflections of Women in Antiquity,* edited by Helen P. Foley, 127–67. New York: Gordon and Breach Science Publishers, 1981.

Franxman, Thomas W. *Genesis and the "Jewish Antiquities" of Flavius Josephus.* Biblica et Orientalia, 35. Rome: Pontifical Biblical Institute, 1979.

Frölich, I. "Historiographie et Aggadah dans le *Liber Antiqui-tatum Biblicarum* du Pseudo-Philon." *Acta Antiqua Academiae Scientiarum Hungaricae* 28 (1980): 353–409.

Gaster, Theodore H. *Myth, Legend, and Custom in the Old Testament.* New York: Harper and Row, 1969.

Gilbert, M. "Ben Sira et la femme." *Revue Theologique de Louvain* 7 (1976): 426–42.

Ginzberg, Louis. *The Legends of the Jews.* 7 vols. Translated by Henrietta Szold. Philadelphia: Jewish Publication Society of America, 1968.

Grant, Frederick C. *Hellenistic Religions: The Age of Syncretism.* New York: Liberal Arts Press, 1953.

Grant, Robert M. "The Problem of Theophilus." *Harvard Theological Review* 43 (1950): 179–96.

Greenspan, Frederick E. "A Typology of Biblical Women." *Judaism* 32 (1983): 43–50.

Griffin, Miriam T. *Seneca: A Philosopher in Politics.* Oxford: Oxford University Press, 1976.

Gry, L. "La date de la fin des temps, sélon les révélations et les calculs du Ps-Philon et de Baruch." *Revue Biblique* 48 (1939): 337–56.

Haas, Lee. "Bibliography on Midrash." In *Midrash in Context: Exegesis in Formative Judaism,* edited by Jacob Neusner, 197–207. Philadelphia: Fortress Press, 1983.

Harrington, Daniel J. "The Biblical Text of Pseudo-Philo's *Liber Antiquitatum Biblicarum.*" *Catholic Bible Quarterly* 33 (1971): 1–17.

———. "A Decade of Research on Pseudo-Philo's *Biblical An-tiquities.*" *Journal for the Study of the Pseudepigrapha* 2 (1988): 3–12.

———. "Interpreting Israel's History: The Testament of Moses as a Rewriting of Deut 31–34." In *Studies on the Testament of Moses,* edited by George W. E. Nickelsburg, 59–68. Society of Biblical Literature Septuagint and Cognate Studies, 4. Cambridge, Mass.: Society of Biblical Literature, 1973.

———. "The Original Language of Pseudo-Philo's *Liber An-tiquitatum Biblicarum.*" *Harvard Theological Review* 63 (1970): 503–14.

———. "Palestinian Adaptations of Biblical Narratives." In *Early Judaism and Its Modern Interpreters,* edited by Robert A.

Kraft and George W. E. Nickelsburg, 237–47. Philadelphia: Fortress Press, 1987.

―――. "Research on the Pseudepigrapha during the 70's." *Catholic Biblical Quarterly* 48 (1980): 147–59.

Hasefarim Haḥiṣonim: Sipure-Aggadah. Translated by A. S. Hartom. Vol. 7, *Sefer Qadmaniot Hamiqr'a.* Tel Aviv: Yavne, 1969.

Heinemann, I. "Josephus' Method in the Presentation of *Jewish Antiquities.*" *Sion* 5 (1939–40): 180–203. (Heb.).

Hengel, Martin. *Judaism and Hellenism: Studies in the Encounter in Palestine during the Early Hellenistic Period.* Translated by John Bowden. 2 vols. Philadelphia: Fortress Press, 1974.

Hoffner, Harry. "Second Millennium Antecedents to the Hebrew '*ob.*" *Journal of Biblical Literature* 86 (1967): 385–401.

James, E. O. *The Cult of the Mother Goddess.* London: Thames and Hudson, 1959.

―――. *Myth and Ritual in the Ancient Near East: An Archaeological and Documentary Study.* London: Thames and Hudson, 1958.

James, M. R., trans. *The Biblical Antiquities of Philo.* 1917. Reprint. New York: Ktav Publishing House, 1971.

Josephus. *Josephus.* 9 vols. Loeb Classical Library. London: William Heinemann. Vol. 4, *Jewish Antiquities, Books 1–4,* translated by H. St. J. Thackeray, 1928. Vol. 5, *Jewish Antiquities, Books 5–8,* translated by H. St. J. Thackeray and Ralph Marcus, 1927.

―――. *Josephus: Complete Works.* Translated by William Whiston. 1867. Reprint. Grand Rapids: Kregel Publications, 1960.

Kaufmann, Yehezekel. *Sefer Šofetim.* Jerusalem: Qiryat Sefer, 1962.

―――. *The Religion of Israel.* Translated and abridged by Moshe Greenberg. New York: Schocken Books, 1974.

Kerenyi, C. *The Religion of the Greeks and Romans.* London: Thames and Hudson, 1962.

Kisch, Guido. "The *Editio Princeps* of Pseudo-Philo's *Liber Antiquitatum Biblicarum.*" In *Alexander Marx Jubilee Volume,* edited by S. Lieberman, 425–46. New York: Jewish Theological Seminary of America, 1950.

―――. "A Note on the New Edition of Ps-Philo's *Biblical Antiquities.*" *Historia Judaica* 12 (1950): 153–58.

————. *Pseudo-Philo's Liber Antiquitatum Biblicarum*. Publications in Mediaeval Studies, no. 10. Notre Dame, Ind.: University of Notre Dame Press, 1949.

————. "Ps-Philo's *Liber Antiquitatum Biblicarum*, Postlegomena to the New Edition." *Hebrew Union College Annual* 23/2 (1950): 81–93.

Klein, Isaac. *A Guide to Jewish Religious Practice*. New York: Jewish Theological Seminary of America, 1979.

Koester, Helmut. *Introduction to the New Testament*. Vol. 1, *History, Culture, and Religion of the Hellenistic Age*. Philadelphia: Fortress Press, 1982.

Kraeling, Carl. "The Jewish Community at Antioch." *Journal of Biblical Literature* 51 (1932): 130–60.

Kraemer, Ross. "Women in Religion." In *Women in the Ancient World: The Arethusa Papers*, edited by John Peradotto and J. P. Sullivan, 129–39. Albany: New York State University Press, 1984.

————. "Women in the Religions of the Graeco-Roman World." *Recherches de Science Religieuse* 9/2 (April 1983): 127–39.

Lacks, Rosalyn. *Women and Judaism: Myth, History, and Struggle*. Garden City, N.Y.: Doubleday, 1980.

Lattimore, Richard. *Story Patterns in Greek Tragedy*. Ann Arbor: University of Michigan Press, 1964.

————. *Themes in Greek and Latin Epitaphs*. Urbana: University of Illinois Press, 1962.

Le Deaut, Roger. "Apropos a Definition of Midrash." *Interpretation* 25/3 (1971): 259–82.

————. "Miriam, soeur de Moise, et Marie, mère du Messie." *Biblica* 45 (1964): 198–219.

Lederer, Wolfgang. *The Fear of Women*. New York: Harcourt Brace Jovanovich, 1968.

Lefkowitz, Mary R., and Maureen B. Fant. *Women's Life in Greece and Rome*. London: Duckworth, 1982.

Levey, Samson H. *The Messiah: An Aramaic Interpretation*. Cincinnati: Hebrew Union College, 1974.

Licht, Jacob. "Taxo, or the Apocalyptic Doctrine of Vengeance." *Journal of Jewish Studies* 12 (1961): 94–103.

Lieberman, Saul. *Hellenism in Jewish Palestine*. Texts and Studies of the Jewish Theological Seminary of America, 18. New York: Jewish Theological Seminary of America, 1950.

————. "Some Aspects of Afterlife in Rabbinic Literature." In *Wolfson Jubilee Volume*. Vol. 1, 495–532. Jerusalem: American Academy for Jewish Research, 1965.

Lightfoot, J. B., trans. *The Apostolic Fathers*. Edited by J. R. Harmer. London: Macmillan and Co., Ltd., 1898.

Loewe, Raphael. *The Position of Women in Judaism*. London: SPCK, 1966.

Lucretius. *Lucreti: De Rerum Natura*. Vol. 1, *Prolegomena, Text, and Translation*. Translated by Cyril Bailey. Oxford: Clarendon Press, 1950.

Lust, J. "On Wizards and Prophets." *Vetus Testamentum Supplement* 26 (1974): 133–41.

McCarter, Kyle. *1 Samuel: A New Translation with Introduction, Notes, and Commentary*. Anchor Bible, 8. Garden City, N.Y.: Doubleday, 1980.

McCracken, G. E. "Review of Pseudo-Philo's *Liber Antiquitatum Biblicarum* by Guido Kisch." *Crozer Quarterly* 27 (1950): 173–75.

Macmullen, Ramsa. "Women in Public in the Roman Empire." *Historia* 29 (1980): 208–18.

Magnetti, Donald Louis. "The Oath in the Old Testament in Light of Related Terms and Legal and Covenantal Context of the Ancient Near East." Ph.D. diss., Johns Hopkins University, 1969.

Marcus, Ralph. "A Hebrew Critique of Philo." *Hebrew Union College Annual* 21 (1948): 29–71.

Midrash Rabbah. Edited by H. Freedman and Maurice Simon. 7 vols. London: Soncino Press, 1939. Vol. 1, *Genesis Rabbah*, translated by H. Freedman. Vol. 3, *Exodus Rabbah*, translated by S. M. Lehrman. Vol. 4, *Leviticus Rabbah*, translated by Judah J. Slotski. Vol. 7, *Lamentations Rabbah*, translated by A. Cohen.

Milgrom, Josephine. *The Akedah: A Primary Symbol in Jewish Thought and Art*. Berkeley, Calif.: BIBAL Press, 1988.

————. "Sacrifices and Offerings, OT." In *Interpreter's Dictionary of the Bible, Supplement*, edited by Keith Crim, 764–71. Nashville: Abingdon Press, 1976.

Mirsky, Aaro. "Biblical Explanations in the *Jewish Antiquities* of Flavius Josephus." *Sinai* 22 (1948): 282–87. (Heb.).

The Mishnah. Edited by Herbert Danby. 1933. Reprint. London: Oxford University Press, 1974.

Moehring, Horst R. "Joseph ben Matthia and Flavius Josephus: The Jewish Prophet and Roman Historian." In *Aufstieg und Niedergang der römischen Welt II*. Vol. 21:2, *Religion (Hellenistisches Judentum in römischer Zeit: Philon und Josephus)*, edited by Hildegard Temporini and Wolfgang Haase, 764–917. New York: de Gruyter, 1984.

Moore, Carey A. "Judith: The Case of the Pious Killer." *Bible Review* 6/1 (1990): 26–36.

Moore, George F. *A Critical and Exegetical Commentary on Judges: Translation, Introduction and Notes*. International Critical Commentary, 7. Edinburgh: T & T Clark, 1949.

Murphy, Frederick J. "Retelling the Bible: Idolatry in Pseudo-Philo." *Journal of Biblical Literature* 107 (1988): 275–87.

———. "2 Baruch and the Romans." *Journal of Biblical Literature* 104 (1985): 663–69.

Murray, D. F. "Narrative Structure and Technique in the Deborah-Barak Story." *Vetus Testamentum Supplement* 30 (1979): 166–83.

The Nag Hammadi Library. Edited by James M. Robinson. New York: Harper and Row, 1981.

Neusner, Jacob. *Midrash in Context: Exegesis in Formative Judaism*. Philadelphia: Fortress Press, 1983.

———. "Varieties of Judaism in the Formative Age." In *Jewish Spirituality from the Bible Through the Middle Ages*, edited by Arthur Green, 171–97. New York: Crossroad, 1987.

Nickelsburg, George W. E. "The Bible Rewritten and Expanded." In *Jewish Writings of the Second Temple Period: Apocrypha, Pseudepigrapha, Qumran Sectarian Writings, Philo, Josephus*, edited by Michael E. Stone, 89–156. Assen: Van Gorcum, 1984.

———. "Enoch, Levi, and Peter: Recipients of Revelation in Upper Galilee." *Journal of Biblical Literature* 100 (1981): 575–600.

———. "Good and Bad Leaders in Pseudo-Philo's *Liber Antiquitatum Biblicarum*." In *Ideal Figures in Ancient Judaism: Problems and Paradigms*, edited by John J. Collins and George W. E. Nickelsburg, 49–66. Society of Biblical Literature Septuagint and Cognate Studies, 4. Chico, Calif.: Scholars Press, 1980.

————. *Jewish Literature between the Bible and Mishnah: A Historical and Literary Introduction*. Philadelphia: Fortress Press, 1981.

Nickelsburg, George W. E., and Michael E. Stone. *Faith and Piety in Early Judaism: Texts and Documents*. Philadelphia: Fortress Press, 1983.

Niditch, Susan. "The Visionary." In *Ideal Figures in Ancient Judaism: Problems and Paradigms*, edited by John J. Collins and George W. E. Nickelsburg, 153–80. Society of Biblical Literature and Cognate Studies, 4. Chico, Calif.: Scholars Press, 1980.

Noth, Martin. *A History of Pentateuchal Traditions*. Englewood Cliffs, N.J.: Prentice Hall, 1972.

The Old Testament Pseudepigrapha. Edited by James H. Charlesworth. 2 vols. Garden City, N.Y.: Doubleday, 1983.

Otwell, John H. *And Sarah Laughed: The Status of Women in the Old Testament*. Philadelphia: Westminster Press, 1977.

Patte, Daniel. *Early Jewish Hermeneutic in Palestine*. Society of Biblical Literature Dissertation Series, 22. Missoula, Mont.: Scholars Press, 1975.

Pearson, Birger A. "Jewish Elements in Gnosticism and the Development of Gnostic Self-definition." In *Jewish and Christian Self-definition*. Vol. 1, *The Shaping of Christianity in the Second and Third Centuries*, edited by E. P. Sanders, 151–60. Philadelphia: Fortress Press, 1980.

Pesikta de Rab Kahana. Translated by William G. Braude and Israel J. Kapstein. Philadelphia: Jewish Publication Society of America, 1975.

Pesikta Rabbati. Translated by William G. Braude. 2 vols. New Haven: Yale University Press, 1968.

Philo. *Philo I–X*. Translated by F. H. Colson and G. H. Whitaker. Loeb Classical Library. London: William Heinemann, 1929–53.

Philonenko, Marc. "Essénisme et gnose chez le Pseudo-Philon: Le symbolisme de la lumière dans le *Liber Antiquitatum Biblicarum*." In *Studies in the History of Religions, 12*, edited by Ugo Bianchi, 401–10. Leiden: E. J. Brill, 1967.

————. "Une paraphrase du cantique d'Anne." *Revue d'Histoire et de Philosophie Religieuses* 42 (1962): 157–68.

Plumpe, Joseph C. *Mater Ecclesia: An Inquiry into the Concept of the Church as Mother in Early Christianity*. The Catho-

lic University of America Studies in Christian Antiquity,
edited by Johannes Quasten. Washington, D.C.: The Catholic
University of America, 1943.

Pomeroy, Sarah B. *Goddesses, Whores, Wives, and Slaves*. New
York: Schocken Books, 1975.

———. "Selected Bibliography on Women in Antiquity." *Arethusa* 6 (Spring 1973): 125–57.

———. *Women in Hellenistic Egypt*. New York: Schocken Books,
1984.

———. "Women in Roman Egypt: A Preliminary Study Based
on Papyri." In *Reflections of Women in Antiquity*, edited by
Helen P. Foley, 303–22. London: Gordon and Breach Science
Publishers, 1981.

Prosak, Bernard P. "Women: Seductive Siren and Source of
Sin?" In *Religion and Sexism: Images of Women in the Jewish and
Christian Traditions*, edited by Rosemary Radford Ruether,
89–116. New York: Simon and Schuster, 1974.

Pseudo-Philo. *Biblical Antiquities*. Translated by Daniel J. Harrington. In *The Old Testament Pseudepigrapha*, edited by
James H. Charlesworth. Vol. 2. Garden City, N.Y.: Doubleday,
1983.

———. *The Biblical Antiquities of Philo*. Translated by M. R.
James. 1917. Reprint. New York: Ktav Publishing House,
1971.

———. *Pseudo-Philo's Liber Antiquitatum Biblicarum*. Edited
by Guido Kisch. Publications in Mediaeval Studies, no. 10.
Notre Dame, Ind.: University of Notre Dame Press, 1949.

Pseudo-Philon: Les antiquités bibliques. 2 vols. Sources Chreti-
ennes. Paris: Éditions du Cerf, 1976. Vol. 1, *Introduction et
texte critiques*, by Daniel J. Harrington, translated by Jacques
Cazeaux. Vol. 2, *Introduction litteraire, commentaire et index*, by
Charles Perrot and Pierre-Maurice Bogaert.

Quasten, Johannes. *Music and Worship in Pagan and Christian
Antiquity*. Translated by Boniface Ramsey. Washington, D.C.:
National Association of Pastoral Musicians, 1983.

Rajak, Tessa. *Josephus: The Historian and His Society*. Philadelphia: Fortress Press, 1983.

———. "Moses in Ethiopia: Legend and Literature." *Journal
of Jewish Studies* 29 (1978): 111–22.

Rengstorf, K. H., ed. *A Complete Concordance to Flavius Josephus*.
Leiden: E. J. Brill, 1973.

Robinson, James M. "Jesus as Sophos: Wisdom Traditions in the Gospels." In *Aspects of Wisdom in Judaism and Early Christianity*, edited by Robert L. Wilken, 1–16. Notre Dame, Ind.: University of Notre Dame Press, 1975.

Ruether, Rosemary Radford. "Feminist Interpretation: A Method of Correlation." In *Feminist Interpretation of the Bible*, edited by Letty M. Russell, 111–24. Philadelphia: Westminster Press, 1985.

Sakenfeld, Katharine Doob. "Feminist Uses of Biblical Materials." In *Feminist Interpretation of the Bible*, edited by Letty M. Russell, 55–64. Philadelphia: Westminster Press, 1985.

Schaff, Philip, and Henry Wace, eds. *Nicene and Post-Nicene Fathers of the Christian Church*. 14 vols. Grand Rapids: Wm. B. Eerdmans, 1964. Vol. 13:2, *Gregory the Great, Ephraim Syrus, Aphrahat*.

Segal, J. B. "The Hebrew Festivals and Calendar." *Journal of Jewish Studies* 6 (1961): 74–94.

Seneca. *Seneca: Moral Essays*. Translated by John W. Basore. Loeb Classical Library. London: William Heinemann, 1958.

The Septuagint Version of the Old Testament and Apocrypha with an English Translation. London: Samuel Bagster and Sons, 1976.

Shinan, Avigdor. "Moses and the Ethiopian Woman: Sources of a Story in the Chronicles of Moses." *Scripta Hierosolymitana* 27 (1978): 66–78.

Skehan, Patrick. "The Hand of Judith." *Catholic Biblical Quarterly* 25 (1963): 94–110.

Smallwood, Mary. "Philo and Josephus as Historians of the Same Events." In *Josephus, Judaism, and Christianity*, edited by Louis H. Feldman and Gohei Hata, 154–79. Detroit: Wayne State University Press, 1987.

Smelik, K. A. D. "The Witch of Endor: 1 Samuel 28 in Rabbinic and Christian Exegesis till 800 A.D." *Vigilae Christianae* 33 (1977): 160–79.

Smith, Morton. *Jesus the Magician*. New York: Harper and Row, 1978.

———. "The Occult in Josephus." In *Josephus, Judaism, and Christianity*, edited by Louis H. Feldman and Gohei Hata, 236–56. Detroit: Wayne State University Press, 1987.

Sperber, Alexander, ed. *The Bible in Aramaic: Based on Old Manuscripts and Printed Texts*. 5 vols. Leiden: E. J. Brill, 1959.

Spiegel, Shalom. *The Last Trial*. Translated by Judah Goldin. New York: Pantheon Books, 1967.

Stone, Michael E., ed. *Compendia Rerum Iudaicarum ad Novum Testamentum*. Sec. 2, *The Literature of the Jewish People in the Period of the Second Temple and the Talmud*. 3 vols. Vol. 2, *Jewish Writings of the Second Temple Period: Apocrypha, Pseudepigrapha, Qumran Sectarian Writings, Philo, Josephus*. Assen: Van Gorcum, 1984.

Suggs, M. Jack. *Wisdom, Christology, and the Law in Matthew's Gospel*. Cambridge, Mass.: Harvard University Press, 1970.

Swidler, Leonard. *Biblical Affirmations of Women*. Philadelphia: Fortress Press, 1979.

————. *Women in Judaism: The Status of Women in Formative Judaism*. Metuchen, N.J.: Scarecrow Press, 1976.

Thackeray, H. St. John. *Josephus: The Man and the Historian*. New York: Ktav Publishing House, 1967.

The Third and Fourth Books of Maccabees. Edited and translated by Moses Hadas. Jewish Apocryphal Literature series, edited by Solomon Zeitlin. New York: Harper and Brothers, 1953.

The Tractate "Mourning": Regulations Relating to Death, Burial, and Mourning. Edited and translated by Dov Zlotnick. New Haven: Yale University Press, 1966.

Trenchard, Warren C. *Ben Sira's View of Women: A Literary Analysis*. Brown Judaic Studies, 28. Chico, Calif.: Scholars Press, 1982.

Trencsényi-Waldapfel, Imre. "Die Hexe von Enrod und die griechisch-römische Welt." *Acta Orientalia* 12 (1961): 201–22.

Trible, Phyllis. *Texts of Terror: Literary Feminist Readings of Biblical Narratives*. Philadelphia: Fortress Press, 1984.

Ulrich, Eugene C. *The Qumran Text of Samuel and Josephus*. Harvard Semitic Museum, 19. Missoula, Mont.: Scholars Press, 1978.

Urbach, Ephraim E. *The Sages: Their Concepts and Beliefs*. Translated by Israel Abrahams. 2 vols. Jerusalem: Magnes Press, 1979.

Vermes, Geza. "Bible and Midrash: Early Old Testament Exegesis." In *Post-Biblical Jewish Studies: Studies in Late Antiquity, 8*, edited by Jacob Neusner, 59–91. Leiden: E. J. Brill, 1975.

————. *Scripture and Tradition in Ancient Judaism: Haggadic Studies*. Studia Post Biblica, 4. 2nd rev. ed. Leiden: E. J. Brill, 1973.

Wagner, Walter H. "The Demonization of Women." *Religion in Life* 42 (1973): 56–74.

Wallace-Hadrill, D. S. *Christian Antioch: A Study of Early Christian Thought in the East*. London: Cambridge University Press, 1982.

Winston, David. "Philo's Ethical Theory." In *Aufstieg und Niedergang der römischen Welt II*. Vol. 21:1, *Religion (Hellenistisches Judentum in römischer Zeit: Philon und Josephus)*, edited by Wolfgang Haase, 372–416. New York: de Gruyter, 1984.

————. "Two Types of Mosaic Prophecy According to Philo." *Society of Biblical Literature Seminar Papers* (1988), edited by David J. Lull, 442–55.

————. *The Wisdom of Solomon: A New Translation with Introduction and Commentary*. Anchor Bible, 43. Garden City, N.Y.: Doubleday, 1979.

Winter, Paul. "*Monogenēs Para Patros*." *Zeitschrift für Religions und Geistesgeschichte* 5 (1953): 335–65.

Wiseman, Donald J. "Rahab of Jericho." *Tyndale House Bulletin* 14 (June 1964): 8–11.

Witt, R. E. *Isis in the Graeco-Roman World*. London: Thames and Hudson, 1971.

Wright, Addison G. *The Literary Genre Midrash*. New York: Alban House, 1967.

Index